MW00675358

5TH EDITION

Up and Running in 30 Days

A PROVEN PLAN FOR FINANCIAL SUCCESS IN REAL ESTATE

CARLA CROSS
CRB, MA

Dearborn
Real Estate Education

This publication is designed to provide accurate and authoritative information in regard to the subject matter covered. It is sold with the understanding that the publisher is not engaged in rendering legal, accounting, or other professional advice. If legal advice or other expert assistance is required, the services of a competent professional should be sought.

President: Dr. Andrew Temte
Executive Director, Real Estate Education: Melissa Kleeman-Moy
Development Editor: Kristen Short; Jennifer Brandt

UP AND RUNNING IN 30 DAYS
A PROVEN PLAN FOR FINANCIAL SUCCESS IN REAL ESTATE,
FIFTH EDITION
©2017 Kaplan, Inc.
Published by DF Institute, Inc., d/b/a Dearborn Real Estate Education
332 Front St. S., Suite 501
La Crosse, WI 54601

All rights reserved. The text of this publication, or any part thereof, may not be reproduced in any manner whatsoever without written permission from the publisher.

Printed in the United States of America

ISBN: 978-1-4754-4544-2

DEDICATION

Up and Running in 30 Days has been inspired by people from two worlds—the worlds of musical performance and real estate sales.

At four I sat down at the piano to pick out the melody and chords to popular songs. That early love of music led to years of performing on piano and flute in front of thousands of people. It also introduced me to the performance concepts that ensure mastery of skills. For those indelible lessons in performance, this book is dedicated to two influential teachers—Stacy Green, University of Oregon piano instructor, and Del Chinburg, my flute teacher in grade school and high school. You'll find in this book references to "perfect practice makes perfect," "precision in following the process," and "improvising after you know the tune." These aphorisms aren't mine. They were taught to me by these master performer-teachers, and I learned them by doing them—the only way we really learn.

I stumbled into the world of real estate sales by chance, simply to help my husband. Although I didn't realize it at the time, the musical performance skills I had perfected as a pianist and flutist were exactly what I needed to hone and master the skills of real estate sales. For believing in my abilities and answering my innumerable questions, I acknowledge my first real estate "boss," Robert Grace, who taught me to "just do it." "Go meet people" was his mantra—so, student that I am, I did just that.

Perfect practice makes perfect. We learn by doing. Mastering something takes dedication, tenacity, and determination over time. These are the lessons my mentors taught me, and these are translated into real estate practice in this book. Thank you for allowing me to pass the lessons of my teachers and mentors on to you.

— Carla Cross

P.S. As I read through my dedication, it may sound to you like mastering performance isn't fun! Not true. There's nothing more exhilarating, more motivating, and more inspiring—plus confidence-building—than doing something well enough that you want to do it again! (That's how you'll feel when you sell your first home.) And that's what I'll help you do as you use this resource.

CONTENTS

PREFACE

Up and Running in 30 Days is dedicated to all the agents who have taught me "what works." I have enjoyed helping great salespeople launch their careers to high profitability—quickly. *Up and Running* is organized to help you do the same.

As I write this fifth edition, I want to add a huge thank you to the many managers who continue to select their real estate agents for success. Armed with that exceptional selection process, these managers are willing and able to dedicate 100% of their efforts to coaching and assuring each agent is successful. I personally appreciate you and your dedication to raising the standards of the industry. As you select carefully, you assure we provide invaluable service to clients—and you assure that your coaching efforts with each agent will pay off. It's a win-win for everyone.

In *Up and Running* you have a personal, detailed, workable business-development plan. It has taken me two decades in real estate sales, management, and training to organize and prioritize this business—so you won't have to.

With *Up and Running* you can start your career today using the same activities top producers use to create multi-million-dollar careers. Congratulations on choosing to become a dedicated, professional, successful salesperson. Before you know it, you will be serving as a success story for the industry!

A C K N O W L E D G M E N T S

To ensure new agents get the technological support they need, as well as the start-up business planning support already offered in earlier editions of *Up and Running in 30 Days*, I called on my friends—and technology and social media experts—Amy Chorew, John Mayfield, Tricia Andreassen, and Scott Pierce. Each contributes greatly to our industry, and I know I can trust their input and advice regarding all things technical and social media.

In addition, thanks to my son, Chris Cross (chriscrossteam@gmail .com) (yes, I know, but we could have named him "Red," "Blue," or "Double"), who is a decade-long, very successful sales veteran and real estate company owner in Bellevue, Washington. Chris provided me a list of what he believes the new agent should have in his technology arsenal. And, he reviewed this entire edition for accuracy and up-to-date information. These suggestions have all been incorporated into this fifth edition of *Up and Running in 30 Days*.

Other reviewers and contributors:

- Carolyn Baran, a designated broker and trainer of new agents (carolynbaran@kw.com). Carolyn coaches new agents to use the *Up and Running in 30 Days* start-up plan, so she had great advice for this edition.
- Cathy Waidelich, founder and CEO of LegacyCaring, a unique program for seniors, assisting them with housing and other needs. Cathy was a managing real estate broker and top producing agent for more than 10 years.

For this edition, I invited newer and seasoned agents to provide you with advice. Plus, I have some observations from team leaders who have worked with new agents consistently. A huge 'thanks' to these contributors:

- Kyle Kovats, a top producing agent and inductee to the National Association of REALTORS® 2016 Class of 30 Under 30—a national group of 30 rising real estate industry stars (kylekovats@ gmail.com).
- Gary Richter, a first-year agent who used the *Up and Running* start-up plan to start his career like a rock star agent (gary@ghrrealty. com).
- Merrilee Prochaska, who is now using *Up and Running* to polish her business plan (merrillee@agtowncb.com).
- Cerise Paton has been in the business for over two decades and has held almost all positions available in real estate—assistant, coach, trainer, and full-time sales agent. She uses *Up and Running* to refocus her career (cerisepaton@firstteam.com).

- Diane Honeycutt, a seasoned team leader with more than 26 years of industry experience and who hires new agents regularly (diane.honeycutt@allentate.com).

Note: I got lots of specific advice, too, from these agents and managers in making choices in your business. I've put them in my ebook, *What They Don't Teach You in Pre-License School* (www.carlacross.com).

There's one other person I want to thank in advance, and that's whoever serves as your coach or mentor. Listen to your coach. Figure out what you need to support your business. And, remember, it's still a relationship, trust-driven business. Here's to your successful career!

■ 13 Tips to Ensure *Up and Running* Works for You as a Coach

Let me begin by saying thank you for choosing to coach your new agents. In this age of complexity and high consumer expectations, I believe it is the only way for agents to thrive quickly. To help you coach your agents effectively through the *Up and Running* program, informational "Manager's Tips" are included. You'll find them in each unit.

How to Coach the *Up and Running* Program

Before you provide *Up and Running* to your agents, there are a few organizational steps you'll want to take:

1. Read Units 1–3 to get an idea of the overall scope of this program. You will assign the introduction and these three units to your agents the first week they are in the business so they'll understand the scope and concepts of the program.
2. Look at the "get ready" list in Unit 3. Look at the list of recommended technologies at the end of this unit. Add the ones you think are important for the new agents.
3. Read through Units 4–7, which outline each of the four weeks' activities. See the assignments in each of these four units.
4. Use Unit 12 to coach the agents to the specific assignments. All the blank forms and assignments you need are there.
5. Look at Unit 8, the skills for lead generation. If you want to supplement the skill development in that unit, create lists and packages to use with each of your agents in *Up and Running*.
6. Note the resources you'll want to provide your agents before their assignment completion. For example, have ready your company or outside resource for your agents before they complete the assignment of assembling a listing presentation. This will be extremely helpful to your agents in getting their systems in place faster, better, and with more confidence.
7. Look at Unit 9 for the resources for business support packages.
8. Take a look at Unit 14 at the end of this program for additional resources.
9. Create a resource notebook in your office or online with articles or blogs on how to contact and recontact the various lead generating sources outlined in this resource.
10. Before your agents start the program, do an initial meeting with them to explain the program and how you will coach them.
11. Get the mutual expectations agreement in this resource signed before starting to coach the agents. You can also request a video

for your agents from www.carlacross.com explaining the program and mutual expectations.

12. Decide where in the program you will review expectations and results and make adjustments.

13. An additional tip: Provide the *Up and Running in 30 Days* resource to your desired recruits, explaining that it is the business plan you use for starting businesses.

14. Use the end-of-program evaluator and the next steps: 60-day planner (introduced in Unit 9) to keep the momentum going. It takes 6–12 months to ensure that the new agent is doing her business as an "unconscious competent." Don't stop coaching to this program until you're sure they have it.

Thank you for your dedication to our industry and especially to that agent lucky enough to have a start-up coach. It makes the difference between a career that barely succeeds (if at all) and an exceptional career start.

INTRODUCTION

Congratulations on purchasing your start-up business plan for your real estate business. There are many books published for new agents about starting your business. They give you good advice. But this resource has a different goal. My goal is to provide you what's missing in 98% of new agents' arsenals: a proven, prioritized performance plan to bring you success in 30 days.

It's a business plan designed to give you specific steps to start your business. In fact, most people would call this a full business plan. But, there are two big differences between this *Up and Running* plan and others' business plans:

- A real business plan has three more parts: vision, review, and mission.
- This plan helps you prioritize what to do on Monday, rather than asking you to create a full picture of your business. (How could you do that? You haven't been in business yet!)

It's great to learn interesting things. It's helpful to get lots of advice. But if you don't know exactly what to do each day to get a sale, what good is all of that advice?

Why this start-up business plan is unique. Besides books with lots of advice, there are also activity plans available to you. But, again, this start-up plan is distinctly different from those checklists new agents are given to complete. The specific structure and foundations of this start-up plan have been carefully created based on my decades of experience as a

- top-producing agent (I sold 40 homes my first year),
- coach to hundreds of new agents who became productive fast, and
- high-level performing musician and music coach.

A message to those in pre-license school. If you're now in a pre-licensing course, you may think that information prepares you to sell real estate. If you haven't found out already—it doesn't. Instead, pre-license courses are designed to help you pass real estate licensing tests. Besides this, though, you need information to

1. interview to choose the right company for you;
2. grasp the importance of time management, self-management, business planning, and how to work successfully as an independent contractor; and
3. identify and plan for stumbling blocks agents face in prioritizing and executing business goals.

As you read here, you will see several references to an excellent study from Inman Select: *How to Fix New Agent Onboarding*. Unfortunately, a vast majority of new agents (estimates are 50%+) fail within their first year in the business. Inman asked hundreds of brokers and agents to pinpoint how agents succeeded—and why they failed. One of the big takeaways of this report is that three-quarters of the respondents said new agents fail in large part because they *are unprepared for the realities for working as an independent contractor.*

That's why I wrote the book that you should read before you start selling real estate: *What They Don't Teach You in Pre-License School*. This text gets you fully prepared to start your career running—not limping or falling by the wayside as way too many new agents do! (I even include a hit-the-ground-running activity checklist for you to complete to prepare to sell real estate while in pre-license school.) Note: If you'd like a copy of my hit-the-ground-running activity checklist to use while you're in pre-license school, email me at www.carlacross.com/contact or carla@carlacross.com.

Big Idea: Advice is useless without the judgment to prioritize it.

Want to know everything before you start? Maybe you're one of those 'thorough' agents who wants to know everything there is to know about selling real estate—before talking to a human being. Give it up! Relax. You don't need to know everything to start lead generating. Evidence: there are thousands of real estate agents with licenses right now who know a lot, but don't sell much real estate. I don't want you to become one of them!

Big Idea: Real estate is a *performance art*, not a *knowledge pursuit*.

■ Five Structural Components Work Together to Get You a Sale

As an agent, you learn that every home must have a firm foundation that is structured against natural disasters of your particular area—flooding, landslides, and so on. (I live in Seattle!) You also learn that some builders are great at building foundations, while others aren't so good. It's the same in a business start-up plan. I've identified the five structural components in a business start-up plan that ensure that you get the best foundation, while protecting you from the pitfalls to which the majority of agents fall prey. Here are the components and why they are so important to your success.

1. Get you to top performance fast. As a top-producing agent, I learned how to put together and implement a start-up plan that worked. Then, I proved this plan works for others, as I used it to coach hundreds of new agents to success fast. Many of the new agents I hired and coached achieved top 10% status their first year

in our company, which consisted of 400 agents, including those who had fifteen years' or more experience.

2. Provide a top-flight "performance plan." More than experience and background have gone into crafting this business start-up plan. I really learned how to craft a good performance plan as a musician and musical performance coach. (I started teaching piano at age 16 and taught private and group piano and flute lessons in colleges for several years.) To learn to do something, you must have a structure that helps you perform correctly from the start. It must give you your next steps—in the right order. It must challenge you at the right times. It must teach you the principles so you can "go on auto" yourself.

Big Idea: This business start-up plan is the foundation for your career success—forever.

Up and Running will:

1. Get you to top performance fast
2. Provide a top-flight "performance plan"
3. Help you consistently get better results
4. Get you a sale in 30 days
5. Protect you from adopting the habits of failure

When a learning experience is badly crafted, you can't perform at a high level. (Think trying to use a computer when too much is thrown at you too fast or when you don't have a chance to get your hands on that computer quickly enough.) When a learning experience is well crafted, you learn well—and fast. (Think Montessori school or the Suzuki violin method.)

I think I learned these lessons so well because I saw how badly my piano students performed when I couldn't lay out a well-structured performance plan! I saw the need to create a very clear, precise performance foundation so those who wanted to learn to play the piano (or sell lots of real estate fast) could accomplish their goals. *Up and Running* integrates these performance principles like no other plan you can find!

Big Idea: Performing well results from a highly organized learning experience.

---

3. Help you consistently get better results. As a musician, I know that in order to get great performance fast, I need a way to measure what I'm doing and make adjustments. In music, we listen to our performances, usually with our coach, and evaluate to make adjustments. Then, we play it again with the benefits of our evaluations. That's how we get higher performance. As a real estate coach, that's what I do with my clients: help them look at their performances and make adjustments for higher performance results. So, another big difference in this resource is that I've built in the measurement tools you'll need to analyze your progress and adjust your activities to get the results you want. I haven't just given you activity plans.

I've given you the means to measure your results. I've given you the analysis tools to make adjustments. I've given you all the tools you need to become a master at self-management.

Big Idea: Measuring what you do frequently propels you to higher results.

---

4. Get you a sale in 30 days. When do you expect to make your first sale? If you're like the majority of new agents, you expect to make a sale in your first 30 days in the business. I discovered those expectations when I did a survey of hundreds of agents who had under three months in the business. (The results of that survey are in my ebook for would-be and new real estate agents, *What They Don't Teach You in Pre-License School*. See the References and Resources unit.) However, most new agents don't achieve that goal. In fact, about half the new agents who start their careers in any year leave the business that same year! Not only do they not make a sale fast, they don't make enough sales to stay in the business. So, if making a sale your first month is your expectation, you need a start-up plan that gets you into the sales game fast and has you talking with (and working with) many people so that you sell fast (remember, sales is a numbers game).

Big Idea: If you want a sale fast, you need a performance plan specially constructed to deliver just that

---

5. Protect you from adopting the habits of failure. As a new agent, at first I honestly didn't know why I was succeeding, but as I began observing the activities of low-producing agents, I noticed they spent most of their time previewing properties to "know the inventory." They also spent a significant amount of time in class learning interesting things and spent less time on the job (National Association of REALTORS® statistics show successful agents spend many more hours on the job). In contrast, my primary priority was finding and showing homes to buyers. I, too, viewed plenty of homes—but took genuine buyers with me to see them. I started contrasting the low-producing agents' plans with mine (although low-producing agents say they have no plan; what they did last week was their plan). My plan was to find and show people homes. Sell as fast as you can! I finally figured out that most new agents avoid the actions that require sales skills. They avoid rejection. They naturally do the activities that are easy: preview homes and sit in class!

Here's a very valuable piece of advice from one of my contributors, team leader Diane Honeycutt: "It's very important to grasp how to organize for the 'long haul,' develop good habits from day one, and be able to recognize and work successfully with all personality types (see information on those personality types in *What They Don't Teach You in Pre-License School*).

Big Idea: Slow starters do activities that allow them to avoid rejection but also have a low financial payoff. If you want to start fast, you need a start-up plan designed for that purpose.

The School of Hard Knocks

You may read this introduction and say, "Who does she think she is? How come she's giving us all this advice? Did she ever make a mistake?" In truth, my whole first year in the business was one mistake after another. I had no training, no full-time manager, and no mentor. I came from a musical background, not a sales or business background. I had never taken a sales skills course. I didn't attend any type of training school. It was really trial and error, and I'll bet I made every mistake in the book! So, just because I'm writing this book with all this advice, you shouldn't think I was ever perfect—or ever will be.

What I did do was go out into the field and sell a house my first week in the business and frequently continued doing that while I made all those mistakes. I learned as I went, and I set about doing it better every day. I think my musical and scholastic background helped me stay motivated through that baptism by fire and caused me to not settle for mediocrity. The reason I'm writing this book is so you don't have to make the mistakes I made, and here you have a wonderful track to run on.

I asked Gary Richter, one of my agent contributors, about his first year in real estate, in which he did exceptionally well. He listed three ways he succeeded as a new agent, and I loved his perspective on the connection between success and failing: "I was not afraid to fail. I'm okay with failing and failing often, as long as I failed fast, and failed forward."

What a great attitude! Too many of us get rejection or failure and conclude that it's just the way it's going to be. People who succeed put aside that failure and just keep going forward. Kyle Kovats said it: "Get out there and just do it. I just dove in head first." My observation is that those who wait and wait until they know everything fail—because action is the best teacher! Have the intestinal fortitude (that's guts, folks) to get out there and make mistakes.

I so appreciate the candor of my agent contributors! It's not always a smooth ride! Here are some comments from Cerise Paton on what she wishes she would have done differently: "Followed up more and more consistently; understood the time and discipline and numbers needed for lead generation and lead conversion; recognized the time it took to build trust; went on more appointments, failed more often, and got better; practiced presentations with friends." Cerise, those are the most common mistakes new agents make. That's why *Up and Running in 30 Days* stresses the numbers over and over, and strongly encourages you to use the plan consistently *and* keep and analyze those numbers so you're in control of your own destiny.

Here's a great question that one of my contributors, Cathy Waidelich, asked top agents when she was new: "What do you wish someone would have told you when you were a new agent?" Cathy related that top agents actually loved being asked this question and her genuine interest in learning from them connected them to her. Another great tip from Cathy: "Surround yourself with the types of agents you aspire to be like."

Finally, a comment from Merrilee Prochaska: "I wish I had understood the importance of a mentor/coach before I began."

I certainly don't want to make this a treatise on all the mistakes new agents make! But, you can bet that's why the business plan in this book is written exactly the way it is—to assure you don't fall into the bad habits and mistakes that result in too many new agents failing.

Every agent who has done well has experienced failure after failure. Cathy Waidelich says, "Every failure gets us one step closer to success." So, what's your attitude about "failing forward," one of author John Maxwell's favorite truisms?

Big Idea: We learn from our mistakes, and we can make mistakes *only* when we're willing to take a risk and get into action.

■ What's New in the Fifth Edition

Up and Running in 30 Days was first published in 1995. Since that time, thousands of new real estate agents have used the program to get "up and running" in 30 days. Every three–four years, I've updated this program so it stays fresh—and practical for each user. I made major changes in my fourth edition, so, in this edition, there are technical updates but no major changes in structure. These updates include the following:

- An update in trends
- Updates in technology with recommendations for the new agent
- Recommendations for using the technology that is most needed by the new agent in order to simplify the myriad choices a new agent has
- Updated statistics from the National Association of REALTORS® and other trusted sources
- Advice on working the market you're given—whether it's a buyers' or sellers' market
- Advice from very successful newer agents on how to succeed right now in real estate
- At the end of your four weeks, an evaluation for you to complete. What are you proud of? What do you want to keep working on? Evaluate yourself on your activities and attitude, and plan your next 6 months in the business. See the end-of-program evaluator in Unit 7.

- At the end of your four weeks, a template to create a 60-day plan to extend your success with the *Up and Running* principles. See Unit 7.

For you managers who have used earlier editions, here are the big changes I made in the earlier fourth edition and that I've kept here:

- I've realigned and added new trends and what they mean to you, the new agent, and as you start your career so you can make performance adjustments.
- I've created a cleaner, more structured road map to use this resource to its fullest potential so you won't get off track. It's also easier for managers to use to coach agents to the plan. For instance, I've added a Technology Budget and Planner so you can integrate technology faster into your business.
- I've added a unit on scripts and letters with examples for you to use. I want to make it easy for new agents to get the sales training support needed to make lead-generating calls their first week in the business (not everything you need to know, but just enough).
- I've added scripts, dialogues, and processes for answering and following up on online leads. Too many are not followed up or are not handled correctly. I want to help you make the most of every lead you get.
- Because social media is becoming a force in marketing, I've added assignments to create a presence in major media, along with a Social Media Planner. Using social media, you can enhance your networking efforts and make them more effective.
- I've added many Big Ideas to ensure that you really grasp and internalize the principles of high performance that so many agents miss, and you get the motivation and inspiration you need to keep on keeping on.
- To help managers coach to the plan, I've added Manager's Tips in every unit. Having a coach and a motivator is essential to starting your career right—and fast.

This edition includes

- Stronger "get ready" directions for the new agent (e.g., information on how to create a budget, how to organize information in three resource manuals, a checklist of "get ready" materials) (it's literally your start-up plan, not just a book or an idea fest)
- Improved clarity in the four-week start-up plan so you'll know exactly what you are to do
- A detailed, highly structured, prioritized system to track your goals and results in each of the four weeks (and great for your manager to use to coach you)
- Explanations of why I've prioritized your sources as "best" to "not so good," so you'll be able to customize your plan to self-manage better and faster
- Built-in caveats, or what to watch for as you start your business so you won't fall into the same failure patterns too many new agents create

New in This Edition

1. Trend update
2. Technology update
3. Recommended technology for new agents
4. Updated statistics
5. Advice on working the market you're given
6. Advice from very successful, newer real estate agents
7. End-of-program evaluation
8. Template for your 60-day plan

- "Big Ideas" to ensure you get the really important concepts of starting and managing your business
- A scripts and letters unit (Unit 13), where the scripts I introduce in Units 8 and 9 are detailed so the new agent can learn, use, and refer to them often
- Summaries in each unit so you can revisit the crucial points

What Kind of Market Are You In?

As I edited the fourth edition, we were in a shifted market—a very challenging market with homes sitting on the market and few buyers. Money was tight, and clients weren't very motivated to make buying decisions. Now, as I prepare the fifth edition, we're in a market where prices are escalating. This can force buyers to make quick decisions and sellers to decide it's a great time to sell. I call this a forgiving market. It forgives agents who aren't very good at what they do—because market pressures motivate buyers and sellers. (I call these agents "on accident" agents because they stumble across some happy sales accidents and assume that's the way it's always going to be.)

In real estate lingo, our market today is called a sellers' market—few homes available, escalating prices, with buyers scrambling to compete with others who want the same home (and are willing to pay escalated prices for it!). A sellers' market is good for sellers but challenging for buyers. A fast market may make it easier for a new agent to succeed fast. But agents can get complacent; it makes it easy to drift along without a plan. So, in this edition, I'll give you advice about how to optimize that great market so that, when the market changes, you're not left like a newbie—no prior business and no thoughts on how to help buyers and sellers figure out it's actually a great time to buy and sell!

Big Idea: Using a great plan to succeed in any market assures you succeed in the long term.

What You *Won't* Find in This Resource

- A lot of training. Why? Because:
  - I don't want to clutter this start-up plan with lots of ideas on how to do things. As previously mentioned, I don't want to distill it to an idea fest. That's not what you need. A business start-up plan needs to be separate from curriculum-based training so the new agent understands the priorities of his business. (Few new agents ever receive or implement a start-up plan because they're too busy "learning important stuff.") New agents actually think that they can just choose any way to start their businesses and that they are all the same. Not true. What is true is there are many methods to call on for-sale-by-owners. But if you don't make the

sales calls to them, it doesn't matter to your income that you have learned three ways!

Big Idea: For real estate success, *action* is more important than *learning*.

- New agents need a clear, separate, prioritized, directive plan telling them what to do every day, week, and month to be successful. They need direction from their *first day in the business*. They don't need to do long-term goal-setting. They need to know what to do on Monday—and why.
- New agents typically can't "see the forest for the trees" and you may receive some bad advice on what you should be doing. After all, most agents don't do lots of business. So, they're going to give you their versions of a business plan . . . a very slow business plan! You want to start fast. You just can't use a slow-start business plan.
- General "get started" advice such as how to choose a real estate company, how to choose a manager, how to interview, how to hire an accountant, auto and dress considerations, and so on—why isn't any of this advice included here? Although these are all admirable topics, they are peripheral to your business plan. Check the bibliography to see the book I've written that addresses many "get started" concerns.

Big Idea: A start-up plan tells you *what* to do and the priorities of your actions. Training shows you *how* to do it.

But What about the How?

It is true that we generally won't start something until we know how to do it. So, in Units 8, 9, and 10, I've provided a start on "how to"—how to make sales calls and how to execute critical sales skills. You will need to supplement the *how* with the training program provided by your office or REALTOR® association. But a new agent doesn't need to know everything about everything to start lead generating. (Remember my comment about mistakes, action, and success?)

References and Resources

Throughout this text and in the References and Resources unit, I've added specific technology tools as they relate to the tasks I've asked you to complete. Please note I am not endorsing these! I just want to provide some examples of specific tools available to you. Check with your broker to find out if there are certain companies' tools your broker recommends.

In addition, some real estate companies have contracted with providers to create a branded version of the generic software.

In the References and Resources unit, I have also provided information to supplement the level of training I'm able to provide you here. There are specific listing tools, selling tools, and sales tools, as well as an online training program that is *Up and Running* on steroids—*Up and Running in Real Estate*. (www.upandrunninginrealestate.com). Why aren't all these tools included in this book? This resource would be 1,000 pages! Also, each of these tools has specific uses. You wouldn't buy a car that was also an airplane, a boat, and a bike, would you? It would just be too weird! Again, don't let those trees get in your way of seeing the forest (your performance plan).

Are you willing to make an investment in yourself? You have the ability to make hundreds of thousands of dollars a year in real estate. Invest in the coaching and training tools you need now to become that professional you want to be. It amazes me when new agents start their careers and tell me they don't have enough money to invest in the tools they need—or they are unwilling to invest in themselves. Successful professionals always invest in themselves because they believe in their abilities to attain their goals. What other field could you enter that gives you the ability to earn six figures while you were investing only a few thousand dollars to attain it? (Yes, I said "thousand.") I have never met a successful agent who refused to invest in himself!

Big Idea: People who are going to be successful invest in themselves because they believe in their abilities to attain their goals.

Learn to Think Like a Top Producer

My long-term goal for you is to teach you how to *think*. I want you to understand the principles in creating a prioritized, successful plan. I want you to implement this plan until you become what some people call an "unconscious competent." Then, no matter the market, you will have the plan and the skills to earn as much money as you want.

Big Idea: Doing this plan for four weeks will teach you how to think like a top producer for life.

■ When and How to Use This Program

When to Start the Plan

Start the plan your first day in the business! Brokers: give this to your new agents during their orientation process. Ask them to read Units 1–3. Then, meet with the agents to start week one of the start-up plan (see Unit 4) within their first week in the business. Why? The new agents expect to make a sale their first month in the business!

Big Idea: Start using this plan your first week in the business.

How This Resource Is Organized

The following table shows a clear idea of how this resource is organized:

How Up and Running Is Organized

Overview	Units 1, 2, 3
Four-Week Plan	Units 4, 5, 6, 7
Training	Units 8, 9, 10
Completed Plan	Unit 11
Forms and Assignments	Unit 12
Sample Letter/Scripts	Unit 13
References and Resources	Unit 14

Overview

Units 1–3. In the first unit of this book, we investigate the trends you need to recognize as you start your business. Then, in Unit 2, I explain the six principles of a high-producing business. This is a very important unit. I want you to know the "why" of your business start-up plan. I'm going to let you in on a secret: this start-up plan isn't just to get you through your first four weeks. It is to set the priorities of your business *forever*. In Unit 3, I prepare you to start your plan, explain the manager's role, and give you an overview of your first four weeks. Read these units right after you finish your orientation with your office so you'll be set to start your week one action plan.

The Four-Week Plan

Units 4–7. Your actual four-week prioritized start-up plan starts with Unit 4, which is your plan for your first week. Unit 5 is your plan for week two. Unit 6 is your plan for week three, and Unit 7 is your plan for week four. This isn't just a book. This is literally your business start-up plan. I didn't write this to give you *ideas* about how to start your business. This is the specific, prioritized, proven action plan for you to dive into and complete each week. This is the action plan your coach will hold you accountable to. This is the action plan that will get you business as fast as you want it! Start your week one action plan in your first week in the business so you'll get a sale fast.

Big Idea: Most people would call this business start-up plan a business plan for *seasoned* agents!

Training: Sales Skills and Marketing Plan

Units 8–10. In Unit 8, I teach you how to contact the four types of lead-generating sources in *Up and Running in 30 Days*. In Unit 9, I show you how to create a marketing plan and a promotional tool to stay in touch for as long as it takes. In Unit 10, we explore the seven critical sales skills that are extremely important for you to master right now! Armed with the sales skills and marketing strategies, along with your lead-generating action plan, you are as educated and trained as many agents in their fifth year in the business in these areas. In addition, you know the priorities of a very successful business, and you've been implementing them automatically every week—because this four-week plan is designed using those priorities and principles. You automatically start thinking like a top producer. These are your resources. Remember, they aren't in the four-week plan because I don't want to clutter up your "forest" with too many trees!

Resources: Sample Plan, Forms, Weekly Action Plans, Scripts, Letters, and Processes

Units 11–13. Here are the *Up and Running* structured forms, scripts, and letters you need to make, implement, and track your plan. I've even included a sample start-up plan for you, along with a sample marketing plan, so you can see how all the pieces of the puzzle fit. These are more training resources for you.

References and Resources

Unit 14. In the References and Resources unit, I have listed various support tools that are appropriate for you to use in your first few months in real estate. They include sources for statistics, marketing, websites, and software. I've provided information about my training and coaching tools for agents and managers as a further support to you. I realize I can't put everything you need to know in one book, and it wouldn't be organized properly to best train you. (Let's take it one step at a time!) So, when you want to dig deep to create complete systems, when you want to train yourself at a higher level to list and sell, look to those specific resources. To keep the text clean and clear, most of the time I will simply point you to references at the appropriate areas in the text by saying, "See the References and Resources unit."

Symbols to Focus Your Attention

I've added more ways to help you focus on what's important:

Big Idea

Caution

Manager's Tip

You've already seen Big Ideas. They're here to draw your attention to major points. You get so much information that I know is very difficult to prioritize. Here's my attempt to help you do so. I've added the caution symbol to provide clarity on the reasons new agents fail. The concepts and skills I'm giving you here aren't just nice to know and do—they're *need* to know and do for you to be successful fast. I've left all the other stuff out! Finally, I've provided tips to managers to use this program, indicated by the Manager's Tip symbol.

How to Use This Resource

1. Read the first three units as soon as you get the book in order to get an overview of the principles and structure. If you're a new agent, you'll want to get these chapters read in your first three days in the business. In Unit 3, I have a list of "get ready to go" materials. Gather them quickly so you're ready to start your four-week plan. (See your manager to refine this list so it's pertinent to your area and your practice.)

2. Start the four-week plan (Units 4–7). Remember, since this is literally your start-up plan, you'll want to start the plan your first week in the business. As you proceed in your plan, the week's assignments will refer to the sales skills you'll need to master as you carry out that week's plan. The explanation of the sales skills, marketing plan, and promotional tools are in Units 8–10.

■ A Perspective about Training Programs and Start-Up Plans

A new agent doesn't have the perspective to make judgments about the quality of her training program or the quality of the start-up plan she is given. In fact, most new agents think all training is the same and that going to the company training program will ensure their success. Neither assumption is true. In addition, new agents think any plan of action given to them by their managers is as good as the next one. That's not true either. In this unit, I'll provide you some perspectives about what training can do for you, and what you shouldn't expect it to do. I'll also provide you some ammunition to judge the effectiveness of any start-up plan you're given. As a lifelong performer and coach, I know that the performance models that you're given, and that you follow, predict the kind of performance you give.

The Limitations of Training Programs

I hope your company has a great training program. However, it won't be enough to ensure your success without your implementation of the business start-up plan for these reasons:

- Training programs tell or show you the *how*. They don't provide a directive performance plan and hold you accountable to it over a period of time so you get your priorities straight. That's coaching, and it must be done by your manager or an outside coach.
- Most company training programs are focused on the technical aspects of real estate (how to write a purchase and sale agreement, all about financing, and so on).
- Most training programs do not teach *sales*. Or, if they do, they don't teach sales using the facilitation skills required to ensure you master the sales skills you need to succeed (role-playing countering objections, role-playing giving a listing presentation, etc.). You may conclude that hearing someone tell you how to do a listing presentation, or seeing someone do one, gives you everything you need to make a great presentation yourself. Only role-play, coaching, and performance evaluation will make you a great salesperson.

In fact, a recent survey of hundreds of brokers and agents from Inman Select (see References and Resources) said that, although some large franchises and boutique companies' training programs were highly rated, it's not enough to ensure success. Other support systems, mainly coaching and mentoring, were deemed as needed to ensure the new agent transferred the knowledge and skills gained in class to real life.

A Big Training Manual: Does It Equate to Success?

You've finished your training program. You have a huge training manual. Now, what do you do? You know a lot of things, and you have a lot of information in that training manual. But, without *Up and Running*, you still don't know what to do on Monday. I learned how new agents get the wrong idea about selling real estate firsthand. As a manager, I sent my new agents to the five-day company training program. When my new agents came back, they would ask, "Now, what do I do?" I would get out *Up and Running*, which I had introduced to them in their interview, and remind them that this is a business plan—a performance plan for real life. Sometimes I wished I just had not let them go to training because they came out of training thinking it was *optional* to start the *Up and Running* plan! Why?

They thought information was all they needed to succeed. They didn't have to actually take any actions!

I told you I would include advice from very successful newer agents. Here's a quote from Kyle Kovats, who is an inductee of the National Association of REALTORS® 2016 Class of 30 Under 30, a national group of agents who are under 30 and very successful in the business.

About training, Kyle advises: "Find a broker who has a comprehensive training program. Ask if you can speak with agents who have gone through it to get the agents' perspective on whether it was helpful."

Critical Analysis: How Good Is That Start-Up Plan?

You know what your training will do for you. So I hope you are convinced you also need to implement a business start-up plan to put all that information into perspective. But watch out—there are more poor ones than good ones out there. As a Certified Real Estate Brokerage Manager (CRB) instructor for 12 years, I taught thousands of owners and managers nationally. I saw plenty of poor plans that managers shared with me. (These were the plans they were giving their agents, too.) Here are some commonalities of them:

- They are laundry lists of busywork activities interspersed with activities that actually make you money, so the agent doesn't get any evaluative perspective to self-manage.
- They *do not* prioritize lead-generating activities, so the agent thinks all types of lead generation have equal payoffs.
- They *do not* have methods of setting goals, keeping track of results, and analyzing results to make changes quickly. (*Up and Running* provides sales ratios so you learn how many specific actions it takes to get the results you want.)
- They *do* incorrectly prioritize actions. For example, as a high priority, they direct the new agent to see all the inventory before doing anything else. The rationale is that it's very important to see all the inventory to build a knowledge base. It is important, but only as it relates to working with buyers and sellers. (It's the means, not the end.) But new agents don't want to do the high-rejection, high-risk activities such as talking to people. So they gladly see all the inventory until it becomes their job descriptions!
- They *do* include plenty of busywork as equal priority to lead generating—such as a broker having an agent visit a title company to learn how it operates. This keeps the agent busy and out of the broker's hair! Also, the new agent loves the broker for a while because the broker isn't asking the new agent to do those high-rejection activities—those activities that lead to a sale!

The bottom line is no would-be-successful agent in his right mind would continue doing this type of plan any longer than he had to because the successful agent recognizes the plan is a poor one.

Big Idea: Be critical before you commit to any start-up plan. It is prioritizing your mind! The start-up plan you may love because it keeps you out of sales activities isn't the plan that is going to love you back (get you the sales you want). What you do every day becomes your job description.

An Effective Start-Up Plan

The following are the seven attributes of an effective business start-up plan:

1. Does not give equal weight to all activities
2. Provides an organized activities schedule with certain activities prioritized first because they lead to a sale (in *Up and Running*, these are called business-producing activities)
3. Includes an organized activities schedule with certain activities prioritized second—and explaining why (In *Up and Running*, these are called business-supporting activities)
4. Provides a road map for a continuing plan
5. Builds in the *why* of the plan structure, so you learn to self-manage
6. Has a method to measure and make adjustments in your plan as you progress
7. Has a coaching component, so someone can coach you effectively to the plan

Business-Producing Activities Get Highest Priority

Your business actions are either:

- Business-producing activities—highest priority
- Business-supporting activities—lower priority

I have to admit that many of the concepts I created in *Up and Running* resulted from my seeing agents fail again and again. One of the ways they failed was that they couldn't differentiate the value of the activities they would complete in a business day. Because they naturally wanted to avoid rejection, they chose to do the low-rejection activities they felt comfortable completing—which didn't lead them to a sale! So, to help "train their minds," I separated those business activities into two categories:

- Business-producing
- Business-supporting

The activities that are highest in priority are those that result in a sale or listing sold. Why? Because those are the only two ways you get a check! These activities are specifically lead generation, presenting and showing, and closing.

These activities, which top agents call "dollar-productive activities," are listed and performed first in your *Up and Running* plan. When I began selling real estate, one of the best agents in the company told me to write at the top of my daily plan, "How will I make money today?" That was good advice. It pays to develop that success habit that all top producers have.

Business-Supporting Activities Get Lower Priority

Activities that are not directly lead generating, presenting and showing, or closing are termed *business-supporting activities*. As you may have guessed, low-producing agents complete a variety of business-supporting activities. (They conveniently run out of time before they can begin lead generating!) *Up and Running* is structured not to let you fall into that bad habit. As you follow the guidelines in *Up and Running*, you will learn to create your daily plan consciously, recognizing the value of your activities.

Don't take my word for it that clearly prioritizing your activities as business-producing or business-supporting is key to success. Hear it from Gary Richter, who used *Up and Running in 30 Days* to start his career. He says his prioritizations are a big reason he's succeeding now: "I am cognizant of my daily activities and recognized them as either business producing or business supporting. I spend the majority of my time on business-producing activities."

And, Diane Honeycutt states, "Take the advice in this plan and be sure you're not a 'secret agent'! Develop a work plan and stick to it."

Big Idea: Schedule and perform business-producing activities first.

Building Success Habits from Day One

The best business-producing plan teaches you to think like a top producer and helps you set the pace for your career. *Up and Running* meets these goals by offering the following:

- The business-producing plan followed by top agents
- The concepts behind the plan, so you can adapt it to meet your needs
- Time management tools, so you can self-manage your time and activities
- A specific plan for your first four weeks in real estate, so you can't get off track
- The support and technical activities you should be doing your first four weeks in real estate
- The sales skills and sales calls, including specific scripts, you need to master to complete the business-producing activities in *Up and Running*
- Advice for your manager or coach, to coach you to the plan

Your Most Important "Success" Ingredient: Accountability

You've heard it before. Businesspeople make fancy, multipage, even excellent business plans and then fail. Why? Because making the plan doesn't ensure success. *Doing* the plan does. (You wouldn't expect that if you studied the life of Mozart you could automatically play a Mozart sonata, would you?)

Big Idea: No success is realized without action.

If action brings about success, why don't people get into action? Because it's human nature not to! So, what is the missing ingredient you need—besides a great start-up plan and action-oriented training—so you have the skills to implement the plan? You need someone to be accountable to. Study after study shows that we attain our goals when we are regularly accountable to someone in the short term. That's because we human beings tend to work on time frames and schedules. (Do you really get your taxes done by April 15 because you love doing them?) Those studies prove we work best on deadlines. We work best when we have a heavy workload. We work best when we have high expectations of ourselves, and we have someone—our coach—who shares those high expectations. (I know this from being a pianist from age four and having the privilege of being taught by exceptional piano coaches.)

Big Idea: People succeed not because they have a plan. They succeed because they get into action and are accountable to the plan.

Keeping priorities straight without a coach is very difficult to do. I know what you're going to tell me. You're goal-oriented. You're a self-starter. You don't need a coach. That's what most new agents say, and over 50% of them fail their first year in the business! Unless you have already attained high performance in music, sports, and the like, how would you realize that you can't achieve those high levels of performance without a coach?

Big Idea: The habits you form your first month in the business greatly influence your career success—forever.

Most agents have never been in a field that requires such a high degree of self-direction and the mastery of many skills to succeed, so they don't know how easy it will be to get priorities all backwards! They also don't realize how difficult it is to change a bad habit. If you want to be a great pianist, you'd find a great teacher, wouldn't you? So, look at starting your real estate career just like you would look at becoming a great pianist or golfer. You need someone to be accountable to. You need a trained, committed coach so you have deadlines, expectations, someone to help you keep those priorities straight, and someone cheerleading and believing in you.

Big Idea: No one succeeds alone.

■ Summary: The Full Scope of *Up and Running*

Up and Running in 30 Days offers you a clear, concise start-up plan built on the six foundational structures conceived by me. It provides the game plan coaches must have in place to coach you to success. It is also built to protect you from failure. It provides you the why, how, how much, and what answers you need to get into action quickly and with confidence.

- **Why.** In *Up and Running*, you get the *why*. You'll be able to discriminate between effective and ineffective plans and actions long after you're not following the *Up and Running* plan to the letter. You've been given the gift of the tools you need to self-manage your career—forever.
- **How.** In *Up and Running*, you get the *how*. *Up and Running* explains critical sales skills and sales calls so you can find a partner and practice until you have mastered these skills.
- **How much.** *Up and Running* shows you exactly how to create sales by the numbers, teaching you to measure success and providing reassurance that you are on target.
- **What.** In *Up and Running*, you get the *what*—what to do each day.

What's next: read Units 1–3 so you have the background to start your four-week plan to success. Prepare to start your four-week plan *now*, so you get into the habits of success. Here's to a thriving career launch!

Real Estate Trends that Mean the Most to You

As I write this fifth edition, we're experiencing a very strong real estate market in most of the United States. I've identified ten major trends that are dramatically impacting real estate sales and will, in turn, dramatically impact how you are going to sell real estate. The reason I've included this unit is because you are going to go into an office that may have many seasoned agents. These agents are influential. They will speak with authority to you. However, I want you to realize that they are speaking to you from a "historical" perspective (e.g., less than 25% of agents have a database or contact management system. That's pretty historical—or old school!). Although I want you to respect the seasoned agent's perspective, you are not seasoned. You are launching your career. You may need to do things differently. You will want to launch your business for the future, not the past! In this unit, I'll give you advice on how to launch your business so you can take advantage of these trends instead of letting them take advantage of you—or discounting the need to plan with these trends in mind.

Big Idea: Launch your business for future success.

These ten trends are as follows:

1. Evolving company economic models (various methods of how you'll get paid)
2. The globalization of real estate and what it means to you, the residential specialist
3. Lead generation is still king
4. Systematizing your business with technology (what you do and don't need to succeed)

Ten Trends That Affect Your Business

1. Evolving company economic models
2. The globalization of real estate
3. Lead generation is still king
4. Systematizing your business with technology
5. Social media as a marketing tool
6. Segmentation of the buying population
7. The advantage of a coach
8. Shrinking commissions
9. Consumers choosing agents differently
10. Advantages and disadvantages of teams

5. Social media as a networking and marketing tool (how much effort and time should you spend)
6. The segmentation of the buying population—how to think about real estate as target markets (how you must niche your business)
7. The advantage of a coach (why more agents are seeking coaches, and what you should watch for)
8. Shrinking commissions (what you must do to gain the commissions you want to charge)
9. Consumers choosing agents differently (what you must manage)
10. Advantages and disadvantages of teams (is joining a team in your best interest?)

Big Idea: Respect a historical perspective, but plan your business to thrive today and compete for the future.

These trends have permanently affected real estate sales; to be successful in the field you must learn to recognize them—and embrace them in your practice. In this unit, I've noted the positives in the trend and the "watch out for" aspects of that trend. I'm not endorsing any particular company, concept, or practice. I want to provide you with the critical analysis you need to make your own best decision about how to do your business.

■ Trend One: Still-Evolving Company Economic Models

This first trend addresses how and what you get paid. When I started in real estate over three decades ago, there was basically one company economic model. Very simply stated, it was this: a person owned a real estate company. We agents worked for that real estate company. For our work, the owner paid us 50% of the commissions. It was our one source of revenue from the company.

Over these past 30+ years, both variations on that theme and other types of economic models have emerged from that model. One of the most important decisions you'll make is to decide which model fits you. I'll give you a short description of these models with the pros and cons of each.

The traditional split fee model. This model is a variation of the 50/50 commission-splitting model under which I worked. Today, companies using this model generally have a sliding commission split. That is, the more you earn, the more of the total commission you are paid. These plans can get quite complex, so be sure you understand the details of this type of plan.
   ■ **Positives:** Generally, the kind of company that collects relatively more of the commissions offers more service and support to its agents. It has spent many dollars and many years creating a solid company name. For the new agent, these can be very important. To

get your money's worth, take full advantage of the company programs, such as training, coaching, and marketing.

- **Watch out for:** Unfortunately, some new agents assume (or are even told) that the company will be responsible for their successes. That's just not true. If it were, then all new agents with a high support company would reach their goals, and no one would fail. What is true is that you, as a new agent, must go out and generate your own leads, no matter the company structure. You may be given some leads from company sources, so you must know what you may be charged for a company lead.

The 100-percent model. About 30 years ago, another economic model emerged in real estate—the 100-percent concept. In this model, agents keep 100 percent of the commissions they earn while paying a desk fee. This desk fee varies from a few hundred to a few thousand dollars a month, depending on the company. (A variation on this theme is a charge for each transaction. Sometimes a transaction charge is coupled with a desk fee, too.) This model was designed for experienced agents who already know how to run their businesses and don't need many company support services, such as training, coaching, or marketing. Today, many 100-percent companies do not allow the new agent to start at 100 percent because they offer additional training and coaching services to the new agent. These companies have learned that new agents need a high level of support to succeed. From an organizational standpoint, these companies are acting more like the traditional model, while keeping their independent instincts.

- **Positives:** New agents are drawn to the independent model because they get to keep 100 percent of the commissions. That looks great to the new agent who is spending a lot more money in the first few months than she budgeted! Having to generate their own leads also forces new agents to be independent, developing the very business habits taught in *Up and Running*.
- **Watch out for:** 100-percent companies assume that an agent has the business skills to run her own business without much support or training. If you're a new agent, that may not apply. Also, there's very little coaching or mentoring in the pure 100-percent model, simply because there is no company dollar to pay for those services. In addition, check out the other fees you will be paying because they could add up to about the same as if you were starting in the traditional model company.

The shared revenue model. This model emerged about 20 years ago, paralleling its introduction to business internationally. Here, the company shares additional revenues to commissions, which are usually paid in splits, just like the traditional split revenue company. These additional revenues may include profit-sharing, stock options, or company-dollar revenues (what the company gets when an agent sells a home). Generally, these revenues are shared as a reward for helping the company grow. To gain these additional revenues, agents must refer another agent to the company. That way, the company grows, creating more revenue and profit, which are then shared throughout the company with those who helped the company grow.

- **Positives:** Sharing revenues can create a sense of excitement, common focus, and camaraderie. This is motivating to a new agent, who can feel lost in a new business with little day-to-day imposed structure! If the new agent takes full advantage of the training and coaching offered, he can benefit from this environment.

- **Watch out for:** Getting carried away with the excitement! Too many times, agents have been sold on that extra revenue, as if no one had to sell anything to get rich. In addition, you don't just get that extra revenue for showing up. You get it for referring (mini-recruiting) agents to the company. Now you've got two lead-generating jobs: finding leads for your business and finding leads for your company (recruits). Before you commit to a shared revenue company, find out exactly what those revenues are and how you are going to earn them. Remember, you still have to start your business by generating your own leads!

Note: Frequently, companies come up with variations on each model. Be sure you understand your bottom line for each of these economic models (few agents understand the impact on their net).

Big Idea: How or how much the company pays you doesn't determine your success. Your actions do!

Choosing a Company to Support Your Career Goals

The main question all serious, determined new agents should ask their prospective company is: "How will this particular office, this particular manager, and this particular company help me achieve my career goals?" Too often, agents choose a company based on how much of the commission they will be allowed to keep. That's the last item a determined new agent should consider. I proved how faulty that logic was while managing a real estate office. I was competing with an office down the street from me (it was the same company, however). The other office charged the agent a desk fee of $1,000 per month. My office took a percentage of the commissions. The difference to a productive agent was about $10,000 a year (with my office charging that $10,000 more). So, why wouldn't any agent go to that other office? Because they made and kept more money with me. My statistics proved I helped new agents make four times more in their first year than did the less expensive office, where most of the new agents failed—quickly—because they did not receive direction or coaching. In addition, my statistics showed many more of my agents' listings sold, at higher prices and at higher commissions. If you want a successful real estate career, you will choose the company you feel is best suited to support your career goals.

Big Idea: What's important is what you keep, not what you make. And, as a new agent, it's very important that you make a sale quickly enough to stay motivated. Stack the deck in your favor!

■ Trend Two: The Globalization of Real Estate

You've read about foreign buyers buying in the United States. You've heard about international trade. But what does the globalization of real estate mean to you, the residential specialist? It means three things:

- U.S. franchises are aggressively pursuing expansion around the world. Several large franchises have international operations, and now the largest U.S. franchise is rapidly expanding in several countries. That can mean opportunities for investment in these companies, referrals, or both.
    - **Positives:** Investment and referral or sales opportunities
    - **Negatives:** As a new agent, you can be drawn into markets and areas where you don't have expertise. If you scatter yourself too thinly, you'll accomplish very little. Keep your focus in the markets where you can benefit over and over—before you expand your reach.
- Agents are roaming far and wide listing and selling. Multiple listing services (MLSs) have combined forces in many areas and allowed agents entry into homes that hadn't been available to them.
    - **Positives:** Agents can show buyers much wider areas. In some states, agents can list homes virtually anywhere in their state (at least in Washington, where I live).
    - **Negatives:** New agents can spend so much time learning each new area and comparables that the new agent can't become an expert at anything, and clients expect a certain level of expertise. New agents waste a lot of time unable to convert buyers to solds and getting listings sold because they don't have the expertise in that area. Also, as a new agent, you have to get name recognition to create your business. If you're always new in an area, you can't create that brand. Be careful not to spread yourself too thin!
- To become a global specialist, an agent needs specialized training. This goes both ways: An agent needs specific training to deal with each culture coming to the United States to buy, and an agent needs special training to work with agents in other countries or to work in another country.
    - **Positives:** Agents with language skills or those with a heritage from another country can specialize successfully with clients from that country.
    - **Negatives:** Agents can look at the international market with hungry eyes, thinking, "I want some of that money." They don't

realize that working with international clients requires special training, expertise, and consistent, tenacious work.

■ Trend Three: Lead Generation Is Still King

In their excellent book, *Game Plan: How Real Estate Professionals Can Thrive in an Uncertain Future*, authors Steve Murray and Ian Morris also name this trend as one of the top ten for the next five years. In my view, lead generation is always king (I can't see how it wouldn't continue to be a number one trend and priority). But Murray and Morris's point is that real estate professionals who want to be successful can't depend on leads just coming their way. Instead, they must actively go after them. That means creating systems, disciplines, priorities, and goals for capturing, working with, and keeping leads—forever. Here's what they say:

> . . . contact management, lead cultivation, and customer relationship management systems can and will play a huge role in determining which agents and companies are most successful.

A recent study by Active Rain (a popular real estate blog and tech information center), showed that agents who spent more money on customer relationship management (CRM) made significantly more money. It just makes sense. Agents who capture their leads via a database and then keep in touch with them via contact management software ensure they keep their names in front of their potential clients and are able to manage and help many more clients. Agents who try to organize their clients via pieces of scrap paper and remember to call them once in a while are woefully inadequate when it comes to staying in meaningful contact with their potential clients. Which agent would you prefer working with as a client? An agent who regularly contacted you and kept you abreast of the market, or one who either never called you or contacted you irregularly? In that Inman Select survey I mentioned earlier, *How to Fix New Agent Onboarding*, 47% of respondents stated lead generation is critical in initial training. And, they observed most new agents struggled with lead generation. That's why this *Up and Running* start-up plan is so important to follow to the letter!

Here's what Kyle Kovats said: "Get out there and just do it. Try different forms of prospecting and see what works. An ounce of action is more powerful than a ton of planning."

- **Positives:** For those of you who intend to be successful in sales, this trend should be a comfort. That means, if you invest in yourself, your work ethic, and your systems, you will be ahead of the pack. In *Up and Running in 30 Days*, I've laid out a plan of action for those of you who do intend this success. I'm not being facetious here. Some agents are surprised that, in fact, one must lead generate to be successful in this business.
- **Watch out for:** Companies or managers who tell you that leads will simply come to you—or that they will provide them to you. That

would include the following reactive (you sit and wait for the lead) lead-generating strategies:

- The traditional ones, such as open houses and floor time or relocation leads
- The technologically driven leads, such as software and programs that capture leads for you (they don't just sell themselves; you must have an effective capture, engagement, and follow-up program)

Unfortunately, interviewers use the "we will take care of you and give you leads" strategy to convince new agents to work with them. Then, after the agent is with that office, the agent learns there is no free lunch. Do I mean that you shouldn't accept various types of leads from others? No; just know that you will be paying for that lead, and consider this. If that lead source goes away, what are you left with? You are a first-day agent all over again! The *Up and Running* program will protect you from that, helping you build your own business so you always rely on yourself, not someone else.

Note: It's extremely important that you capture your leads in a database, or better yet, in a customer relationship management (CRM) program from your first week in the business. Why? Because you can't remember who those people are, and you certainly can't remember how and when to stay in touch with them! I've provided a list of various databases and CRMs in Unit 14: References and Resources. I'm not endorsing any one of them; I'm just providing you several to research and to choose. See your manager for recommendations.

When I asked those agent and team leader contributors what technology is important to incorporate, here's what they said:

"CRM and lead management tools"—Diane Honeycutt

"A really good and easy-to-use CRM"—Cerise Paton

"A good CRM"—Chris Cross

So, don't be like the majority of new agents (and even seasoned agents!): Start using a database or, better yet, a CRM your first week in the business.

Big Idea: To build a strong long-term business, order takers need not apply. To be successful, you must create relationship continuance, no matter your lead-generating sources.

■ Trend Four: Systematizing Your Business with Technology

To be more effective, you need to duplicate and delegate. The trend today is for agents to move faster and better by systematizing what they do and using technology to do it. The first step is to create checklists and processes for everything you do. These become your systems. For you new agents, take full advantage of every checklist and presentation your company offers—and those here in *Up and Running in 30 Days*. You'll save hundreds of hours of time and energy, because these resources are the result of experts' work. Your clients want to know that you have systems so that you provide a high quality of work every time.

Big Idea: It's much easier to refine a ready-made system than to create one from scratch.

Your second job is to find some technology to support these processes. Your company may have already done that research work for you. It is amazing to me the number of agents who do not take advantage of the technology their company has paid for in research, development, or partnering costs. For example, one large franchise had partnered with a lead followup company to ensure that their agents had a simple, effective method to follow their online leads. The franchise spent thousands of dollars and hours researching companies to ensure that they chose a company in the agents' best interests. They negotiated a great price for their agents, too. However, only about half of the agents in that franchise took advantage of the thousands upon thousands of dollars their company spent to create that partner agreement. I just can't see any reason not to take advantage of such a great opportunity—unless the agent just didn't care to be successful!

Look at the References and Resources unit. I've asked experts in the real estate field to name their favorite technology and I've provided their recommendations.

Gary Richter advises: "Get off your computer and go out into the areas. Focus on business-producing activities."

Big Idea: Use the technology and systems your company has invested in for your convenience.

- **Positives:** You're going into the industry as it has matured in its choices for needed technology. It will be easier for you to choose those that are important to your career success.
- **Watch out for:** Invest quickly enough, but don't invest in gimmicks. Also, don't let yourself think that if you have all the technology toys, you'll be successful.

Big Idea: Duplicate and delegate.

From Recipe Box to Software

As a new agent, I was handed a recipe card box and recipe cards and advised to keep all my prospect and client names on those cards. Organizing and tracking contacts with a system is one of those models I've been telling you about. Because my boss directed me to organize and keep track of my contacts, I started that lifelong habit. Although recipe and card files are passé, when you go into your office, you probably will still observe some agents trying to keep track of all the names they gather on scraps of paper and in card files—if they keep track of them at all! Why don't they? They haven't gotten into today's world of relationship marketing, or they didn't have a boss like mine, who directed me to start this way. They're still selling a new client every time. Or, as the owner of a very successful real estate company told me, some agents say they're in the business 20 years, but they're operating like they're in the business the first year twenty times!

When to Start Gathering Contacts into Your Database

Your first day in the business! Agents constantly tell me they'll put their contacts into a database later. So, these agents are unwittingly dropping thousands of dollars along the wayside because they just can't type a name into a blank! *Up and Running in 30 Days* has suggestions for various CRMs. It has assignments for populating your database each week. This is critically important for you to do if you intend to be successful!

According to Gary Richter, having a CRM is critical to his success: "For me, having a CRM to track my leads and contacts is absolutely critical. I live in that database daily."

Picture this: You meet a potential client, and a competing agent like Gary meets that potential client, too. The other agent consistently followed up and kept in touch; you didn't. Who would finally earn the commission from that client? Don't lose out because you are trying to operate without a CRM and have a haphazard follow-up marketing plan!

Big Idea: If every time you sell a home you sell it to a new customer, every year is your first year all over again!

Your Technology Needs

1. A laptop computer
2. Database of prospects, clients, and affiliates
3. Customer relationship management (CRM)
4. Online lead follow-up technology
5. Program to measure your business goals
6. Smartphone
7. Cloud-based file-storage service
8. Personal website and/or blog
9. Digital camera
10. Camcorder
11. Financial management with software

Use technology to support your dynamic business. The easiest way to organize the names of prospects and clients is on a computer. If you're not in the technology world now, jump in. You'll need technology to do a number of tasks (these are not my priorities, just a list):

1. Work from wherever you are with a **laptop** so you can find properties, do market analyses, and create presentations anywhere, anytime.
2. Organize your prospects, clients, and affiliates (such as mortgage lenders) in a **database** (if you're not extremely computer literate, start with Microsoft Outlook, which almost everyone already has on their computers).
3. Organize your follow-up programs for specific target markets via **customer relationship management** (CRM).
4. Capture and follow up on your online leads with **online lead follow-up technology** designed for that purpose.
5. Measure your **progress to your goals** with specific software.
6. Keep in contact with your customers via smartphone (you will find it truly amazing how few agents return phone calls).
7. Store your contacts (database), schedule, and so on using a cloud-based file storage service like Google Drive or Dropbox.
8. Create a personal **website**, **blog**, or both that promotes you and provides your prospects and clients access to information they value, such as updates on their property, marketing, or transaction progress.
9. Take pictures with a **digital camera** and add them to your website or your flyers.
10. Invest in a camcorder so you can promote yourself and your listings via video.
11. Budget for your expenses; track expenses; and create, implement, and analyze your profit and loss statements with **financial software** (such as QuickBooks, Quicken, or Mint).

See the References and Resources unit for more information about these valuable tools.

These include only a few of the technologies agents use in business. Before you buy anything, interview three technology-savvy, high-producing agents in your office and identify the technologies they consider important. Don't expect your real estate company to provide them, although seasoned agents within your organization may be willing to provide direction on the best use of technology. Also, see your manager for advice on the most up-to-date technology you need to perform.

Caveat: Don't run around buying every marketing program and tech tool from vendors. As Gary Richter advises, "There are many different programs and systems that vendors will try to sell to you as a new agent. Many overlap in capabilities. Pick one that works for you and stick with it."

That's why I've given you tech recommendations from agents I trust.

Your Technology Budget and Planner

Using technology to support your business has become a much higher priority than it was when I wrote earlier editions of this book a few years ago. So, I've created a Technology Budget and Planner for you to use to plan your technology acquisitions and implementation. The planner is in Unit 12 and is an assignment for you to complete during your first week in the business. Your assignment will be to decide which technology is most important to you now and when you're going to purchase and implement it. That way, you can progress in your technology plan every week during *Up and Running*.

Here are suggestions for the technology needed by new agents and a couple of very helpful programs to use from technology expert John Mayfield:

- A portable scanner(HP 1000 mobile scanner is an example) is a must.
- A good printer with duplex capability allows for printing just-sold and listed postcards.
- A small video camera allows you to record testimonials, information about homes listed and the local area, and tips on buying and selling. Video blog everything! (See the References and Resources unit for various video blogging tools.)
- Google tools are free, and tools like Google Docs, Google Sync, Google Picasa, and Google Voice are especially helpful.
- Cloud sites like Dropbox or Google Drive allow you to store and share client files, listing presentations, photos, and more.

Big Idea: Invest *now* in the technology you need, not later.

By the way, I've included biographies and contact information about my tech advisors in the References and Resources unit.

People want to be sold homes by people, not by computers. Your biggest value is not just that you have information (so does the computer). You will develop judgment and priorities. These are your value to the client. That's true of the value of professionals in any field. Don't hide behind your computer learning new technologies. Don't think you're going to be successful because you know more about email than anyone else. And don't judge start-up plans such as *Up and Running* as less than complete because they don't include details on all the latest technology. What matters is that you stay with the start-up plan, adding your improvisations as you go.

Make a draft using your Technology Budget and Planner and see your manager. Your manager knows the programs that work and can help you decide on those you really need in order to run your business (and those you don't need now—or ever!)

Big Idea: Prioritize it right: Technology provides *support* for relationship marketing. See your manager for refinements to the technology list on page 10.

■ Trend Five: Social Media as a Networking and Marketing Tool

The average real estate agent is in his 50s. Social media has become a huge concern of real estate agents: how to use it and how much time to spend on it. In addition, results are difficult to measure. Agents are asking themselves, "Is the investment in time (and perhaps money) worth the results?"

As I prepare this fifth edition, I noticed that two social media and technology experts I referenced in the fourth edition are no longer specializing in tech talks. Why? I think it's because agents are more tech savvy, and tech is easier to use. (Although my observation is that less than 20% of agents regularly use a database or CRM!)

I'm going to simplify the mystery of social media. The key word here is *media*. What is media? Those are the marketing delivery methods marketers use to communicate their marketing messages. Traditional marketing medias include newspaper ads, television, and direct mail. Digital marketing tools include websites, social networks (e.g., LinkedIn, Facebook, YouTube, Twitter, Instagram), and email. Think of social media as several media choices you can use to promote yourself and your listings.

Just think of social media as another way to network. In fact, it's a method of social networking.

Do you have a marketing plan? If you're like most agents, you don't have a marketing plan as part of your business plan. That's why I've included one in *Up and Running in 30 Days*. When you create this marketing plan, you'll have many media choices to make. A good plan mixes traditional and digital methods. *Up and Running* will help you create your social media presence and integrate it into your marketing plan.

Using Social Media

1. Integrate it into your marketing plan
2. Restrict yourself to business communication
3. Remember your goal is to form warm relationships—in person (not distant relationships based on keyed-in words)

- **Positives:** Social media is either low cost or free. It allows us to communicate and stay in touch with those who like to follow us. It expands our choices of media for marketing.
- **Watch out for:** It's easy to spend too much time online. In fact, some types of agents would rather spend time on their smartphones or computers than go meet people. After all, it's safer. But, as you'll learn in *Up and Running*, successful sales consists of engaging people, earning their trust, and communicating "until they buy or die." High trust is earned face-to-face, not online.

Tip: In that Inman Select survey, respondents observed agents spending too little time on lead generation and too much time on marketing. Why? It's easy to spend time online or send out cards; it's more challenging to actually talk to people! (But, the payoff comes when you talk to people!)

Big Idea: Integrate social media into your business marketing plan, and choose your media wisely.

■ Trend Six: Segmentation of the Buying Population

As a new agent, I know you're just concerned about finding someone who wants to purchase or sell a home! Yet, let's think past that. There are now four distinct segmentations of buyers (meaning those who want to buy our services of buying or selling a home). As you think about these distinct groups, ask yourself, "How do I have to adjust my selling style, my technology, my communication, and my expectations for each of these distinct groups? Which groups will I naturally relate to?"

1. Traditionals—those older baby-boomers who have retired
2. Baby boomers—enjoying retirement or getting ready for it, these folks make up the second largest buying population and have the greatest assets
3. Gen X—these folks have purchased first homes, but because of the housing bust, haven't been able to move up
4. Millennials—(Gen Y) first-time homebuyers, typically looking for starter homes, condos, co-ops, and so on

In NAR's *Home Buyer and Seller Generational Trends Report 2016*, Gen Y (millennials) comprises the largest share of home buyers, at 35%. This trend will continue, as their large numbers combined with improving personal financial conditions will enable these buyers to move the market. Gen X has the largest share of sellers at 25%. Read this report to see buyer and selling habits of these various target (segmented) markets, and choose your markets carefully.

■ **Positives:** If you are able to adjust in the areas mentioned here, you can relate and sell to more people. To be successful, you must be flexible and sensitive to these differing needs and desires.

■ **Watch out for:** Don't try to lump all these needs into one. The average real estate agent is in his 50s; the average buyer is in his 30s. Also, minorities will account for many more clients in the future, yet minorities are a small part of the real estate community. In many areas, buyers are frequently more tech-savvy than agents (that's generally true in the Seattle area because of Microsoft® and related businesses). Also, agents tend to work the market as they've known it. They are relating to the past rather than accessing trends and working the market they're given. Be sure to stay updated on where the market is going (your manager is a great source of this information).

Big Idea: One size fits all is no longer applicable to real estate sales. Agents must specialize in each of the niches they want to serve.

■ Trend Seven: The Advantage of a Coach

Coaching is:

1. Directed
2. Regular
3. One-on-one
4. Planned communication
5. Focused on action

Coaching is *a directed, regular, one-on-one planned communication focused on action* in which the coach

- directs action following a particular agreed-on game plan (like *Up and Running*), and
- holds the person coached accountable to that particular agreed-on game plan.

Coaching is needed today because of the skill level required of an agent to be successful. In addition, it is difficult to find adequate skills training. As you will see when we talk about consumer demands and expectations in this unit, consumers are expecting and demanding much more than agents are delivering.

Think of coaching like a piano or golf lesson. You take a piano lesson because you want to play the piano. You play for your teacher and you practice outside class (your action).

Does everyone in real estate sales need a coach? My short answer: yes, but not for the reasons you may think. Often, new agents think they need a coach because they must have all the answers to succeed. They wrongly consider a coach an "answer man." These agents are correct in that they won't have all the answers—but no agent I have ever known failed from lack of answers. What agents do need to succeed is direction and focus. A coach can help an agent with direction—what to do daily, how to implement a plan, how to measure success, and how to stay focused on what's important.

In the Inman Select study, respondents said having a generous mentor or coach is very important to the new agent's success. (See *What They Don't Teach You in Pre-License School* for tips on how to choose a coach or mentor—and what to avoid.)

Big Idea: A coach's main function is to hold the agent accountable to his goals.

Big Idea: No one ever failed because she didn't *know* enough.

Choosing a Coach

There are three important points you should consider as you search for a coach:

1. The specific program should be highly organized and precisely outlined with checklists and systems. Ask, "What system are you going to use to coach me?" You need a specific plan because you are new. You have no history.

2. The specific program should be related to a game plan—a business start-up plan. Ask, "What game plan are you going to use?"
3. The coaches should be trained and coached themselves. Ask, "What's your coaching background, and what sales principles do you believe in?" For example, each of our coaches in the Carla Cross Coaching program has been trained by me and coached regularly by me.

    ■ **Positives:** Having a coach keeps you on track, motivated, and, ideally, inspired to reach your goals.
    ■ **Watch out for:** Your coach is trained and dedicated to your success, and is following a proven game plan (otherwise you'll be paying just to talk to someone every once in a while). You're probably saying, "I'm new. I can't afford a coach," but did you know that it's estimated 50% of new agents fail their first year in the business? So, is investing in a coach worth it to you to succeed? It may be that simple!

Note: See *Up and Running in Real Estate*, my online coaching and training program for new agents. It's *Up and Running in 30 Days* on steroids. It combines my start-up plan with a coaching component at a very affordable price.

■ Trend Eight: Shrinking Commissions

Commissions are going down and have been for the past several years. We've gone through a boom period of real estate, during which hundreds of thousands of new agents entered the business. Although some of them did quite well quickly, they may have not provided the level of customer service the consumer expected. Why? Because they were new. When the market is really great, agents don't have to offer exceptional service to make money! Then, as the market turned, many agents were caught with little expertise in foreclosures and short sales. Yet, they still tried to work that market. Client surveys showed a high level of dissatisfaction. No wonder many clients today don't want to pay many thousands of dollars for service they deemed inferior years ago.

Earning a generous commission. Don't just rely on a fast market to get you sales. Build your business with an eye to maintaining and growing it with valued customers. Remember, it costs six to nine times more to get a new customer than it costs to keep an old one. Your job is to find potential buyers, qualify them, sell to them, and then keep in contact with them regularly to show you care more about them than just their money. The consumer wants a predictable experience coupled with high trust. They want you to save them time, help them prioritize information, and share your judgment with them. That's what you'll get paid the big bucks for.

■ **Positives:** A shrinking commission means agents will have to provide true value-added service to be paid what they feel they are worth. As a new agent, you can start that way.

- **Watch out for:** Don't settle for cutting commissions because you don't know how you're worth a larger commission. In *Up and Running,* we help you provide dozens of pieces of evidence to buyers and sellers to show them why you're worth the commission you want to charge (and show you, too!).

Big Idea: Don't take for granted the fact that you are value-added. The consumer expects more than agents think. Be honest with yourself and work on yourself so that you're worth more than you charge.

■ Trend Nine: Consumers Choosing Agents Differently

Traditionally, consumers either stumbled upon an agent (e.g., going into an open house) or got a referral from a friend. Although that's still true, consumers have another powerful method to choose an agent: online agent reviews. Increasingly, consumers are looking at evaluations on sites such as Zillow, Trulia, realtor.com®, Yelp, or LinkedIn to find out what other clients thought about that agent. Take a look yourself. Some of the evaluations are wonderful. Some are stunningly awful. And all are very public! There are even specific agent-rating sites such as www.realestateratingz.com and www.incredibleagents.com. Bank of America and USAA are also getting into the game. You must work for long-term customer engagement and great ratings to sustain your real estate business. This will continue as a trend and, I believe, change the way consumers choose and keep their agents!

Big Idea: It costs six to nine times more to get a new client than to keep an existing client. Retention is king, and reputation is key.

- **Positives:** It will be great for those competent, caring agents who really take care of their clients. It is easier now for potential clients to get feedback from third-party sources, clients just like them.
- **Watch out for:** Doing a *next* kind of business, where you don't care what happens after the sale, may have negative repercussions. The client has recourse now, of the most expensive kind—a poor review!

Tip: Always use an after-sale survey to find out what your clients thought of your service. If you'd like a sample survey form, go to www.carlacross.com/contact or email me at carla@carlacross.com and request my survey form.

■ Trend Ten: The Advantages and Disadvantages of Teams

What are the benefits of joining a team? When you join a team, you affiliate yourself with a rainmaker agent, an agent who will deliver leads to you, for which you'll pay a portion of your commission. You're teaming up with that agent to do the work that the rainmaker agent doesn't have time to do. First, joining a team doesn't mean partnering—two agents working together. If you join a team, you are working for that rainmaker agent. Generally, agents who grow teams have been in the business at least a few years. They've developed a large business. To grow their businesses, they need to duplicate and delegate, so they hire assistants and buyers' agents—agents who work with buyers who the rainmaker agent has generated. Many times, they hire new agents and train them in their methods.

How Joining a Team Can Help a New Agent

Joining a team helps agents obtain leads as they start up business. While agents earn the most in commission dollars when they generate their leads themselves, a new agent may need to pay for someone else's lead generation to begin to develop business. There is a downside to this approach, however. Agents can become complacent and sit and wait for leads. They won't generate—until they get tired of paying for someone else's leads.

- **Positives:** You may be able to jump-start your career with leads given to you.
- **Watch out for:** Be careful to choose a rainmaker who really has enough good leads to distribute to you. Sit in on her team meeting to see how she manages the team. Find out if and how the rainmaker will train you. Find out how much turnover there has been on the team. Find out whether you can sell and list houses outside the team and how much the rainmaker would charge you if you did. Read the contract the rainmaker asks you to sign and be sure you understand the consequences of your involvement.

Evaluate how good a leader that rainmaker is. Some rainmakers are great salespeople but lousy leaders, so their team never gels. Most team leaders ultimately expect their team members to generate their own leads, in addition to team leads. If you can't meet the rainmaker's expectations, you are terminated. Be willing and ready to take the responsibilities of team membership seriously.

Questions to Ask the Rainmaker

1. How many leads will I get per week?
2. How do you manage the team?
3. How will you train me?
4. How much turnover has the team had?
5. Can I sell homes from my own leads, and what will you charge me?
6. Do you expect me to generate my own leads? How many?

Big Idea: If they aren't your leads, you're starting the real estate business all over again when you leave the team.

■ Summary

Major Real Estate Trends that Mean the Most to You

The ten major trends discussed here have significance on your business as a new agent:

1. Company economic models are still evolving. No matter which model you choose, the lesson here is that you must generate your own leads to ensure that you create your own real estate business at the income level you desire. Be aware, too, that there is no free lunch. Figure out whether you want the benefits of a specific company structure before you commit.

2. Real estate is local but also global. Real estate franchises are playing an increasingly large role internationally. This means the real estate agent can more easily buy and sell homes to international clients. MLSs have combined forces so an agent can roam far and wide selling homes. These trends have advantages for agents but can lead to wasting time and lack of focus.

3. Lead generation is still king. Be sure you understand your responsibilities to generate leads and are willing to do the business this way. In a fast market, you may sell a few homes as an "on accident" agent, but you can't sustain that when the market changes (and it always does). Organize and work your business for the long term, not just for the next sale.

4. You can systematize your business with technology. Too many agents are still doing business "by the seat of their pants." So it's not a business; it's not even a career; it's just a vocation. As a new agent, you must invest in technology to systematize your job so you can do it faster and better. You have a technology planner here to get the technology you need and budget for it. Be sure to review your technology plan with your manager.

5. You can leverage social media as a networking and marketing tool. Make social media a part of your media marketing arsenal. Discipline yourself to concentrate on social media for only a small portion of your day—and be sure it's business, not pleasure.

6. Today's real estate buyers can be segmented in terms of their needs and interests. Educate yourself to handle specific buyer niches. Decide which of these four client segments you're comfortable with. Develop skills and technology to match the needs of your chosen buyer segment(s).

7. Coaches offer a lot of advantages. More and more agents are seeking out independent coaches to fill in the gaps left by the constraints most companies and offices face (time, expertise, and money). Most important for new agents is to find a coach who can hold new agents accountable to their business start-up plan. Over 50% of new agents don't make it through their first year. Be part of the half that does!

8. Agents compete for shrinking commissions. Consumer demand for better service, coupled with less service provided by generous-commissioned agents, has pushed commissions downward. To earn the commissions they are worth, new agents must get really good really fast.

9. Consumers choose agents differently. Monitor your online evaluations; decide to work for repeat and return business; accept that exceptional customer service is worth more to you than one quick sale.

10. Teams have advantages and disadvantages. Joining a team within an office is a choice that may be good for the new agent because the new agent will receive leads from the rainmaker, plus high direction and structure. However, there is a high cost for those leads, which must be weighed carefully by the new agent. Not only that, when you're accepting someone else's leads, you're not creating a business for yourself. If your lead source leaves you, you're a new agent again!

With that background, you're ready to learn the six principles of a high-producing business. Armed with the *why* of prioritizing your start-up plan in the manner described in *Up and Running,* we know you'll not only implement this plan correctly, you'll have the invaluable skills to continue these principles throughout your career.

Manager's Tip: Be sure to get the *Swanepoel Trends Report* by Stefan Swanepoel each year. You can see it at www.retrends.com. I also recommend the book *Game Plan,* by Morris and Murray, where these industry experts analyze what they believe are the ten trends for the coming five years.

The Six Principles of a High-Producing Business

✓ **Manager's Tip:** Ask the agent to read the Introduction and Units 1–3 the first week in the business, while the agent is completing your orientation process.

Too often new agents receive some sort of activity plan from their managers without an explanation of the principles behind the plan—that is, the why. They just get a list of activities and are told, "Do these things." As soon as they get them done, they think they're off the hook! They don't see that activity plan as a basis for their long-term business habits. *Up and Running* isn't just an activity plan. It's a prioritization of the actions you need to take every day of your career life. It is your business plan for your start-up.

The Six Principles of a High-Producing Business

1. Start the business cycle by talking to people
2. Stay on the business path
3. Prioritize your activities
4. Lead generate like the pros
5. Work the numbers
6. Be accountable to your plan

✳ **Big Idea:** The *Up and Running* concepts are business-planning priorities for all your career life.

I'm afraid if you don't know the why, you may ignore or change some of the parts of my *Up and Running* plan. My friends' child constantly asked, "How come?" (Only it came out of his four-year-old mouth as "How tum?") Even then, he wanted to know why. As an adult, you also deserve to know why each part of this plan has been created. You need the *why* so you can learn to self-manage.

The six principles in the box to the left form the foundation of the whys—the recommendations and priorities in *Up and Running*. In this unit, I'm also going to give you the other side of the coin: the major reasons new agents fail. I told you I would protect you from failure, and I will! When you see this symbol, you'll recognize when to use caution.

!

■ Principle One: Start the Business Cycle by Talking to People

The most important principle in the *Up and Running* business start-up plan is this: your business starts when you start talking to people.

> . . .the only message that needs to be stressed is to prospect a major portion of your day. Get the scripts and dialogues needed to cold-call, door knock, work expireds and FSBOs. Do the work, and you'll become a great, consistently high-producing agent.
> —Rick Franz, top-producing agent

To be successful quickly, the most important activity you need to accomplish every day—at least four hours a day—is to talk to people to get a lead. This activity starts the business cycle (see Figure 2.1).

FIGURE 2.1   The Business Cycle

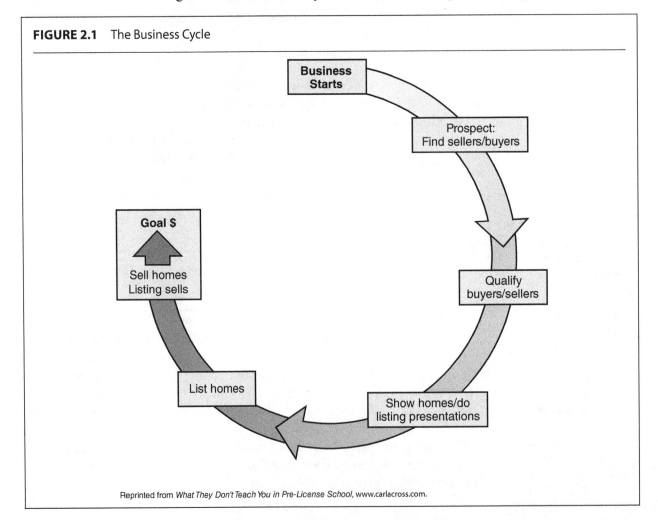

Reprinted from *What They Don't Teach You in Pre-License School*, www.carlacross.com.

The more often you talk to people, the greater your chances to continue the business cycle, to work with and sell someone a property. *Up and Running* will ensure that you spend enough time in the sales cycle to reach your monetary expectations.

Big Idea: The business starts when you start talking to people.

Caution: The biggest reason new agents fail is that they don't contact enough people frequently (too little lead generation—not only my opinion but the observation of hundreds of brokers and agents, as stated in the Inman Select Survey, *How to Fix New Agent Onboarding*).

■ Principle Two: Stay on the Business Path

> If you don't prospect, the potential for failing in this business greatly increases. I wish I knew how to tell other agents, in a nice way, to get the hell out of my way when they try to discourage me from proactive prospecting!
>
> —Brian Orvis, top-producing agent in his first year

Your objective in real estate sales is to get on the business path and to stay on it every day until you get to the end of the road—a sale or a listing sold. Figure 2.2 illustrates the business path. It's simply made up of the activities that lead to a sale!

Seems simple, doesn't it? However, many obstacles get in the way—anxiety over making sales calls, fear of not knowing enough, dread of rejection, need for more organization, quest for more knowledge—the list is endless. *Up and Running* will help you stay on the business path, while filling some of those other needs in the correct relationship to your mission—to sell real estate.

Caution: New agents fail because they let fear create their "safe" version of the start-up plan (doing lots of business-supporting activities and very few business-producing activities).

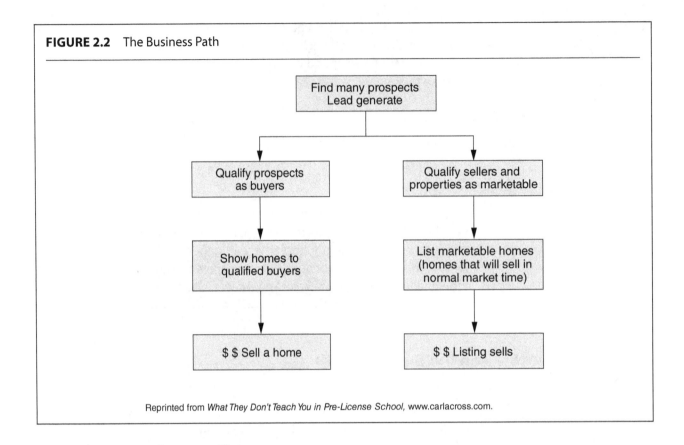

FIGURE 2.2   The Business Path

Reprinted from *What They Don't Teach You in Pre-License School*, www.carlacross.com.

■ Principle Three: Prioritize Your Activities

What I would have given to have had a job description indicating a plan of attack. For example, this is how your day must be scheduled: prospecting three hours, follow-up, clerical, etc.

—Rick Franz, now a very successful agent, formerly in hotel management

It's all here, Rick, in *Up and Running*—the hours, the prioritizations, and the concepts behind the schedule. First and foremost, you must spend at least four hours a day starting the sales cycle by lead generating. Where do the other activities fit in? To teach the habits of successful agents, this system has been prioritized for you. As you plan each day, you'll see that your activities fall under two categories:

1. *Business Producing* (activities in the sales cycle)
   - Lead generating
   - Following up on leads
   - Qualifying buyers
   - Showing homes to qualified prospects
   - Writing and presenting offers to purchase
   - Giving listing presentations to qualified sellers
   - Listing marketable properties
   - Presenting offers to your seller clients, either via phone or in person, and explaining the pros and cons

> **Big Idea:** Lead generation starts your sales cycle.

2. *Business Supporting* (activities that support the sales activities)
   - Previewing properties
   - Following up on transactions, making flyers, etc. (marketing)
   - Sending out emails and mailings (this is not lead generating; it's supporting—marketing)
   - Talking to loan officers and title companies
   - Attending meetings
   - Furthering education
   - Website maintenance
   - Social media plan implementation (marketing)

> **Big Idea:** Learn fast to prioritize your activities as business producing or business supporting.

> **Caution:** New agents who fail think that any activity will get them a sale. (They're the ones in the office "playing computer" or sorting paper all the time.)

This list could be exhaustive. It's common for agents to hide out in support activities because they think they are not ready to talk to people. Watch out. This is a sign of creating the *wrong* activities in the business plan. These agents could end up becoming their own assistants—or someone else's!

According to the respondents in the Inman Select survey, new agents spent too much time on marketing and not enough time on lead generation.

> **Big Idea:** Actions don't have equal consequences.

How Should You Allocate Your Time?

The resources in *Up and Running* are arranged to help you keep these activities in the right priorities. I want to train your brain so you can prioritize for yourself long after you've passed your first few years in the business. Figure 2.3 illustrates a prototype schedule that shows how much time you should be spending on each category. Use this schedule to check against the actual plan you design each week. Also, on your weekly schedule, which you will start creating yourself in your week one plan, I have put a reminder of how many hours you should be spending on each category of activities. That way, you can check the "ideal" with your "real" each week. It's another time management tool to help you create the kind of time management habits you will carry with you throughout your career.

Big Idea: Lead generate in the morning as much as possible; you are fresh and there's no competition because the other agents are still in bed! Remember: the plan you use predicts the results you get.

■ Principle Four: Lead Generate Like the Pros

One of the foundations of *Up and Running* is the *30 Days to Dollars* prioritized lead-generating plan. This plan is built on the solid lead generating principles that make real estate superstars successful. It uses the same target markets (sources of business) and numbers that superstars rely on to build a professional career. To create a high-number, highly profitable career, superstars do the following:

- Secure at least 50% of their business from people they know (called referrals). In fact, NAR research indicates that 52% of all buyers are referred to an agent or used the agent previously. That's why I stress keeping in touch with people you know and your prior clients (you will have many prior clients who refer you if you follow *Up and Running*).
- Gain business by promoting themselves on their successes
- Create a lead-generating plan that meets their monetary goals
- Secure the majority of their business through proactive lead generation (they find people—they don't wait for people to come to them)

Gary Richter commented on what he would do differently, which could apply to most new agents: "Contact all of my sphere and ask for business." Gary admits he was reticent to ask them all for business. Aren't we all? From coaching thousands of new agents, I learned that asking your business contacts for referrals is more productive when you're new than asking for referrals or business from your close friends or relatives. (Maybe those friends and relatives are like mine were—they didn't think I'd stay in real estate sales and would return to a musical career.) It will take a while to convince friends and relatives you are serious and committed. That's why you create that marketing plan to constantly remind them you're a full-time, serious professional real estate salesperson. (See my marketing plan suggestions and planner templates later in this program.)

FIGURE 2.3 Prototype Weekly Schedule

Time Commitments: How to allocate your time to ensure quick success.

Activity	Daily	No./Week	Hours
Proactively lead generate	4 hours	5 days	20 minimum
Open house		Once a week	3–4
Floor time (if scheduled)		1 day	3
Business meeting	1 hour	Once a week	1
Office education	1 hour	1 day	1
Manager/agent coaching		Once a week	1/2
Previewing homes	2 hours*	5 days*	10

(*first month only to learn your inventory, then preview as needed)

Schedule

Mon.	8:00 – 8:45	Meet with manager if in a coaching relationship
		Paperwork/calls/emails/social media/answer online inquiries
	8:45 – 9:30	Business meeting (if scheduled in your office)
	9:30 – 12:30	New office listing tour
	12:30–1:30	Lunch
	1:30 – 5:30	Proactively lead generate (better in the morning if no other commitments)
Tues.	Day off—take it!!	
Wed.	8:00 – 9:00	Paperwork/emails/social media/answer online inquiries
	9:00 – 12:00	Proactively lead generate
	12:00 – 1:00	Lunch
	1:00 – 2:00	Lead generate
	2:00 – 4:00	Preview
	4:00 – 5:00	Paperwork/emails/social media/answer online inquiries
Thurs.	8:00 – 9:00	Paperwork/emails/social media/answer online inquiries
	9:00 – 11:00	Proactively lead generate
	11:00 – 1:00	Lunch
	1:00 – 3:00	Floor time/buyer tour
	3:00 – 5:00	Lead generate
Fri.	8:00 – 8:45	Paperwork/emails/social media/answer online inquiries
	8:45 – 9:30	Office class
	9:30 – 12:00	Lead generate
	12:00 – 1:00	Lunch
	1:00 – 3:00	Lead generate
	3:00 – 4:00	Office class
	7:00 – 8:00	Listing presentation
Sat.	9:00 – 12:00	Lead generate
	12:00 – 1:00	Lunch
	1:00 – 4:00	Listing presentation/buyer tour
	4:00 – 5:00	Paperwork/emails/social media/answer online inquiries
Sun.	12:00 – 2:00	Lead generate
	2:00 – 5:00	Open house or buyer tour
	5:00 – 6:00	Listing presentation
	7:00 – 8:00	Paperwork/emails/social media/answer online inquiries

Reprinted from *What They Don't Teach You in Pre-License School*, www.carlacross.com.

> **Big Idea:** (1) The *30 Days to Dollars* prioritized lead-generating plan is your sales-generating goldmine map. (2) Producers spend much more time each day lead generating than do non-producers.

But you're not a superstar yet. *30 Days to Dollars* takes the superstars' business principles and translates them to your situation:

- You should work your best source of prospects. At this point, you have no past customers. But you do have a great network of people you know. Start with them. (They are your "past client" category until you get a real "past client" category. Why? Because they already trust and like you!)
- Whenever possible, you should promote your success. Next, superstars create more success by promoting their success. If you are a new agent, find someone in your office who will let you promote yourself on her success: a new listing taken, a sale, a listing sold, an open house. This method is called *circle prospecting*. (Refer to Unit 8 for an explanation of this process.)
- You should choose lead generating methods that match your style. The *30 Days to Dollars* lead generating prioritized plan provides several methods for meeting prospects. But you can't reject all of them because you don't like any of them! Remember, it's a numbers game. (Refer to Unit 8 for more information on these methods.) During the program, just do the four-week plan so you'll have the experience of making several kinds of sales calls, and you'll have met lots of people!

30 Days to Dollars translates these concepts that successful agents use to create high-producing businesses to your situation so that you can create the same kind of career base quickly.

> **Caution:** New agents fail because they start with the hardest, most expensive, smallest-payoff lead-generating sources—which causes them to give up fast.

What about Cold-Calling?

Cold-calling means picking up the phone, dialing a stranger, and asking for a lead. Although cold-calling is the quickest way to get a lead if you're willing to make lots of sales calls, it isn't the most common way successful agents build their businesses. Why? The biggest reason is that real estate, over time, is a relationship continuance business. Agents just don't have the time and energy to get a new customer over and over. The second reason is that most successful agents are intuitive and emotional types. (See the References and Resources unit for more information.) They truly like people. They don't like to get a "no." They don't like the rejection they encounter making those hundreds of cold calls. They hate being rejected. They tend to get their feelings hurt! So, they avoid those situations where the likelihood of being rejected is high—situations like cold-calling.

Conversely, since they are intuitive and like to form and maintain relationships, they naturally enjoy working with those they know, and will work to maintain those relationships. The *30 Days to Dollars* plan, which does not include cold calls, is modeled after the *best sources* of business for the typical agent's behavioral profile. Part of the reason these sources are prioritized as best is that most real estate agents like to do them and become good at them. So, start with the best source of prospects—people who already know you. Remember, *the warmer the relationship, the better chance you have of getting a lead.*

What works. Too often, agents want someone to give them one lead-generating method that is guaranteed to work. However, what always works is the numbers. Not only that—as you start selling, you'll discover that you are naturally drawn to certain types of lead generating, while you are repelled by others. That's your behavioral profile speaking! That's why we use a behavioral profile in our coaching company—to help people discover their best sources of business and help them interact with people who have profiles that are different from theirs. In addition, relying on only one lead-generating method to pull you through even tough times is dangerous. Again—it's a numbers game!

The pros and cons of cold-calling. Cold-calling does provide more contacts in the least amount of time, but it also brings more rejections and tougher contacts to convert. So, if you run out of people to talk to in the target markets recommended in *30 Days to Dollars*, go ahead and make cold calls—to anyone—using any method you want.

A script for cold-calling. A sales skill called *craft a sales call script* is described in Unit 10. Using this technique, you can craft a sales call to any target market. If you want to cold-call in an area, just put together a script using this crafting technique. You will become a master cold caller because you not only have a script; you have the methodology behind the script. I've also put a script specifically designed for cold-calling in Unit 13 for you, so you can cold-call as you need to.

If you don't know anyone. If you are new to your area, you will need to start with colder calls. However, before you begin true cold-calling, take another look at the people you come in contact with weekly. Make a list of the service people you meet each week. Remember, every time you talk to someone, find out if he has a real estate need. These people are categorized in *30 Days to Dollars* as "people you know and meet"—and they are your best source of leads.

Look at cold-calling this way: it increases your repertoire. Being able to make several kinds of sales calls and mastering the sales skills in this program ensures that you have the repertoire.

But I don't wanna! Of course you don't want to do certain types of lead generating, but don't restrict yourself to only one type of lead generating unless it is paying off big from the beginning. Develop the "chops" so you have them when you need them. When I played piano bar to put myself through college and graduate school, I didn't want to play a lot of those old warhorse songs! But, the customers wanted to hear them—and I got tips when they heard what they wanted to hear! You know we all do things we don't love to do in our businesses. So, bite your tongue and master the lead-generating sales strategies!

Later in this unit, I'll explain the numbers game: how many lead-generating contacts you must make weekly to get the weekly appointments you need to sell the number of homes you want to sell in a year.

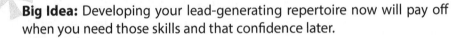

Big Idea: Developing your lead-generating repertoire now will pay off when you need those skills and that confidence later.

"It won't work for me in my area." If you find yourself saying that to an idea, an action, or a method I've given you in this resource, stop and ask yourself these questions:

- "Why am I resistant to this idea?"
- "How can I make this principle work for me?"
- "Is there something about my confidence level that's stopping me from taking this action?"
- "What am I trying to protect by being negative to this?"

In other words, don't throw the baby out with the bathwater! I am giving you the template, the process, the principles, the system, and the examples. I am giving you enough information for you to get started. You *can* improvise on this tune. The principles here are proven; this is a system. Use it as a basis to improvise.

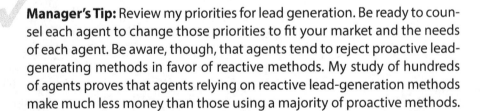

Manager's Tip: Review my priorities for lead generation. Be ready to counsel each agent to change those priorities to fit your market and the needs of each agent. Be aware, though, that agents tend to reject proactive lead-generating methods in favor of reactive methods. My study of hundreds of agents proves that agents relying on reactive lead-generation methods make much less money than those using a majority of proactive methods.

Complying with Do-Not-Call Legislation When Cold Calling

In 2003, President Bush signed into law federal do-not-call legislation, and real estate professionals are expected to comply with the provisions of the National Do Not Call Registry. Federal law requires that telemarketers and sellers, including real estate professionals who cold-call, search the National Do Not Call Registry at least every 31 days and remove the phone numbers of registered consumers from their call lists. Most real estate companies have adapted their practices and procedures regarding the scope of this law. Failure to comply with do-not-call legislation can result in fines up to $16,000, so it is important to check with your broker to stay updated on this law and its rules. Information is also available on the National Association of REALTORS® website (www.nar.realtor). A *Field Guide to Do Not Call and Do Not Fax Laws*, with multiple listed resources, is available to NAR members. With that amount of information available from a source that has been double-checked by your professional association's attorneys, you can see why I need not say more about it here!

Understanding the Habits of Online Buyers

The percentage of buyers who start their home search online has steadily increased over the years. Now, 42% of home buyers look online for properties for sale as their first step in the home buying process, while 14% of buyers first contact a real estate agent. Not only do online buyers start their home search process by researching via the internet; more and more buyers are finding the home they purchased online. According to a survey from the National Association of REALTORS®, 44% of buyers found their homes online, compared to only 8% in 2001. Websites were judged by buyers as the most useful information source during the home search process (82%).

For the majority of buyers, looking online at homes has replaced contacting a real estate agent as the buyer's first step in their home purchasing process. Because of this change, agents have had communication challenges in tracking and communicating over time with potential buyers—to turn those buyers from information junkies to trusting clients. That's why it's extremely important today that agents have effective websites and a seamless, continuous communication process. This should be facilitated by a good CRM. Unfortunately, the vast majority of agents have neither of these tools and lose a majority of their leads. That's why this edition of *Up and Running in 30 Days* has strong recommendations for website and CRM solutions. See the References and Resources unit for suggestions.

As you can see from these statistics, our mindset should be capture and keep, not meet and close. Unfortunately, most agents are still in the "next" communication mode. They meet someone and think that person will buy from them in the next 30 days. If that person doesn't buy, they drop the person and go on to the next. They have neither the system nor the technology backup to keep in contact with potential leads.

The interesting news about the online buyer. Once an online buyer finds an agent and starts looking at houses, he again acts differently from a traditional buyer. Look at this research:

- Online buyers take twice as long to search for homes compared to traditional buyers. According to the most recent survey from the NAR, overall, home buyers took 10 weeks to find the home of their choice. However, this varied between online and traditional buyers. Those who used the internet for research searched 10 weeks and looked at 10 homes. Those who did not use the internet searched only five weeks and visited five homes.

■ Buyers typically choose the agent referred to them by a friend, neighbor, or relative and don't generally shop agents. That's why it's so important that you have a capture and keep system to stay in touch.

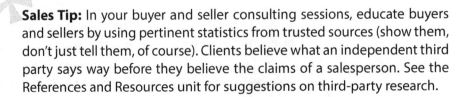

Sales Tip: In your buyer and seller consulting sessions, educate buyers and sellers by using pertinent statistics from trusted sources (show them, don't just tell them, of course). Clients believe what an independent third party says way before they believe the claims of a salesperson. See the References and Resources unit for suggestions on third-party research.

Today's Successful Agent Profile: Short-Term Lead Generator and Long-Term Communicator

New agents expect a sale quickly—quicker than the online buyer typically buys. So, you need to get into action quickly using the *30 Days to Dollars* prioritized lead-generating plan. But to get a bigger payoff from all that lead generating in the future, you must (1) capture all your leads in your database so you won't lose them, (2) apply a contact management system so you'll follow up on your leads, and (3) make a marketing plan for these leads and drive it with your contact management (what you'll do to contact them and when you'll do it).

The best business strategy for the future. The successful agent of tomorrow will create a marketing program to keep in touch until their contacts "buy or die" so that when online buyers are done with their research, the buyers and the agent will work exclusively together to make a quick buying decision.

Big Idea: Tenacity always wins. Stay with them until they buy or die.

Business planning tip: Use the marketing plan explained in Unit 9 to ensure you're not a "love 'em and leave 'em," short-term–thinking agent.

It's Still a Relationship Business

Relationship marketing creates the most business in the shortest amount of time with the least cost. In fact, relationship marketing has always been the method great salespeople use to create long-term business. Businesses internationally have discovered that it is the best way to market their businesses because it costs less and delivers better results.

An example of how companies have changed their strategy and their training is how car salespeople treat customers. A good car salesperson today actually keeps in touch with you after you have bought the car! Although that used to be rare, it's more common today because car company surveys have shown that people buy the same car again not because of mechanical service excellence but because they feel the people in the car dealership cared for them.

How many agents do you think keep in contact with the buyer and seller after the sale? Not many. In fact, a recent study showed that less than 40% of real estate agents ever contacted their buyers after closing! (The buyer thinks we took the money and ran. . . .) Many agents still think that their job is to find strangers, sell them something, and then move on to the next stranger. Remember, it's nine times more expensive to advertise to find strangers (e.g., by placing ads in newspapers) than it is to keep the old customer and get referrals.

More great advice from Kyle Kovats: "Be relentless. Follow up with handwritten letters rather than the generic form letters and cards most agents send people. Be unique."

Big Idea: Communicate regularly with your best source of business (your clients and your sphere of influence).

Create your marketing plan and systematize it. Don't think that you can keep your relationships by ignoring the people you have talked to. You must create a marketing plan to communicate with them regularly. One of your business-supporting assignments will be to create that marketing plan and do a marketing action weekly. In Unit 9, I'll give you information on how to create a marketing plan, along with a sample plan and a marketing planner that covers all the bases.

Use technology to systematize your marketing plan. After you've made your marketing plan, systematize it by putting it in your contact management system. Now the system will remind you when to implement the action you've planned.

Many companies will provide postcards and mailing services to keep in touch. See your manager or company catalog for lists of these companies and services. You can easily create a call or postcard program to let these people know you care about them. If you prefer creating a program yourself, see senior agents in your office. They can help you create simple postcards with current or sold listings. You can also send flyers or brochures of homes you've recently listed and sold. At first, your list will be small, so write a personal note on each mailing to let the buyers and sellers know you are thinking about them. Companies like the Personal Marketing Company (www.tpmco.com), QuantumDigital (www.quantumdigital.com), MyRealEstateTools (www.myrealestatetools.com

or www.crosscoachingtoolbox.com), Sendsations (www.sendsations.com), and ProspectsPLUS! (www.prospectsplus.com) all have affordable marketing programs that are turnkey. (See Unit 14, References and Resources, for more information.)

What Information Do You Need?

You will need the following information about your contacts:
- All of the person's contact data, including email and website information (it's especially important today to get email addresses so you can send updates and newsletters electronically)
- Personal preferences and personal information, such as birthdays, children's names, pets' names, and so on
- Information regarding each transaction

Real estate–specific CRMs already have these fields built into their programs. For a person new to real estate or databases, these customized databases are useful. The downside is that the real estate–specific programs are more expensive. (See more information on these programs in the references unit.)

Two other bonuses that real estate specific programs offer are
- letters for many contact occasions and
- marketing plans for specific target markets (identifiable groups of people with common needs), such as people selling their own homes (for-sale-by-owners) or people who have tried to sell their homes through real estate agents but failed (expired listings).

A fellow board member of a company that specializes in online real estate training—and a founder of the largest contact management software company for real estate professionals—tells me that agents who buy his programs use only a fraction of the features. He also knows a top-producing agent who closes about $20 million of properties a year and has been lauded for his innovative marketing programs. In fact, all this agent is doing is using the programs provided in his software! (If you decide to use one of these real estate–specific CRMs, take advantage of the marketing tools, including marketing plans, wording, and scripts they provide.)

As a new agent, unless you are very contact management–savvy and have been in sales before, I caution you against using a generic contact management program. Instead, buy or lease real estate–specific software and learn all the features. Use the letters and marketing programs in the software until you are comfortable customizing them or creating your own programs. Using these programs will be a self-training tool. Take advantage of the thousands of hours of expertise that went into creating those programs for real estate agents!

Big Idea: It's better to start with *any* database than with none. The potential clients you *don't* capture will cost you your success!

Big Idea: Get into the habit of "meet up, put them in your database, and contact them"—all within one day of meeting them, so you won't lose those precious contacts, and they won't forget you! They are your gold-mine! (And my informal surveys show less than 10% of first-year agents establish a database and use contact management—no wonder there's such a high failure rate for new agents!)

Lead Generation: *30 Days to Dollars* Prioritizes Your Best Sources

Lead-Generating Sources in Priority

1. People you know
2. Circle prospecting
3. FSBOs and expired listings

Reactive sources: open house, online leads

Agents who didn't learn the business with the *Up and Running* concepts constantly ask me, "What are the best sources of leads?" In this program, I have given you the answers. I have prioritized the best sources of leads for the new real estate agent. *30 Days to Dollars* (see Figure 2.4) is the most important part of your *Up and Running* program. Why? Because it is the lead-generating plan component of *Up and Running in 30 Days.* It consists of the following:

- Your **best sources of business**, prioritized for you
- The **numbers of contacts** you need to make
- The **time frame** in which you need to make them

It is structured to ensure a sale in your first 30 days in the business. Take another look at *30 Days to Dollars* (Figure 2.4). You'll see four sources of leads and the numbers of contacts recommended per week in each source. Those are the sources you'll be using to get leads during these four weeks. But you won't be contacting all those sources in week one. That would be overwhelming! You'll start with one source and keep adding sources. Each week, a new source of leads will be introduced to you so you can expand your repertoire for getting leads. Doing the numbers of contacts recommended in this plan gets you a sale in a month.

Big Idea: Your four-week business start-up plan introduces you to the lead-generating sources gradually so you can build your repertoire.

FIGURE 2.4   *30 Days to Dollars* Lead-Generating Plan

These lead-generating activities are assigned in a prioritized order each week of your four-week plan.

Lead-Generating Source	Weekly Minimum
1. Contact people you know/meet (best source)	
In-person calls	20
Phone calls	30
2. Circle prospect in person (next best source for new agents)	25
3. FSBOs In-person or phone contacts	25
or	
Expired listings In-person or phone contacts	25
4. Hold public open houses (reactive)	1
5. Initial contact online leads take 200 leads to equal 1 sale (reactive)	25*

*If you are on a team that accepts online leads, or have purchased an online lead-generation program, your number of initial online lead follow-ups will have to be much higher. Ask your manager how to set reasonable numbers for yourself.

Total leads per week:

100–125

Why I Have Chosen These Lead-Generating Priorities

Too many lead-generating plans are just an unprioritized laundry list of all the things you could do to generate business. I don't want you to waste time and energy pursuing sources that don't give you a high payoff. I have chosen those activities because they are perfect for new agents. They are *low cost*, both in energy and money. Best of all, they're *high payoff*. I've created this *30 Days to Dollars* prioritized lead-generation plan with the new agent specifically in mind. In addition, my research with experienced agents shows that the best source of business is always people they've sold to and people they've met. Because you've not sold any real estate, I will give you your best source in your terms: people you know or meet.

Now, you know that this 30-day plan is just not for 30 days. It is a prioritized plan that should last you your whole real estate career! In other words, it is a model for the successful real estate agent.

Big Idea: Know your best lead-generating sources and create a repeating lead generating plan with high numbers. It's your assurance of success.

Why "People You Know" Is Top Priority

Simply, these people already like and trust you! They want to do business with you. They just don't know you're in real estate. Your job is to contact them, let them know you're in real estate, and ask for their business or referrals (see Unit 8 for the process and script). There are four other reasons why this source is your best:

- It is very low cost with high return.
- It requires little skill.
- It is inexpensive.
- You have no competition for this market—these people already love you!

Why Circle Prospecting Is Next Highest Priority

Circle prospecting means going door to door in a neighborhood to announce a "home happening"—that is, a new listing, a sale, a listing sold, a price reduction, an open house, or a closing. (See Unit 8 for how to circle prospect.) There are four reasons why circle prospecting is so powerful for the new agent:

- It is easy to do—it requires little skill.
- It is "low rejection"—most homeowners are glad you informed them.
- It is inexpensive.
- It has little competition—most agents will not bother to personally contact homeowners.

Why For Sale by Owner and Expired Listings Are Lower Priority

For-sale-by-owner listings—listings by owners attempting to sell their own homes—and expired listings—listings that didn't sell—can be immediate sources of business. Why? Because these sellers have told us they want to sell. That's the good news. The bad news is that these sellers don't have a high opinion of real estate salespeople. Perhaps they've had a bad experience in the past and decided that selling their own home is preferable to working with a bad agent. Perhaps they had their home listed by an unscrupulous agent who overpriced it just to get calls on the sign. The reason that I've prioritized these sources as third on the list is that they

- require skill,
- are high-rejection sales activities, and
- require you to have the kind of behavioral profile to accept and deal with high rejection and tough sellers—and stay in the game! Only about one-fourth of the population is wired that way. See more on behavioral profiles in *What They Don't Teach You in Pre-License School.*

We will teach you how to contact these best sources of business. Information on contacting and working with these sources is in Unit 8. See the References unit for more help on sales skills.

Why Open Houses Are Included

The first three sources are proactive (i.e., you go out and contact these sources). This puts you in the driver's seat because you have control over the number of people you contact. The last source, open houses, is reactive (i.e., you sit and wait for a potential client). You can't make them come to your open house (but you can up the odds by putting out more signs). You can also up the odds by circle prospecting around that home a day before the open house. I've included open houses here because new agents generally have many opportunities to hold homes open. Before you commit to an open house, though, be sure it is

- in a well-trafficked area,
- you have access to plenty of open house signs (6–8) (most people come as a result of well-placed signs, not ads), and
- the home is attractive inside and out to draw lookers in.

Caution: You need sales training to ask the right questions during your open house to capture that lead.

Why Online Leads Are Included

Online leads (website, commercial lead-generating sources, social media, and so on) are of varying importance to real estate salespeople. However, the one commonality is this: you must answer that online lead within eight hours to have a chance to move that lead forward into a prospect. In this program, I'll provide you a system to do just that. Unfortunately, surveys show that only half of agents ever follow up on their online leads. The half that do take 54 hours on average to do it! No wonder agents don't think online leads are a good source of business. Warning: Do not rely strictly on reactive (they come to you) business. Do a mixture of proactive and reactive sources, and prioritize your sources correctly.

Note: I've placed initial online lead contacts as a reactive source in your 30-day plan. The ongoing follow-up of these leads is in your business support assignments. Skills for both initial contact and follow-up schedule are included in your skill-developing units.

Big Idea: Recognize whether you are lead generating proactively or reactively. Proactive lead generation is king, not reactive.

Other Reactive Sales Activities

You may be getting leads from your relocation service (or *relo*). This is a service, usually owned by your real estate company, that has affiliate relationships with national or international relocation services. These services interact to find and provide leads to real estate agencies, which then distribute them to agents for a fee ranging from 20% to 45%. You may be working as a buyer's agent and getting leads from your head agent. These are all reactive sources. If you don't intend to hold open houses, you can substitute your other reactive sources instead. The following is a huge caveat: do not expect to create a career from reactive sources. If that was possible, every agent in the business would be making the money of his dreams!

Mix and Match

The important message here is to use both traditional and contemporary methods to lead generate. Measure your results. Make adjustments. Always remember that your goal is to create long-term, committed, professional relationships you can count on for future business.

> **Big Idea:** The methods that work best for you are the methods that create trusting relationships. Don't worry if those methods are traditional. There's a reason—they work! You're contemporary enough because you're using technology to support your business, track your business, and market your business.

Top Agents' Best Sources of Leads

A survey by Baylor University of hundreds of top agents showed their best sources of leads were the following:
- Referrals
- Interactive voice response (IVR) technology (your customer calls an 800 number on your For Sale sign; you are sent a text of the potential client's phone number and you call them back immediately. See the References and Resources unit for more information.)
- Repeat business
- Open houses
- FSBO and expired leads
- Face-to-face networking

Isn't it interesting that almost all of the best lead sources were traditional? In addition, with the exception of open houses, the majority of leads were generated proactively. I believe it will shift over time to more success with online leads as agents invest in lead-generating programs (e.g., Market Leader, Listings-to-Leads) and learn how to follow up with these leads effectively.

> **Big Idea:** All lead-generating sources are not equal. Follow my priorities as you start. Measure your successes with each target market. After your initial 30-day program, analyze your best sources and continue working them.

> **Manager's Tip:** Work with each agent to help him analyze his best sources of leads and customize the *30 Days to Dollars* plan.

How These Priorities Are Introduced During the Program

Figure 2.5 shows you when each new lead-generating source is introduced to you during your *Up and Running* plan. Take a quick peek at Units 4–7. Look at the action plans for week one, week two, week three, and week four. You'll see your lead-generating assignments there, just as they show up in Figure 2.5.

FIGURE 2.5   Time Line: When New Lead-Generating Activities Are Introduced

Each week during the *Up and Running* plan, you will be lead generating at least 100 contacts. The schedule of when *Up and Running* introduces and expects these lead-generating sources to be implemented is as follows:

Week One	Week Two	Week Three	Week Four
People you know	Add expireds	Add FSBOs	You choose your best sources
Circle prospecting	Continue people you know	Continue people you know	Continue initial online leads
Initial online leads	Continue circle prospecting	Continue circle prospecting	
	Continue initial online leads	Continue initial online leads	

More sources are added to your lead-generating plan assignments each week of the program. We start with the best and easiest sources for you and progress to the more difficult (requiring more sales training) sources. By the time you've been in the business four weeks, you'll have sampled the major types of lead-generating activities and done them in high enough numbers to see your results. In addition, you'll have found which sources you like best—and which bring you the best results. Now, longer term, you can put into your plan more work in these best sources. At the same time, because you'll have practiced the sales skills of all the major sources (by lead generating in real life), you'll have the skills to implement any of these sources any time you need them. Remember, it's first a numbers game!

> **Big Idea:** Sales is a numbers game. If your lead generating numbers are small, you aren't able to analyze what's right and what's wrong with your business.

What about Short Sales and Foreclosures?

Should you specialize in short sales or foreclosures? Before you jump to one or both of those sources, find out the number of transactions in your area from those sources. Your manager can help. In some areas, the numbers are declining because the numbers of short sale and foreclosures have diminished. In addition, you must become an expert in these areas to be effective—and to help clients successfully. You must create relationships with banks and other institutions, pay for leads, or both. If you decide one or both of these sources is for you, find courses and coaching in these areas and dedicate time and dollars to becoming an expert.

My advice is to leave these sources for later because they require true expertise and experience; too many agents are dabbling in them, hurting the consumer in the end, and wasting time, money, and their reputations. Remember, you need immediate, low-cost, friendly sources of business to start your career. You are competing for short sale and foreclosure leads with agents who have spent years cultivating those sources of leads—along with thousands of dollars in education.

Other Sources of Leads

I have created an area called "other" on your *30 Days to Dollars* spreadsheet. If you have other favored sources of leads, set goals and track them there. Be sure to categorize them as proactive or reactive. Remember, proactive leads put you in control because you're going out to find the lead. Reactive leads (e.g., open houses, floor time, online leads given to you, and relo leads) are not lead generating numbers that you control.

What about Paying for Leads?

Should You Pay for Leads?

- How many leads will you receive in a specific time period?
- What is the cost per lead?
- What is the ratio of leads to sales?
- What is the cost per sale?
- What is the time frame required for follow-up?

Today, there are a multitude of companies asking agents to pay them for leads. Should you do that? Perhaps. But before you leap into the fray, find out the following information as listed in the box to the left.

Here's the sad truth: Agents resort to paying for leads because they can't or won't lead generate using the methods in *Up and Running in 30 Days*. They think it will be easier to convert information queries into loyal clients than to go find those who want loyal client relationships.

Easy sales? By the way, don't think that the majority of those leads will easily and even magically turn into sales! (According to businesses generically, the rate for online lead conversion ranges from 1–5%). I'm afraid too many agents think that these lead-generating companies are going to provide ready and willing buyers and sellers. We wish!

Not only that, there are two big obstacles to lead conversion that most agents don't take into consideration:

- They don't have a lead-conversion system—a method to track those leads until they buy or die.
- They don't have the skill to turn a "cold" communication into a warm relationship. That is, people communicate via the web or email to get information—that's all they want from the agent. But the agent wants to establish a relationship. How does the agent turn

that cold communication into a trusting, long-term relationship? See the References and Resources unit for a suggested script.

Online leads: you need a long-term approach and a great screening method. That means that you'd better be ready to

- have a rapid response to online or any lead-giving inquiries, especially if you're paying for them;
- implement a fail-safe contact management system to capture all those leads and categorize them;
- have a tight, systematized follow-up plan for all those leads; and
- have the skills to convert that online inquiry into a client (see Unit 8 for online sales skills).

Caveat: Be careful of accepting leads as your major source of business! For example, one newer agent got one-third of her business from her company's relocation service. She paid 40% of her commission to get those leads. In a fast market, she did pretty well. However, when the market slowed down, she got many fewer relo leads and hadn't implemented her own lead-generating plan; she never really created her business. She was simply the recipient of the company's relo business and found herself really as a "day one" new agent—no business! So, she had to start from scratch and proactively lead generate. Don't let that happen to you. Just think of the marketing power and real estate business she would have had if she spent 40% of her commission dollars marketing to her best sources of business instead of accepting those relo leads.

As I surveyed newer agents, a theme developed. Many of them cautioned against paying for leads and various marketing programs that promised leads.

Here's some advice from James Pierce, a top-producing agent: "Don't pay a dime to sites like Zillow, etc."

According to Cerise Paton, "You will get a lot of calls to sell you leads, Google placement, banner ads, shopping carts, you name it. Don't do it. It either has no value, or you're not ready for it, or you can't afford it."

Here's my take: I've watched thousands of newer real estate agents try to avoid proactive lead generation! Instead, they believe there must be some other way. They are, as my dad would say, "pigeons" for companies selling leads. What agents don't realize is that it takes hundreds of these leads to turn into a transaction. And, once the agent stops paying, the lead source stops, too. Instead, if you cultivate leads using the principles of *30 Days to Dollars,* you're in control of your own destiny—and you're not spending dollars you don't have.

Big Idea: Reactive leads aren't any good to your long-term career success until you create a long-term relationship with each of them and they become your referral sources.

Substituting Lead-Generating Activities

What if you don't know enough people to fill a week with 50 contacts from this source? Just choose another source. The number of people you contact is the most important factor in your plan's success. What you can't do is have low lead-generating numbers and expect sales!

What If You're Assigned Other Lead-Generating Sources Out of Order with *Up and Running in 30 Days*?

If you're working with a rainmaker or on a team, you may be starting to follow up on online leads your first week in the business. If so, just go to the unit on skill development for that lead source. Adjust your lead-generating priorities to reflect your personal plan.

Big Idea: Most new agents fail simply because they fail to contact enough people fast enough.

The Spreadsheets: How the *30 Days to Dollars* Lead-Generating Plan Looks Each Week

I've taken the *30 Days to Dollars* plan in *Up and Running* and put it in a spreadsheet format for you so you can see your lead-generating assignments (your goals) and track your results (actuals). Look at Figure 2.6 and Figure 2.7. Figure 2.6 shows you the lead-generating sources you are assigned each week. In this example, the agent has done every part of the plan. Figure 2.7 shows you the sales activity this agent generated as a result of his lead-generating work. These are the projections for you during the four weeks. Now flip ahead for a minute to Unit 4. You will see that your first week's lead-generating assignments are the same as the ones for week one on your spreadsheet. This is to make it easy for you to follow a proven start-up plan, so you won't have to figure out priorities or needed numbers. You will also see that your result projections are stated as goals for you in week one. Although we can't guarantee results, working these high lead-generating numbers will ultimately result in sales for you much faster than if you had started with a "slow" plan!

Blank spreadsheets are provided for you to use each week in Unit 12. I've already put in the lead-generating assignments and results projections to make it easy for you to keep your results.

FIGURE 2.6 Your *30 Days to Dollars* Lead-Generating Plan

Set your goals and track your results ("actuals")

Month: _____

Proactive Activities	Week 1 G	Week 1 A	Week 2 G	Week 2 A	Week 3 G	Week 3 A	Week 4 G	Week 4 A	Totals G	Totals A
People you know/meet [50/week]	(50)	50	(25)	25	(25)	25	25	25	125	125
Circle prospect [25/week]	(50)	50	50	50	(25)	25	25	25	150	150
FSBOs [25/week]	0	0	0	0	(25)	25	25	25	75	75
Expireds [25/week]	0	0			25*	(25)	25*	25	50	50
Reactive Activities										
Open houses [1 minimum]	0	0	(1)	1	(1)	1	(1)	1	3	3
Online leads	25	25	25	25	25	25	25	25	100	100

G=Goals
A=Actuals

Circled are the numbers of lead-generating activities from each source–in the specific week they are assigned in your *Up and Running* plan.
*By Week 3, you get to choose your favorite methods among those listed.

FIGURE 2.7   Your *30 Days to Dollars* Lead-Generating Results

Month: _____

Buyer Activities	Week 1		Week 2		Week 3		Week 4		Totals	
	G	A	G	A	G	A	G	A	G	A
Qualifying interviews w/buyers	(2)	2	(2)	2	(2)	2	(2)	2	8	8
Qualified buyer showings	(2)	2	(2)	2	(2)	2	(2)	2	8	8
# sales							(1)	1	1	1

Listing Activities	Week 1		Week 2		Week 3		Week 4		Totals	
	G	A	G	A	G	A	G	A	G	A
Qualified listing appointments	(1)	1	(1)	1	(1)	1	(1)	1	4	4
Marketable listings secured	0	0	0	0	(0)	0	1	1	1	1
# of listings sold	0	0	0	0	0	0	0	0	0	0*

G=Goals   A=Actuals

Note the results projected through time. These results are in your four-week *Up and Running* plan.
*Depends on your normal market time.

Track Your Results and Make Adjustments

Each week, use the spreadsheets to track your results. Look at the results you're getting from your lead generating and make adjustments in your plan. I'll share much more about that in the *Up and Running* plan.

After *Up and Running* Is Over

Don't stop using those spreadsheets! At the end of four weeks, you'll see which have been your best sources of business. Now, you're ready to make your own plan from scratch using the principles you've already learned.

Best advice: don't make your own plan your first four weeks. Use my plan until you get the success habits you need to succeed. Then you can alter the plan.

At the end of Unit 7, Week Four of your *Up and Running* plan, you'll be making a plan for next steps. You'll also be evaluating your progress during your first four weeks. Now, you're set to launch the next 60 days of your career and beyond.

■ Principle Five: Work the Numbers

Do you want to make a sale in your first month in the business? If so, you need to make at least 100 lead-generating contacts (in person or on the phone) each week for the first four weeks you're in the business. This is your insurance plan. The *30 Days to Dollars* lead-generating plan has 100 contacts per week built into the program. But, you say, that's a lot of contacts. Yes, but you want to sell a home quickly, don't you? And you have plenty of time to make those contacts, don't you? And you don't have enough money not to sell a home soon. Finally, you want to keep your enthusiasm high, don't you? Those are all the reasons to make those contacts.

So, get to it. You will use and assess this program each week. With this method, you will learn an important self-management tool—the ability to measure and analyze your activities and the results of those activities.

More Numbers: High Activities Reap High Rewards

The majority of new agents have no faith that the activities they are doing on a given day will bring them results. That's because they don't know the *Up and Running* plan. Here are the very important contact ratios you need to learn so you will know that you are doing what it takes to succeed.

On the sales side, 400 contacts per month will return to you 8 qualifying appointments that will result in 8 showings that, if averaged over time, will result in 1 sale.

This means if you want to sell one home per month, you need to talk to 400 people in that month, find 8 people to qualify, and show homes 8 times. You will, averaged over a few months, sell 1 home for every 8 times you put people in the car (not necessarily the same people—this is just a law of averages).

The Numbers in Up and Running

On the sales side,

- 400 sales calls per month will return to you
- 8 qualifying appointments that will result in
- 8 showings that, if averaged over time, will result in 1 sale.

On the listing side,

- 400 contacts a month will result in
- 4 seller-qualifying appointments that will lead to
- 1 qualified listing, which will sell in normal market time.

On the listing side, 400 contacts a month will result in 4 seller-qualifying appointments that will lead to 1 qualified listing.

The *Up and Running* plan has these numbers built into each week's business-producing activities. You will set a goal for one sale and one listing during the first four weeks of your business. In addition, you'll be setting standards for your business that will ensure you will make a good living and build a solid career from day one. As we progress in *Up and Running*, I'll remind you to review your ratios to make certain you are doing the lead generating and getting the appointment numbers you need to reach your goals.

■ Principle Six: Be Accountable to Your Plan

Don't just write some numbers and forget about them. Write your goals, and track your actual activities and results. That's how you learn to control your income. Through analyzing your own success ratios, you'll be able to truly self-manage.

One of the questions new agents always ask is, "How much work will I have to do?" *Up and Running* certainly lays that out, doesn't it? But that's not the whole story. You just saw the ratios above, but those aren't yours. Ratios can vary dramatically. For example:

- George goes into the business with a mastery of sales skills. When he makes a sales call, it takes him fewer calls to get a lead than it does Sally, who came into this business without any sales skills.
- Martha goes into this business and, although she knows lots of people, is reluctant to talk to them about real estate. Instead, Martha, who is very sociable and hates rejection, decides to call on for-sale-by-owner listings. She experiences high rejection, so she decides she doesn't like real estate. Her ratio of calls to leads is terrible!
- It's a very fast market in Seattle when Chris starts in the business. He finds it very easy to get a lead and very easy to sell that lead a house because the lead is afraid he'll lose the house if he doesn't buy today! In contrast, John starts selling in Florida in a very slow market. John has to make many sales calls to find a good lead.

So quit worrying about my conversion ratios. Start tracking your leads, appointments, and sales. Find *your* conversion ratios. As a musician, I practiced as long as it took to play well. I've never understood the kind of person who thinks she'll just do enough to get by. High achievers don't think like that. Aim high! You're worth it.

■ *Up and Running:* A Start-Up Plan Built in the Six Principles

With these six principles, you have the groundwork of an effective start-up plan, but you don't have to create your plan from scratch. To make it easy for you to launch your business, I've done it for you. *Up and Running* provides a highly structured four-week plan built on those principles (see Units 4–7). The plan includes the *30 Days to Dollars* lead-generating plan (business-producing activities) and the business-supporting actions you'll want to take to become great at sales—and explains how to package your presentations so you can compete with seasoned agents.

Big Idea: The *Up and Running* plan is designed with the actions future top producers take in their first month of the business to make money fast and get good at selling fast.

How the *Up and Running* Plan Gets You to Your Goals

The *Up and Running* four-week plan tells you what to do from your first week in the business to ensure you start your business fast and right. That's the short-term, immediate look at your business. But how is it going to extend to get you to your yearly goals? Now I'll show you how it's built to continue to get you the results you want in your first year. Figure 2.8 is a yearly goal planner filled out by our *Up and Running* agent.

First, I want to show you the relationship between your yearly goals and what you do today. This goal-setting planner helps you set your year's goals, and it breaks your goals into monthly goals and the specific activities you need to do every day to achieve those goals (broken down by the month). Look at month one. You'll see our *Up and Running* plan numbers for the first month. This plan contains a commission to the agent of $6,000 per transaction (listing sold or sale). Yours will probably vary, so find out from your manager what the average commission to the agent is in your area—and in your office. Now, look at month two. See how the number of contacts goes down a bit as the results remain steady. That is how you will continue your *Up and Running* plan through time. The activities you do those first few months get you the transactions you want to achieve at the end of the year. Look at the rest of the figure, which shows the relationship between your activities and your results.

Big Idea: A high activity level of lead generating, coupled with your ever-increasing skill, results in growing sales, listings, and listings sold throughout the year—and you've reached your goals!

Goals Without Knowing What to Do Every Day Is Useless

Activities → Goals

To have faith in a plan, you want to know how the activities you do today ensure the results you get at the end of that year. Most new agents can tell someone how much money they want to make their first year, but they have no idea what they're going to do every day to make it. I found that out when I surveyed hundreds of new agents for my ebook *What They Don't Teach You in Pre-License School.* You need both views of your business—short term and long term—to launch into these activities so you have confidence in your ability to reach your goals.

Caution: Agents fail because they don't create a lead-generating plan to support their goals.

The Five Steps to Create Your Effective Yearly Plan

Steps to Set Your Goals

1. Plan your yearly goals
2. Break down yearly goals into monthly goals/actions
3. Create a weekly schedule that reflects your monthly goals and actions
4. Create your budget
5. Forecast your profits

So you can project your success one year from now, here are the steps to create your yearly plan. I've put a sample of all of the completed *Up and Running* plan forms in Unit 11 so you can see how all the forms filled out work together. I've put all the blank forms you'll need to plan and measure your short-term and long-term results in Unit 12:

1. Plan your yearly goals (see the sample plan in Figure 2.8).
2. Break down your yearly goals into monthly goals and actions (a blank form of your yearly goals and monthly activity plan is in Unit 12).
3. Create a weekly schedule that reflects your monthly goals and actions so your goals are really your action plan (I'll give you a sample weekly schedule and a method to create an effectively weekly schedule in Unit 4, Week One).
4. Create your budget (see the sample budget in Figure 2.9 and the blank budget planning sheet in Unit 12).
5. Forecast your profits (see the sample forecast in Figure 2.10 and the blank forecast in Unit 12).

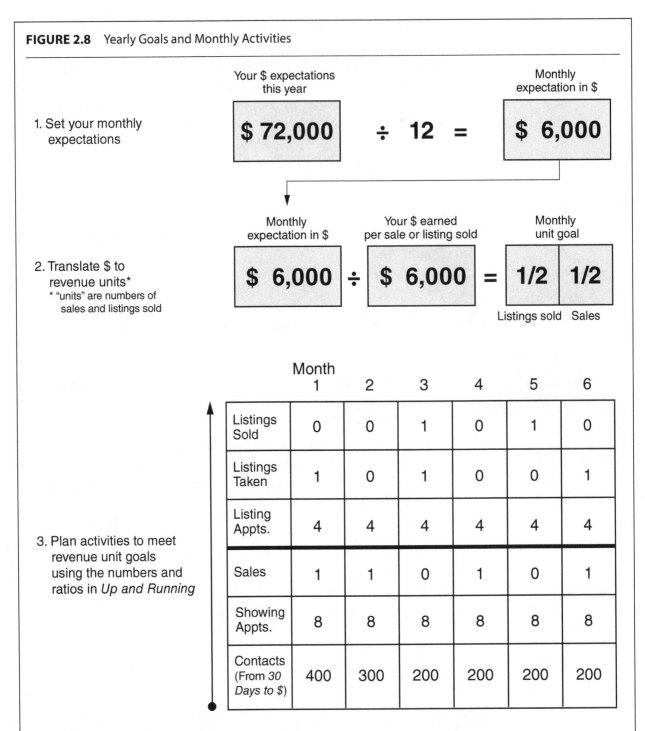

FIGURE 2.8   Yearly Goals and Monthly Activities

1. Set your monthly expectations

Your $ expectations this year		Monthly expectation in $
$ 72,000	**÷ 12 =**	**$ 6,000**

2. Translate $ to revenue units*
   * "units" are numbers of sales and listings sold

Monthly expectation in $		Your $ earned per sale or listing sold		Monthly unit goal	
$ 6,000	**÷**	**$ 6,000**	**=**	**1/2**	**1/2**
				Listings sold	Sales

3. Plan activities to meet revenue unit goals using the numbers and ratios in *Up and Running*

Month	1	2	3	4	5	6
Listings Sold	0	0	1	0	1	0
Listings Taken	1	0	1	0	0	1
Listing Appts.	4	4	4	4	4	4
Sales	1	1	0	1	0	1
Showing Appts.	8	8	8	8	8	8
Contacts (From *30 Days to $*)	400	300	200	200	200	200

The first month activities coincide with the *Up and Running* plan. Our agent follows the same contact plan she used for her third month onward to schedule her contacts and business results for the remainder of the year.

FIGURE 2.9 Sample Budget for the New Agent

**Sample Real Estate Budget
Real Estate Operating Expenses**

Projections: 6 sales this year
6 listings sold this year
8 listings taken this year

Check with your manager for the average expenses in your area as you make your real estate budget.

	YEARLY ($)	MONTHLY ($)
Total marketing budget ($400 per listing or sale—includes postcards, online marketing, sphere marketing, after-sale present)	4,800	400
Professional fees (REALTOR® association dues, MLS)	1,000	83
Business car expenses (gas, oil, tools, repair)	2,400	200
Communication expenses (smartphone, data plan)	2,000	166
Labor/mechanical (unless you have an assistant)	1,200	100
Professional development	600	50
Supplies	1,200	100
Business insurance (L and I)	300	25
Legal fees/E&O	300	25
Licenses, permits	300	25
Other (website, blog, IDX technology, software, and so on)	1,200	100
TOTAL	15,300	1,275

FIGURE 2.10 Sample Budget Forecast for Year One

Month	1	2	3	4	5	6	7	8	9	10	11	12
Sales	1	1		1		1			1			1
Listings Sold			1		1		1		1		1	1
Income (closings)		6,000*	6,000	6,000	6,000	6,000	6,000	6,000	6,000	6,000	6,000	6,000
Expenses Out ($)	1,275	1,275	1,275	1,275	1,275	1,275	1,275	1,275	1,275	1,275	1,275	1,275
Profit ($)	(1,275)	4,725	4,725	4,725	4,725	4,725	4,725	4,725	4,725	4,725	4,725	4,725

Total income: $66,000

Total expenses: − $15,300

Profit: $50,700

*Note: If you make a sale in month one, that sale will be in month two, when the home closes. There is also a month lag from a sold listing to a closing.

1. Plan your yearly goals. Let's work from your yearly goals to the activities you'll need to do and results you want to achieve each month. First, using Figure 2.8, the *Up and Running* agent sets her monetary goal for the year. For her, that's $72,000 her first year in real estate. (This, by the way, is higher than the median income for all REALTORS® according to the latest National Association of REALTORS® survey. I'm assuming that you intend to really work at real estate in a planned way to exceed the median.) Because the average income per sale for the agent in her market is $6,000, this means that she'll need to sell one home per month (or have one of her listings sell). In the real estate industry, each sale or listing sold is termed a *revenue unit*. You will note that she will create one-half a revenue unit per month from a sale and a listing sold.

2. Break down yearly goals into monthly goals and actions. This *Up and Running* agent went to her manager and found out that, in her area, it takes approximately four listing appointments to list one home that sells in normal market time. It takes eight showing appointments to sell one home. This means eight groups of people in the car, not number of homes shown. They don't even have to be different groups; it's just the law of averages. Because our *Up and Running* agent wants one transaction per month, she knows she will have to put people in her car and go to a listing presentation at least four times per month to ensure that she reaches her goal. As she knows her fastest method of getting a check is through a sale, she sets a goal of eight showings per month. She also knows that her skill level isn't high at the beginning of her career, so she sets higher showing and listing presentation goals for herself than she will need to set later in her career.

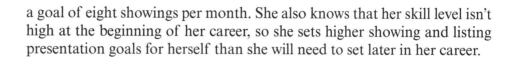

Big Idea: Tracking your lead generating, interviewing and presenting, and showing results gives you the information you need to analyze *your* conversion ratios and project your income.

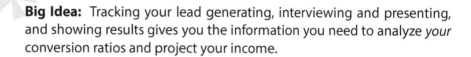

Big Idea: If you want to make lots of money your first year in real estate, you must lead generate your heart out every day!

3. Create a weekly schedule that reflects your monthly goals and actions. Here's where the rubber meets the road. Your plan is not a practical tool for you to use unless it directs you in what to do each week—and every day. Your *Up and Running* four-week plan gives you the specifics— what to do each week to reach your goals. In week one of your plan, you'll be putting together your weekly schedule based on the activities in the plan for week one. There is an example schedule for week one in Unit 11. After you've gained the time management skills in *Up and Running*, you'll be able to make your own weekly schedule.

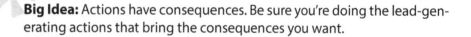

Big Idea: Actions have consequences. Be sure you're doing the lead-generating actions that bring the consequences you want.

4. Create your budget. Figure 2.9 provides a sample budget for the new agent. You will get some budget numbers, too, from your Technology Budget and Planner. Knowing what you need to close each month is a motivator to get out there and lead generate! See your manager for estimates in your specific area.

5. Forecast your income. Figure 2.10 is an example time line, which shows you the *Up and Running* plan sales results for each month, plus your outgo (the budgeted dollars you're spending each month to launch your career). To find out more about what you should be spending, see your manager. Costs vary greatly from area to area, and your company may provide many or none of the materials and services you need to launch your career. (See the References and Resources unit for much more on budgeting and projections.)

Breakeven. Figure 2.10 shows you when your income and outgo are at "breakeven." This usually happens in an agent's business by the fourth to sixth month.

What happens if you don't start lead generating *now*? Very simply, your money will run out before enough of your income comes in!

Caution: Too many new agents fail because they run out of money and time just before they get that first sale! (And, without success, they run out of self-esteem and motivation, too.)

From Unpredictable to Predictable Results

Now go back to Figure 2.8. Note the *Up and Running* agent doesn't get a sale or a listing sold every month at first. Why? Because she's generating hundreds of leads, some who won't buy from her in the first few months. However, she's sowing the seeds of success by contacting those hundreds of people. In addition, at first this new agent, like most new agents, has few sales skills. It takes her more contacts to get a good prospect. As her sales skills and the quality of her contacts grow, she'll enjoy more success with less effort.

Big Idea: Predictability comes with repetition.

Don't Concentrate on the Results; Concentrate on the Lead-Generating Activities

New agents expect to make a sale fast. However, they don't know the work required to make that sale. You do now, but don't be tempted to think that because you said you wanted to make a sale in the first month, you will! Stop thinking about those sales. Instead, concentrate on those lead-generating activities. I'll make a musical analogy. If you wanted to learn to play the piano, would you expect to have to practice daily or just sit down and play that pop tune without rehearsal? Of course you would expect to practice. Think of lead generation as the practice that leads up to the recital—your sale.

Your friend the new agent may make a sale in his first month because of dumb luck. That won't happen often. The worst thing about dumb luck is that it makes the agent think all he has to do is sit around and someone will force the agent to sell him a home. I've seen many new agents who had that dumb luck early in their careers, and that's the last home they ever sold! Selling isn't magic or just dumb luck. It's work. It's predictable. It's a business.

Big Idea: New agents fail because they have no plan—and take no focused lead-generating action—to get to their goals.

Your Lead-Generating Plan after Your First Month

Notice that the *Up and Running* agent reduces the number of contacts she's making after her first month. That's because she is getting the number of leads she needs to convert them to the number of appointments she needs—and ultimately, the number of sales and listings sold. By month three, she's learned that she needs 200 contacts a month to get the appointments she needs to reach her goal for the number of sales and listings sold annually. How does she know these ratios? She has tracked her goals and actuals and analyzed her progress. You should do the same with the spreadsheets I've provided you. That way, you won't be guessing at whether you are on track to your goals or not. You'll know!

How Many Lead-Generating Hours after Your First Month?

This *Up and Running* agent now knows she doesn't need to devote four hours a day, five days a week to lead generating anymore. She now has appointments to schedule. So, she reduces the amount of hours she lead generates a week to ten and continues to do that throughout her career.

If the *Up and Running* Agent Hits a Slump

Too many times, agents stop lead generating because they "get too busy," and then they find they are in a slump. Unfortunately, few of them started with the clarity of an *Up and Running* plan, so they don't really know why they're in the slump. It's different when you start with *Up and Running*. If our *Up and Running* agent doesn't reach her monthly sales goals, she knows exactly what to correct. She knows her conversion ratios—the number of leads she must get to interview, the number of showings she must get to sell, and the number of listing appointments she must make to get a marketable listing. So, she cures her "slumpitis" by increasing her lead generation to three–four hours a day, contacting 300–400 people a week again. That's your cure, too!

Big Idea: Slumps are caused by inaction or wrong actions (using all your time on business-supporting activities). Few results cause low motivation, low self-esteem, and then your activity levels plummet further.

■ All Your Self-Management Tools Are Here

1. *30 Days to Dollars*—provides a monthly and weekly lead-generating plan and spreadsheets to track activities on the sales cycle
2. Your yearly goals and monthly activity plan—plans your one-year goals so you can then plan your month, your week, and even your day
3. *Up and Running* budget—so you can budget enough dollars to start your career right
4. Budget forecast—shows the relationship of income to expenses, and when you break even

All of these blank forms for your use are in Unit 12.

■ Summary

We explored what I've identified as the six major principles of a high-producing business and what they mean to you:

1. Start the business cycle by talking to people (lead generation). Unfortunately, most new agents wait months to start lead generating. They are frightened, feel the need for more education, or are looking for a better way. In fact, they wait themselves right out of the business! If you want to make a sale in your first month, you need to start lead generating your first day in the business. You can see from the business projections that the longer you put off starting your lead-generating plan, the more in debt you get!
2. Stay on the business path. That means you should spend the majority of your day doing business-producing activities like lead generating and working with buyers and sellers. Unfortunately, many new agents spend most of their day getting ready to get ready!
3. Prioritize your activities. I have come up with the concept of prioritizing all activities as either business producing or business supporting. Now you have the skills to direct your own activities toward—or away from—productivity. But I haven't left it up to you. I've scheduled you for your first month so you will have complete clarity of what a successful real estate agent does every day to succeed.
4. Lead generate like the pros. My 30-day prioritized lead-generating plan, *30 Days to Dollars,* shows you which are your best sources for leads and how many of them you must contact each week to get a sale your first month. I don't want to leave it up to you to decide on your lead-generating sources. One new agent in my office thought that if he just sent out postcards to those he knew, he would sell lots of houses. Wrong!
5. Work the numbers. Too many times, agents tell me they "tried that once." It's a numbers game! Trying something once is just telling me you really aren't committed. What if you wanted to learn to play the piano, yet you practiced only once? Keep working those

numbers. You'll get better at sales. You'll see your progress get faster. Analyze your numbers so you can self-manage.

6. Be accountable to your plan. Treat your plan with respect. Measure your actual activities and results against what this plan projects. Find your own conversion ratios. Now you're on your way to creating the kind of business results you want—and you now have the skills to measure and adjust your plan as needed. I'll let you in on a secret, too: you know 98% more about managing your business than other agents, no matter how long they've been in the business. Just think what you're going to accomplish!

Big Idea: These principles aren't just for newbies. These principles are for every type of salesperson building and maintaining a career.

Now, let's go on to Unit 3 to get the overview of the *Up and Running* plan so you can start your week one.

Four Weeks to Becoming a Successful Agent

In the previous unit, you learned the six principles of successful business development. These principles are the ones I used to create the *Up and Running* four-week plan. Units 4–7 are the plan, a week at a time, along with the measurement tools you and your manager need to manage your plan.

In this unit, I'll give you a successful new agent's job description so you can see the job you are filling. Your *Up and Running* plan makes this job description "live" in your actions each day. You'll get an overview of the plan to get you ready for Unit 4, your first week of the plan. In addition, we'll talk about management. You may not think you're in management because you're a new agent, but you really are because you must manage your plan while also managing your attitude. For most new agents, the hardest part of implementing this plan is managing their attitudes! I'll give you some pointers about enlisting your manager in your plan and some suggestions if you're working with a coach so you can get the best results possible. Finally, I'll give you checklist of the materials you need as you enter the business so you're ready to get started selling real estate. Then you're all set to start your plan.

■ What a Successful New Real Estate Agent Does

When you apply for a job, you're generally given a job description so you know what's expected of you. Were you given a job description when you applied to become a real estate salesperson? Probably not. No wonder few new real estate salespeople know what to expect when they started their careers! No wonder they often get their priorities wrong and unwittingly create a business plan for failure! Figure 3.1 is my job description for a successful agent. Notice that it's prioritized using the categories from *Up and Running.* Not all activities are equal. That's exactly what the *Up and Running* plan teaches, too. As you start your *Up and Running* plan with week one, you are fulfilling this job description, just as those who fail are fulfilling a "failed agent" job description. Keep my job description at your desk in front of you to remind you of your priorities.

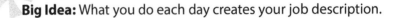

Big Idea: What you do each day creates your job description.

Manager's Tip: Give this job description to each new agent candidate during the interview. Ask each if he is willing to do this job description. You'll weed out those who aren't interested in being successful.

FIGURE 3.1   A Successful Agent's Job Description

A successful agent consistently completes large numbers of business-producing activities.

1.   Lead generates. Finds potential customers and clients by lead generating with the best sources daily.

     An agent's income is greatly determined by the number of people contacted consistently.

2.   Completes a high number of the following activities:
     - Shows homes to qualified clients
     - Sells homes
     - Lists marketable properties to sell in normal market time

3.   Makes money by:
     - selling homes and
     - selling listings.

     (The only two activities that get you a paycheck)

4.   Completes the following support activities with lower priority:
     - Preview properties
     - Paperwork/sales follow-up/emails/answering online inquiries
     - Education/training/coaching
     - Meetings
     - Marketing, including social media

■ The Priorities of *Up and Running*

The most important part of *Up and Running* is the *30 Days to Dollars* prioritized lead-generating plan. During your first 30 days, you will do the following:

1.   Complete 400 proactive lead-generating contacts with the priorities of *30 Days to Dollars*
2.   Get eight qualified appointments to show
3.   Get one sale
4.   Get four listing appointments
5.   Get one marketable listing

Doing these actions in the order and number assigned will get you into production fast. But that's not all you need to do to sell lots of houses.

Business-Supporting Activities Give You Sales Mastery

Besides making those sales calls and doing presentations—plus showing and listing homes—you need to develop your skills. Why? You'll be working smarter, not harder. Why go to ten listing presentations to get one marketable listing if you could go to four to get one? You'll increase your success ratios by practicing and packaging to become a competent salesperson fast. That way, you'll be able to compete with salespeople who have been in the business much longer than you. In addition, you'll have the self-confidence to tackle any sales situation, knowing you have the sales skills and sales packaging to go into the fray and compete with the best. I've chosen the business-supporting activities because you need them right now! I haven't chosen a myriad of other activities because you don't need them right now to succeed in the short term. Here are the business-supporting actions you will complete:

Sales presentations
- Create a visual listing presentation and process so you can prove you're worth the commission you want to charge, and you can get a listing at a marketable price.
- Design a buyer qualifying and counseling presentation and process so you can create buyer loyalty and get the commissions you feel you deserve.

Time management and professional advancement tools
- Create and evaluate your weekly schedule.
- Implement the Listing Presentation Qualifier (set your standards and qualify sellers).
- Implement the Buyer's Potential Evaluator (set your standards and qualify buyers).

Tracking and contacting potential buyers and sellers
- Implement Tracking Qualified Buyers for time management.
- Create a database and contact management system.
- Consistently enter contacts into your database or CRM (customer relationship management).
- Complete your marketing plan and implement it weekly.
- Implement your social media plan daily.
- Follow up with all potential buyers and sellers.
- Implement your online contact follow-up plan.

Technical skills and knowledge
- Complete a listing form.
- Do a market analysis.
- Complete four purchase and sale agreements.
- Learn the basics of financing and qualifying.

Sales skills

- Observe your office's floor time (or observe an agent answering phone inquiries).
- Observe an agent answering online inquiries.
- Observe open houses.
- Practice the four lead-generating scripts.
- Practice the seven critical sales skills.

Why these particular sales skills? Because these skills are the ones you must master right now to convert leads to sales.

But How Do I Make Those Contacts and Work with Buyers and Sellers?

Even though this isn't a training program, I have included enough of the *how* to get you started. Units 8 and 10 contain the critical sales communication skills, forms, and scripts needed to ensure your success. Unit 13 has the scripts and letters in its own unit for you to practice and apply. If you're like many agents, you don't just want to read about it; you want to hear it.

The Four-Week Plan: This Is Your Life—Not Just an Activity Plan or Assignments

Even though I may call the activities in the four-week start-up business plan "assignments," they are not just scholastic. They are the business activities successful agents do each day. You are starting your business with this business start-up plan. However, you can't do and learn everything at once. That's why I've allocated certain lead-generating and business-supporting activities to certain weeks. At the end of the four weeks, I want you to be a salesperson in the swing of things who has contacted hundreds of people. I want you to be "packaged" and "practiced" so you are gaining skill with people and enjoying more success from your lead generating.

Learning the Ins and Outs of Social Media

Because social media has increased in value for business marketing, I've added assignments for setting up your Facebook, Twitter, LinkedIn, and YouTube accounts and establishing a blog. Each week during this plan, you'll add one social network. By the end of four weeks, you'll have a social media strategy and will have implemented it using the Social Media Planner in Unit 9.

Additional Social Media and Online Support

In the References and Resources unit, I've listed several people and resources that will help you get the training and support you need to implement a social media plan and integrate technology into your plan. My technology experts offer specific technology and media training, and they are experts in their field. See more in Units 9–12 and in the References and Resources unit.

> **Big Idea:** Who's your manager? Look in a mirror!

■ Managing "You"

The following are two parts to managing your *Up and Running* program:

1. Managing the activities in the program
2. Managing your attitude during the program

Guess who manages these two parts: you do. You are in business for yourself, with your office and manager supporting you. This program is driven by you. If you want to capture the support of your manager, meet with her weekly. Go over your accomplishments in your business plan. In order to progress faster, get help in your support areas.

> **Big Idea:** Your goal is to understand and apply effective self-management techniques to create dynamic, professional, long-term business success.

■ Getting Help from Your Manager

It's tough out there. Agents enter the real estate business with enthusiasm, hope, and determination. Then they find out what rejection means, and their enthusiasm quickly withers under the stress of starting anew.

Managers can help. This resource offers new agents (and those attempting to re–jump-start their careers) a game plan that will ensure a successful career. However, to start and continue a challenging program (whether it's a diet or a new job), every person needs encouragement—not just "atta boy, keep going" kind of support but real, specific, constructive guidance and feedback that will help the agent build a successful daily plan and know that it is working.

Managers Can Provide Emotional Support and Coaching Focus

In the quest to make a profit, managers must do everything from counsel agents to run the administrative part of the office. It's difficult for managers to provide new agents the guidance needed to get their careers off to a quick, successful start. *Up and Running* relieves managers' concerns because it provides the plan and resources new agents need to begin a successful career.

> **Big Idea:** Managers *support* an agent's business; agents drive it themselves—with their managers as coaches.

Agents are responsible for completing each weekly plan. Managers who want to provide the highest level of support will meet with the agent weekly (the agent sets the appointment) to review the agent's accomplishments, provide encouragement, and add their expertise to the actions the agent is taking. The weekly checklists entitled "Your Start-Up Plan and Accomplishments" for Units 4–7 have been created for just that use and are in Unit 12.

Armed with the *Up and Running* game plan, the weekly accomplishments, and the other measurement tools, the manager and agent can partner for the agent's quick success.

Manager–Agent "Success" Agreement

As in any successful partnership, the new agent has the best chance to succeed when the agent and manager work closely together. To ensure that the manager and agent are sharing mutual expectations, use the Agreement to Ensure You're *Up and Running* (see Figure 3.2). Not only does your manager need to know your level of commitment; you want to know your manager's level of commitment, too.

FIGURE 3.2   Agreement to Ensure You're *Up and Running*

I, _____, agree to complete all the business-producing and business-supporting work in the *Up and Running in 30 Days* start-up plan. I understand each aspect of the plan and that it is constructed to help me get a fast start.

I want support from my manager, so I agree to make an appointment with my manager weekly. During that appointment, I will review the work completed for that week and my plan for the next week. I agree to
- keep each appointment,
- be on time, and
- be prepared.

To ensure that I get the most from my plan, I expect my manager to
- meet with me weekly for at least one-half hour,
- help me keep my activities prioritized correctly,
- provide assistance in my development of specific business methods,
- provide me any resources necessary to complete the work in this program, and
- provide the support and encouragement necessary to begin a successful career.

I understand it's my business, and I agree to manage it according to the principles in *Up and Running in 30 Days*.

Agent _____ Manager _____

Date of this agreement: _____ End of program: _____

Manager's Tip: Introduce this agreement during the interview process to ensure you and the agent share mutual expectations.

Assertively Demanding Your Manager's Attention Is a Good Thing

If your manager doesn't come forward to ask to coach you, go to her! As a manager, I have come to recognize common success traits in agents. One distinguishing quality is the ability to demand a manager's assistance. Inversely, agents who hang back, afraid to ask for the manager's guidance, will be less successful. I really appreciate new agents who consistently make appointments with me to let me know what they are doing, how they are doing it, and how I can assist them. That's called managing the manager! Obviously, these new agents get much of my attention, concern, and positive strokes—the fuel for motivation.

How to Get the Best from Your Manager

New agents want all the support they can get. Sometimes, though, they don't realize they may inadvertently be acting in a way that doesn't get the best from their managers. Their actions are training their managers to react to them differently than how the agents really want their managers to act. For example, if you only come into the manager's office when you have a gripe, you are training your manager to run the other way when she sees your frowning face! If you don't take part in your team's activities, don't attend office meetings, and only appear when you want the manager's help, you are training that manager to believe you aren't a team player. If you don't get into action quickly, you're training your manager to think that her job is to constantly motivate you—not to support your action efforts. (And motivating someone who won't get into action becomes a very difficult and energy-expending job!)

Ten commandments. To ensure you get the best from your manager, I've created ten commandments. I don't mean your manager will play unfair favorites. I mean your manager will get the cooperation and attitude she needs to help you best. Here are the commandments:

1. Do the work.
2. Don't argue.
3. Don't make excuses.
4. Don't tell the manager you've been in the business two weeks and you have a better way.
5. Do thank your manager.
6. Do tell other agents that you appreciate your manager's efforts.
7. Do tell other new agents you meet in other companies that you have a great manager.
8. Don't bug other people in the office to find another answer because you didn't like your manager's answer.
9. Don't change the program because you don't like it.
10. Don't miss a coaching appointment.

■ Should You Find an In-Office Coach?

Coaching fills the gap between the training room and real life. You may be able to find someone in your office or company who's willing to coach you if your manager is unable to do so. In a recent survey conducted by Inman Select, hundreds of brokers and agents said the best thing a new agent can do is find an excellent agent mentor or coach.

A good in-company coach can do the following:

1. Hold you accountable to the goals you say you want to accomplish
2. Share how-tos and packaging (such as listing packages)
3. Let you shadow her on a listing, buyer presentation, or sales negotiation
4. Accompany you on presentations or sales negotiations
5. Remind you if you're off track—tell you the truth because your goals are important to you
6. Use good coaching skills

However, don't expect a coach to be an answer man. Moreover, don't expect a coach to coach you if you don't have a specific game plan—such as the *Up and Running* start-up plan.

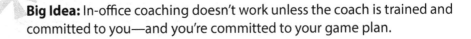

Big Idea: In-office coaching doesn't work unless the coach is trained and committed to you—and you're committed to your game plan.

Why Would Someone Want to Coach You?

You should be able to answer that question. And the answer isn't because you need lots of help! It's not all about you. Ask yourself, "What's in it for the coach?" (Heads up: attaching benefits to features is an important sales skill you'll be learning. See Unit 10.)

In my opinion, you should expect to pay your coach (unless your coach is your manager). You should expect to sign a mutual expectations agreement. You should also expect that, if you don't follow your plan, your coach will fire you.

If coaching fails, it's usually because of three reasons:

1. The coach and agent had different expectations of each other. The contract needs to spell out exactly what is expected of each party.
2. The coach and agent didn't agree upon a game plan. If you want a coach, be prepared to get into action fast so the coach has something to coach you to! Don't expect your coach to motivate you to do the activities you know you should do but won't!
3. The coach wasn't trained. Before you sign up with a coach, see the whole coaching program—in writing—to ensure it's really a program, not just an afterthought.

■ Watch Out Now for Dependent Tendencies

As you start your real estate career, it's inevitable that you will be feeling insecure of your abilities to sell real estate. All of us have felt that way. It's at this time you may start feeling dependent—your company owes you something. That something is probably a lead. Remember, however, leads aren't free. They cost money in terms of either commission splits or referral fees. You make the choice. Either you can work an aggressive lead-generating plan like *Up and Running in 30 Days,* or you can sit and wait for leads (and take the control for your success out of your hands). When you are wondering if you are starting your business correctly, read this again.

Big Idea: Successful salespeople generate their own leads because they want to control their destinies.

■ Managing Your Attitude

We've talked about managing your *Up and Running* plan. That's the hard side of the business—the facts, figures, and activities. However, there's something else you must manage: the soft side of the business—your attitude.

How Our Attitudes Change with the Challenge

One of the things we managers love about a new agent is the enthusiasm with which they start. You're excited to jump into sales. Sometimes you're even overconfident. You tell us managers you are tenacious and that you can handle rejection. You describe yourself as a self-starter; you assure us you can motivate yourself. Then, reality takes over. You've always thought of yourself as a good communicator. However, as you lead generate, you find it difficult to convince people to work with you. People somehow create many ways to reject you. You've always liked people, and you sense they like you. Yet they act differently with you now that you're in sales. People make up stories to avoid you, say they "have a friend in the business," secure information from you but do not give you information, or promise to meet with you at the office—but don't show up. You experience these feelings:

- Rejection
- Frustration
- Impatience
- Self-doubt
- Inadequacy

FIGURE 3.3   Managing Attitudes

Your image of yourself is tested. Who is the real you? The one who feels confident, tenacious, and is a self-starter? Or the one who feels rejected, frustrated, inadequate, and full of self-doubt? Your attitude about the business—and yourself—is in danger of shifting from positive to negative.

Big Idea: The best way to change your attitude from negative to positive is to get a sale.

Attitudes can change in seconds. Each day, hour, and minute, you evaluate your feelings about the business. Your *experiences* as you perform the activities in this plan fuel this evaluation. Your *conclusions* are based on your personal belief system. It's not the activities that cause you to have a certain attitude about the business, but the conclusions you draw from your experiences with these activities. Let's say you have knocked on 50 doors without getting a lead. What do you conclude? Agents who will fail conclude that "this won't work in this area." Agents who will succeed imagine themselves one step closer to a lead with every rejection. These agents realize that they must experience many rejections to get success.

Big Idea: Tenacity is the one character attribute that is 99% of an agent's success.

Big Idea: My survey showed the majority of new agents expect a sale in the first month. Not getting one puts their attitude in the dumper. A protection plan against an in-the-dumper attitude is to go out and talk to lots of people—fast. That is, lead generate!

Managing attitude shifts. Managers can teach new agents what activities to do, how to do them, and how to monitor them to evaluate effectiveness. Using the forms provided in this book, managers and agents can track agents' actual behaviors each day. But who will keep track of changing attitudes? Who will manage the conclusions about these activities? These emotional evaluations flit through a new agent's head hundreds of times a day. *How* these constantly changing attitudes are managed determines whether the agent will succeed.

What agents want. According to a recent survey of real estate salespeople, one of the most important services agents want from their manager is to provide positive motivation. Sounds easy, doesn't it? Part of it is. It's not difficult to create a positive atmosphere in the office. It is difficult to find out what motivates each individual (everyone has different motivators). And it is more difficult to design a motivational program to fit each agent's needs—time in the business, motivators, outside influences, and so on. Moreover, it's difficult for a manager to manage the constant flux of attitudes to catch agents when they are falling into depression and to pump them up. Agents' attitudes change hundreds of times a day. When agents get down, they usually talk to themselves—negatively. How can managers manage agents' ups and downs? They can't—but they can teach new agents how to manage their ups and downs.

Recognize →
Acknowledge →
Develop New Conclusions

Becoming a managing master of your attitudes. Managing your attitude requires three steps:

1. Recognize your attitude about the business will change as you do the activities in the business.
2. Acknowledge each time you draw a conclusion about your activities.
3. Develop a process for drawing a positive, motivating conclusion.

Make an attitude notebook. To evaluate and manage your attitude, try this simple, effective method. In a notebook, divide each page into the following six columns:

1. Self-talk
2. Conclusions of your self-talk
3. Positive attitude
4. Negative attitude
5. Revised conclusion or revised attitude
6. Belief

As you go about your business day, keep your attitude notebook handy. Write down each time you talk to yourself—positively and negatively. Let's say you just held an open house. As you are leaving, you say to yourself, "What's wrong with me? I thought I was a good communicator, but these people coming into my open house won't tell me anything." Write down the conclusion you drew: "Maybe I'm not cut out for this business." Note these thoughts in the proper column—*positive* or *negative*. Obviously, the above comment and conclusion would go in the negative column.

Drawing a positive, motivating conclusion. Studies show that most self-talk is negative, which naturally leads to a negative conclusion. People will talk to themselves about this conclusion 10 to 20 times and convince themselves that this conclusion is true. Thus, when agents conclude that they cannot be successful in open houses, that idea plays again and again in their minds until they change their positive attitude about their success in the business and form a new belief about their ability to communicate.

You can stop this insidious—although natural—process by replacing it with a new process. To do this, you must replace your natural inclination of negative self-talk, repeated again and again, with some positive self-talk, repeated again and again.

FIGURE 3.4   Attitude Notebook Excerpts

Negative Self-Talk	Positive Self-Talk
I can't do this.	I learned a lot from this one.
I'm not cut out for this.	One down, one to go.
Why did they do that to me?	I'm getting better every day.
What's wrong with them?	I'm learning what I need to learn to succeed.

Retraining your brain. Is this the conclusion about open houses that you really want to draw? Is this the attitude that will ensure your success in this business? Can you change your conclusion and attitude? Tough-minded, success-oriented people can adjust their conclusions and attitudes about their experiences to reach their goals. They experience the same rejection, self-doubt, frustration, and anxieties that failure-oriented people do. The only difference is that these tough-minded people have developed a mental system to reinterpret their conclusions. It's as simple as substituting a different conclusion, along with a change in attitude. So, go back to your attitude notebook and write a new conclusion to your experience. For the example above, it might be the following: "Based on my results, I'm not as good a communicator as I thought I was. I need to improve my communication skills. I can get these skills by taking a sales skills course, by observing agents who are successful at open houses, and by practicing my new skills."

> **Big Idea:** Tough-minded people retrain their brains to draw the best positive conclusions for their success.

Making your new conclusion believable. The last column in your attitude notebook, *belief*, is very important. If you don't believe that you can create a new conclusion, you will not take the action steps. In the belief column, add a statement that backs up your opinion about skills enhancement. It might be phrased like this: "I know that, if other agents can be successful getting appointments at open houses, I can be, too. It's just a matter of my learning, practicing, and perfecting the skills required."

Being tough-minded enough to succeed. The ability to consciously control your attitude is a skill that can be learned. To ensure your success in real estate, assume that you need to develop tough-mindedness. By following the steps outlined, you can become tough-minded enough to succeed in real estate.

There are many excellent self-help books on how to create a positive mental attitude, as well as courses and videos on self-esteem. One of the best courses, developed by Lou Tice, is offered at his Pacific Institute in Seattle, Washington.

Controlling your attitude is simple if you recognize that it's a skill that can be learned. It takes practice, tenacity, and patience. But isn't it worth it if it ensures your success in real estate? You have a proven, successful, activity-based, business-developing program in *Up and Running*. You have a manager committed to your success. You have the tools to retrain your mind and control your attitude. You are set for success!

> **Big Idea:** Start your *Up and Running* plan to get success fast; your attitude will take care of itself!

■ *Up and Running:* An Overview of Your Four Weeks

You've gotten lots of advice on starting your career. You know how to manage your actions—and your attitudes. Now you're ready to start your four-week plan. Each week, for four weeks, you will complete the following activities:

1. Create your weekly and daily plan. Use the provided planners; refer back to the Prototype Schedule and *30 Days to Dollars* plan. Be sure to keep a balance of business-producing activities and business-supporting activities. Ask your manager to assess the balance of your plan. Creating your plan and assessing it, two of the most valuable self-management tools in *Up and Running,* provide

the basis for making good business judgments throughout your entire career.

2. Complete the business-producing activities in the *30 Days to Dollars* lead-generating plan. See each week of the four-week plan. It's all outlined for you. Use the provided spreadsheets to measure your results weekly.

3. Complete your weekly schedule and daily plan using the provided planners so you can stay on track daily and weekly.

4. Practice and apply new sales skills. New sales skills are assigned each week to prepare you for sales activities with buyers and sellers.

5. Complete business-supporting activities, such as preparing packages and presentations, evaluating buyers and sellers, implementing your marketing plan, putting clients in your database and updating it, and following up with buyers and sellers, to increase your confidence and help you manage your time better.

6. Meet with your manager for support, information, and encouragement. It's difficult to go it alone, and your manager is committed to your success. *Up and Running* provides a solid foundation for communication between you and your manager.

■ Get Ready—Get Organized

I've provided a list of the materials you'll need to start your first week in the business in Figure 3.5 (there is a blank form for you to use in Unit 12.) See your manager to see if there are other materials you need, too.

These include three three-ring notebooks, each at least one inch thick. You'll see how you're going to use them in week one, discussed in Unit 4. So, your assignment before starting your week one is to do two things:

1. Finish your orientation with your manager and staff and complete all the actions requested of you (if you've already started or done your orientation). I've also assigned this in week one because I don't know how long you've been in the business at this point.

2. Go through the Get Ready checklist in this unit and gather all the materials you'll need. When you get the three-ring notebooks, name one attitude notebook, one office notebook, and one resource notebook. You'll see in Unit 4 (week one) how you're going to use them.

Big Idea: Finish all the actions asked of you by your manager and staff within your first week of the business so you can launch your career with the support you need.

FIGURE 3.5   Get Ready: Gather the Tools of the Trade and Get Ready to Sell

Briefcase	**Car**
Smartphone	Sold signs
Pen	Tape measure
Pencil	Mallet and nails
Colored pen or pencil	Screwdriver
Calendar (or on your smartphone)	Flashlight
Highlighter	Coveralls
Scratch pad	Overshoes
Post-it notes	First aid kit
Daily planner	**Forms****
Access to your MLS	Purchase and sale agreements
Street map	Wording for contract forms
Paper clips	Other contract addenda
Tape measure (100 ft or 30.5 m)	Listing agreements
Staple gun	Other forms pertaining to listing
Laptop computer	**Be Sure You Have**
Handheld calculator	Adequate car insurance (check your agency contract)
Digital camera	A method to keep tax records (see your accountant before you become an independent contractor)
Other Materials	Joined your REALTOR® organization
Attitude notebook*	Completed your manager's orientation
Office notebook*	Chosen a database or contact management program
Resource notebook*	

*These notebooks are assignments in *Up and Running* to ensure you are tracking your attitude, your office resources, and other resources.

**Many of the forms you need are available online. Be sure to have your laptop with you everywhere and be able to access the internet.

Manager's Tip: Help your agent clear all the bases in the "get ready" checklist. Be sure your agent has a database and contact management before starting her start-up plan. Recommendations for these are in the Resources unit.

Manager's Tip: Be sure your orientation has an action plan of the items you expect agents to complete and a method to check off with them to ensure they've been accountable—quickly—to accomplish what you and your staff expect. This way, your agents get the support you promised during the interview, and they're ready to get to work. Visit www.carlacross .com for a prototype orientation checklist.

Get Ready with the Technologies You Will Need

Although you won't be using all these technologies right away, I'm providing you with a list to keep for when you need these tools. See the References and Resources unit also. And, very importantly, see your manager or coach!

- Database and contact management—Take a look at Wise Agent, Top Producer®, or www.crosscoachingtoolbox.com. See other programs in the References and Resources unit, too. Some companies have branded versions of popular software. Don't reinvent the wheel! Use the resources your company provides or endorses. (If you just can't bring yourself to purchase any of these, at least learn and populate a Gmail or Outlook account. However, you'll save thousands of dollars in lost contacts if you step up to the plate at the beginning of your career and invest in some robust CRM. Many of the programs I'll mention offer several services. Pick and choose the ones that fit your needs.)
- A place to store your files in the "cloud"—www.Dropbox.com, www.Box.com, or Google Drive
- A method to send large files—www.Hightail.com
- A program so that you can send offers, contracts, and disclosures electronically and obtain digital signatures—www.DocuSign.com or www.DotLoop.com
- An inexpensive method to print postcards and flyers: www.express-copy.com
- A resource to share files—Google Drive
- Program to edit photos—Google Photos
- An IDX solution so that buyers can search your website for listings and contact you (these all have follow-up programs, too, to make it easy to capture and keep leads):
  - www.marketleader.com
  - www.boomtownroi.com
  - www.idxcentral.com
  - www.diversesolutions.com
  - www.placester.com
  - www.zurple.com

See all my recommendations in various categories in the References and Resources unit. Also, see your manager!

Here's some specific advice for new agents from technology and website expert Tricia Andreassen, tech expert, author, and certified executive coach:

1. Make sure you secure your own domain name. It's important to have a domain name that either you have that you can put with your company-provided site or a site of your own. That way you start branding from the beginning and get the foundation in place.

2. Make sure you have a stand-alone website that can easily grow with you. Ask the Web provider if you can add unlimited pages, photos, video, social media elements, and even your own links and PDFs. This allows you to have a solid foundation in place even if you end up moving companies down the road.

3. Have your own IDX (multiple listing service [MLS] search tool). There could be rules in your MLS that prevent you from having your own MLS search, but you'll want to investigate this. Your broker may give you a link or the MLS may also provide a free MLS search link, but you want to have a search tool that brands you as the agent of contact for every listing. It should have a built-in lead capture element as well so you can generate as many leads as possible and ensure that you are the one getting the lead.

4. Secure additional domain names that provide you extreme target market reach. This is a powerful way to kick up additional leads. For example, potential sellers will be drawn to an ad that indicates they can get information on their local market conditions. Having a domain name like www.FortMillHomeValues.com will compel the homeowner to visit. Have the domain name point to a page within your site or, even better, point to a specific landing page.

5. Get to know craigslist. This is a free way to run ads and drive traffic to the pages within your site as well as search properties on the MLS. Post in the real estate services section as well as the for sale sections.

■ Summary

Live each day as closely to that successful agent's job description as you can. Doing the *Up and Running* plan ensures that.

Your goal throughout this four-week plan is to develop the skills to self-manage your business. To do that, you need to

- follow the *Up and Running* plan to the letter;
- use the measurement spreadsheets and checklists I provided to help you self-manage;
- rely on yourself, not on anyone else, including your manager, to hand you leads or keep you motivated;
- manage your attitude with your attitude notebook—the best way to do that is to get out in the field now and go to work;

- recognize you will underestimate your resilience to rejection and develop the mind skills to accentuate the positive and keep going; and
- enlist your manager as your coach so you'll have an accountability partner.

Now, let's jump right into your week one start-up plan!

Week One Start-Up Plan

Note to managers:

Your new agents should be starting week one of the start-up plan the second week they are in the business. The first week should consist of your orientation. In addition, your new agents should have read the first three units of this resource.

Let's start the first day of your successful career! Units 4–7 are literally your start-up plan. In this unit, you'll get the activity plan for your first week in the business. Also, because you're just starting this plan, I'll explain how to use the various tracking forms I've created. As you use these forms, you'll be developing exceptional time management skills. You don't know it yet, but time management is rated as the number one challenge agents have!

Throughout your four-week plan, you'll have a very detailed, precise weekly plan to follow.

Your activities are divided between

- business producing and
- business supporting.

They're divided and prioritized this way to train your mind to think like a top producer. Business-producing activities involve directly finding and working with potential buyers and sellers. Business-supporting activities are those "get ready" and "practice" activities—packaging your presentations and processes, practicing your sales skills, and learning the technical aspects of the business.

■ Regular Activities Create Success Habits

Every week, you will have certain regular activities, so you'll develop automatic, unconscious success habits. Don't look for new stuff every week. What you need to do is create the routine top producers use to generate and regenerate their businesses.

77

Weekly Regular Business-Supporting Activities

1. Create your weekly schedule in advance of the following week
2. Add at least 50 contacts to your database
3. Write at least 15 follow-up notes
4. Add one social network
5. Evaluate your buyers and sellers using the buyers and sellers evaluation sheets
6. Work your marketing plan
7. Work your social media plan
8. Work your technology plan
9. Practice the sales skills assigned in week one
10. Apply the sales skills that are assigned for week one in real life
11. Add to your resource, attitude, and office notebooks
12. Plan and measure your results: for the day-to-day measurements, use the Daily Planner; for week-to-week measurements, use the Weekly Accomplishments; also use the spreadsheets to compare your goals to your actuals (what you actually did)

In the "business producing" category, every week you will

1. implement your *30 Days to Dollars* lead-generating plan by contacting at least 100 people using the methods introduced in that week,
2. get two qualified seller leads,
3. get two qualified buyer leads,
4. show homes to two qualified buyer groups, and
5. go to at least one listing appointment.

That number of business-producing activities ensures you are on the road to quick success. To make certain you are being accountable to your success, you will be setting goals in each of the areas above and measuring your successes.

Every week, you will have certain regular business-supporting activities to create the systems and processes you need to be trustworthy to buyers and sellers—and to raise your confidence.

Separating these activities into clear categories gives you focus. Doing these activities in sufficient numbers and in the right order creates success habits for you. These are the success habits of a top producer.

How Do I Do These Things?

There is a lot of training in this edition of *Up and Running*. In each week's activities, I have told you the time for that particular skill training. For example, in week one, you will be circle prospecting to get leads. The how-to is in Unit 8, so don't worry that you'll have an action expected of you that you don't know how to do. Units 8–10 have all the how-tos, scripts, and forms you'll need. If there's additional training you want, ask your manager! In addition, your company training program may train you in sales skills and systems. I'll also provide you additional training resources in this business start-up plan. They are referred to in the body of this resource and also listed in the Resource unit.

Manager's Tip: Look through each week's assignments. Have a list of office and outside resources for your agent to help your agent accomplish these support activities.

Scripts, Letters, and Processes Unit

Unit 13 includes the scripts and letters introduced in this program so you can find them easily. These scripts and letters provide you the information you need to lead generate and master those critical sales skills.

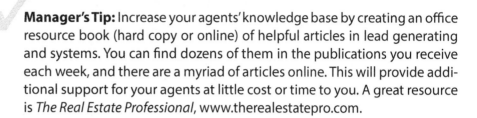

Manager's Tip: Increase your agents' knowledge base by creating an office resource book (hard copy or online) of helpful articles in lead generating and systems. You can find dozens of them in the publications you receive each week, and there are a myriad of articles online. This will provide additional support for your agents at little cost or time to you. A great resource is *The Real Estate Professional*, www.therealestatepro.com.

Organizing All the Information You'll be Getting

We've already talked about your attitude notebook, which you'll be writing in daily. Weekly, you'll see adding to it is a regular business-supporting assignment. In addition, there are two other notebooks I want you to create to organize all that information you'll be getting:

1. Office notebook
2. Resource notebook

I'll be reminding you weekly to add to them so you can find that valuable information you need—when you need it!

Why notebooks, not files? Because I want you to immediately see that notebook in a prominent place. I don't want you to agonize about what to call a file. I don't want you to file it away so you can't find it! I've tried it both ways, and a notebook is better. Also, some of these notebooks you'll want to carry with you. With small laptops and iPads today, you can carry the electronic version with you!

Why not just keep these things in a computer folder? With some of them, you can. Make a folder called "Office Communication" and put all your office communication there. The challenge with that is you may forget to do it, put it in the wrong folder, and so on. I find that most people don't remember where they filed a document in their computer. Also, we're visual people, and we're tactile. Organizing hard copies of these things in notebooks means you have to look at them before you put them in your notebook. It means you look at them again naturally as you're searching for something in that notebook.

Big Idea: Use hard-copy notebooks to start your career. They'll remind you of the many details you're bound to forget!

Office notebook. As you join your office, you'll be given all kinds of information about the office. You'll probably attend an office orientation. Where will you put all this information so you'll be able to find it when you need it? In your office notebook. This would include all the information you got from orientation, your office meeting agendas, phone system how-tos, and anything you need to be able to locate later.

Resource notebook. Put all your information from your business-supporting activities in this notebook. For instance, when you talk with a loan officer, put all the information you got from her about interest rates, points, and so on to qualify a purchaser in this notebook. Take the notebook with you in the field! This will be a lifesaver for you when you're in an open house and a buyer asks, "What's the interest rate today?" Believe me, you will be getting so much valuable yet disparate information, you will not know what to do with it. Then, when you need it, you won't have it! So start your resource notebook today. You can make sections for the following categories:

- Finance
- Inspections
- Title insurance
- Attorney's closing fees
- Escrow fees
- Home insurance
- Law updates
- Short sales
- Foreclosures
- New multiple listing service (MLS) rules

Keeping this information in a folder in your computer for reference is acceptable, but keep in mind that you won't look at it, compare it, delete it, or have it handy when you need it.

Definitions, definitions, definitions. One of the confusing things a new agent has to contend with is the many new terms thrown at him. For example, there's home insurance and mortgage insurance. What's the difference? You should have all those definitions in your resource notebook so you'll know and be able to explain them to buyers and sellers. Don't always believe those seasoned agents when they explain things. They may not really know, either!

Big Idea: Start organizing now. *Any* organization is better than none.

■ Week One *Up and Running* Plan

Note to managers:

Use Unit 12 to coach and hold your agent accountable. Every assignment is in the checklist for each week.

These activities are all listed in your week one accomplishments document in Unit 12 with the week one forms.

Business Producing

Implement your *30 Days to Dollars* lead-generating plan. Contact at least 100 people using the following methods:

- Call or contact 50 people you know (see Unit 8 for a script)
- Circle prospect 50 people (see Unit 8 for definition and operation)
- Follow up on initial online leads—at least 25 (reactive)
- Get two qualified seller leads
- Get two qualified buyer leads
- Show homes to two qualified buyer groups
- Go to at least one listing appointment

These assigned activities are already in your spreadsheets, your *30 Days to Dollars* lead-generating plan, and *30 Days to Dollars* lead-generating results for your week one in Unit 12. All you need to do is log your actuals.

Business Supporting

Regular actions include the following:

- Create your weekly schedule in advance of the following week (a blank form is in Unit 12 for you, marked "Week One")
- Add at least 50 contacts to your database
- Write at least 15 follow-up notes
- Continue to follow up on contacted online leads
- Add one social network each week; this week, it's your website and blog
- Implement your social media plan (in Unit 12)
- Evaluate your buyers and sellers using the buyers and sellers evaluation sheets (in Unit 12)
- Do the activities in your marketing (follow-up) plan for that first week
- Practice the sales skills assigned in that particular week
- Apply the sales skills that are assigned for that week in real life
- Add to your resource notebook
- Add to your attitude notebook
- Add to your office notebook

At the end of the week, before your appointment with your manager, measure your results using the four measurements below:

1. Daily, use the Daily Planner
2. Evaluate your time management on your weekly schedule
3. Check off your completed activities on your weekly accomplishments
4. Weekly, complete the goals/actuals spreadsheets

The following are additional business-supporting activities for your first week:

Sales skills

- Using sales skill 1, craft a sales script to call on people you know (see Unit 8).
- Using sales skill 1, craft an initial contact to online leads (see Unit 10).
- Using sales skill 3, ask for a lead (see Unit 10).
- Create three visuals to counter seller's objections to pricing (see your manager or three agents in your office for suggestions; see Unit 10 for training on answering objections).

Sales opportunities

- If you're going to hold an open house or take floor time, get information from your manager on how to do each of these reactive lead-generating activities.
- Observe two public open houses this weekend; interview the agents who hold them open about their methods.
- Observe at least one hour of floor time this week (or, if you don't have floor time, observe three agents handling incoming calls).
- Observe an agent answering initial online leads; interview the agent.
- Interview the agents who take floor time about their methods.

Technical information

- Complete all your office orientation duties (get your business cards, etc.) and put all the information in your office notebook.
- Meet with a loan officer and have that loan officer teach you the basics of financing (get a loan officer referral from your manager); put all that information in your resource notebook.
- Ask three experienced agents to see their comparative market analyses (CMAs). Take notes so you can compile your own. Then, complete a market analysis on your own home. Practice presenting it to a "seller" so you'll be comfortable with the format and information.

Planning

- Complete your real estate budget using the form called Budget for the New Agent in Unit 12.
- Make your technology plan using the Technology Budget and Planner in Unit 12.
- Create your marketing plan (see Unit 9 for how to create your plan and a sample plan) using the Your Marketing Plan form in Unit 12.
- Implement the social media planner in Unit 12.

Your Website and Blog

Ask your manager for recommendations on agent websites. Your company may offer website templates or branded versions of website builders. View at least three agents' websites that you believe are good. See the References and Resources unit for companies that build websites.

Do you want to include IDX technology (all MLS listings appear on your website and you capture leads)? You should! Remember that almost half of all buyers look at websites to view potential homes, and almost half purchase a home they see on a website! So, be sure your website provider includes IDX, or add it with Market Leader, BoomTown, IDXCentral, or Diverse Solutions. See the References and Resources unit for more suggestions.

For expert help in creating your website, blog, or both, see the descriptions of my online, technology, and social media gurus in the References and Resources unit. Check out John Mayfield's resources at www.businesstechguy.com. John has given you recommendations here, and he is a wonderful, patient, clear teacher. The National Association of REALTORS® two-day e-PRO® certification program is comprehensive (www.epronar.com). Of course, see your manager for recommendations, too.

Planning and Measuring Your Results

You know the importance of planning and measuring the plan. I've created the planning and measurement tools to make it easy for you to become a master of planning and measuring.

Every week, you will be using four methods to plan and measure your results:

- Your weekly schedule. You'll set your schedule and evaluate it each week for effective time management.
- Your *Up and Running* Daily Planner. You'll use one page per day to self-manage effectively. At the end of the day, you'll evaluate the effectiveness of your day.
- Your weekly accomplishments. You'll check off your assigned actions and do a self-evaluation for effective time management.
- Your goals/actuals spreadsheets. You'll keep your completed businessproducing actions on these spreadsheets so you can see your progress through time.

Unit 12: All Your Blank Forms Ready to Use

To make it easy for you to use the forms, I've put them all in Unit 12, with one set of forms for each week. Most of the forms are already filled out with that particular week's activities. All you have to do is make alterations (we hope you won't make any) and log the actions you accomplished that week.

Why set your goals and track your accomplishments so frequently? Because you want to get into the habit. Most agents don't do this, so they have terrible time management problems.

Manager's Tip: Review all the forms in Unit 12 so you're confident in coaching to them.

How to Create Your Weekly Schedule

You have your start-up plan for your first week. Now you need to make a weekly schedule that integrates the action steps in your plan. I've made a sample weekly schedule for you so you can see how your plan should look for its first week (see Figure 4.1).

Using the blank weekly planner for week one in Unit 12, plan your first week. Create your plan in the following order:

1. Log office-scheduled events (e.g., office meeting, tour)
2. Log assignments from office (e.g., floor time, open house)
3. Log your coaching meeting with the manager
4. Log business-producing activities and those on business cycle (e.g., showings, listing presentations, writing offers)
5. Log lead-generating activities
6. Log support activities, including inspecting inventory and support assignments given here

FIGURE 4.1   Sample *Up and Running* Weekly Schedule for Week One

Week: _____ One _____   Name: _____ Joan Smith _____

Time	Monday	Tuesday	Wednesday	Thursday	Friday	Saturday	Sunday
7–8	Organize desk		Day off	Write 40 follow-up cards			
8–9	Office meeting	Paperwork			Meet w/ mgr	Paperwork	
9–10	Office tour	Call 20 people I know		Call 10 people to ask for leads	Call 20 people to ask for leads	Show homes	
10–11							Show homes
11–12	Lunch	Floor time		Paperwork	Inspect		
12–1	Office orient.	Lunch		Lunch	Lunch	Lunch	Lunch
1–2	Inspect inventory	Start market analysis		Inspect inventory	Inspect	Floor time	Follow up
2–3					Bus. support work		In-person visits to five people
3–4	Call 20 people I know	Follow up		Follow up		Inspect inventory	
4–5	List 100 people to ask for leads	Inspect inventory		Meet with loan officer	Circle prospect 25 homes	Circle prospect 25 homes	
5–6							
6–7							
7–8							Do listing presentation
8–9							

Suggested Hours Weekly:

Lead generating

Qualifying buyers/sellers

Show properties/listing properties

Purchase/sale agreements

How could you improve your schedule?

What You Did

10 _____ hours

5 _____ hours

5 _____ hours

5 _____ hours

Evaluate Your Weekly Schedule

Rate yourself in the effectiveness of your weekly schedule: _____

1–10 (10 is high)

Note: You may choose to enter your schedule into your smartphone. This will allow you to view your schedule at any time, along with your contacts and other pertinent information.

At the end of your week, evaluate how you did, using the evaluators in your weekly schedule. Note the suggested hours weekly of various business-producing activities. How did you compare? Rate yourself on how effective you believe that particular weekly schedule was for you. Now you're developing the time management tools other agents will envy!

Why Evaluation Is So Important for You

Unfortunately, most people think the first time they do something is as good as it's going to get! Why? Because they don't know how to get better at something. As a lifelong performing musician, I know you don't have to settle for a mediocre performance. I know the first time I do something isn't as good as that performance will be later. I know how to get better. I've built evaluators into this program because it's one of the methods I use as a performance coach to increase my clients' confidence and help them get performance mastery.

Big Idea: Evaluating how you did automatically creates better performance next time. Those who learn to self-manage control their success.

■ How to Create Your Daily Plan

You've created your weekly schedule. Now, manage your actions daily by using the Daily Planner shown in Figure 4.2. (Blank daily planners are included for each of the four weeks in Unit 12. You will copy these so you have one for each day of the week.) Why do it daily? To ensure you are establishing top-flight time management habits! Also, by tracking your accomplishments daily, you'll be able to congratulate yourself as you go—and quickly make the needed adjustments in your plan.

How to Use the Week One (and Ensuing Weeks) Accomplishments

I've put all the actions in your start-up plan for each week into your weekly accomplishments document. There is one for each week in Unit 12. All you have to do is complete the actions and log them. Now, meet with your manager weekly to review your accomplishments and challenges.

FIGURE 4.2   *Up and Running* Daily Planner

Date: _____

Priorities: **Accomplished**   **Notes:**

1. _____   ☐   _____
2. _____   ☐   _____
3. _____   ☐   _____
4. _____   ☐   _____
5. _____   ☐   _____
6. _____   ☐   _____
7. _____   ☐   _____
8. _____   ☐   _____
9. _____   ☐   _____
10. _____   ☐   _____

	Lead Generating	Qualified Leads	Listing Appointments	Home Showings
Activity				
Hours Spent				

	Listings Obtained	Sales	Listings Sold
Results			

Rate your efforts on a scale of 1–10 _____

How can you improve your rating? _____

At the end of the week, transfer your numbers of activities to your spreadsheets in Unit 12.

Note: Make six copies of this sheet per week.

How to Use the Goals/Actuals Spreadsheets

Figure 2.6 and Figure 2.7 are a concise way to look at your goals and accomplishments for each week. In Unit 12, I have created a goals/actuals spreadsheet entitled "Your *30 Days to Dollars* Lead-Generating Plan" with the assignments in your *Up and Running* plan. All you have to do is to log your results. Take these tools with you when you meet with your manager, so you can see your progress over this four-week time frame.

> **Big Idea:** Tracking your goals and actuals in lead generating and the results of lead generating allow you to see your own success ratios and work from them long term.

■ Final Thoughts for Week One

If you are like many new agents, at the end of week one, your brain feels like mush. New words, new systems, unfamiliar territory—no wonder new agents may reevaluate their charge-ahead attitude and decide to ease into the career! They reason that they must spend more time on learning, research, and organization—instead of talking to people so quickly. Their confidence decreases as rejection increases. New agents conclude that to increase their confidence they need more knowledge.

Build Real, Lasting Confidence

Up and Running is designed to build your confidence the right way—through increasing your skills. Real estate is a performance art, not a knowledge pursuit; true confidence in real estate is built from successful performance. However, until you perform, you have only your practice and imagination to build your confidence. Although there are methods to increase your confidence mentally, they pale before the reality of a great performance.

> **Big Idea:** Confidence and motivation are built from practice and performance.

The Value of Practice

It's painful to learn from your mistakes with real clients. However, there's an additional way to learn skills—practice. All too often, the value of practice is underestimated by both agents and managers, but it's worth the effort to role-play each segment that follows requires sales communication with people:

- Lead-generating scenarios
- Following up with online inquiries
- Counseling and qualifying buyer scenarios
- Showing and closing buyer scenarios
- Negotiating offer scenarios
- Qualifying seller scenarios
- Marketing and presentation scenarios
- Price reduction and review scenarios

Agents believe that because they can talk, they can sell. But we have already discussed the realities of conversation versus the special communication skills required for sales success. I guarantee that if you take seriously the practice asked of you in *Up and Running*, your performance with people will improve quickly and your confidence will soar. Every successful salesperson I have known who started quickly in this business organized, systematized, practiced, and perfected each step in the sales cycle.

> **Caution:** A reason new agents start slowly or fail early is that they underestimated their need to develop a mastery of sales skills in their first months in the business. So, they fail to convert those leads!

Perfect Practice Makes Perfect

The best kind of practice increases your skill and results. Back to my piano-practicing days: as a four-year-old, I picked out tunes on the keys and added the chords. I could play pop music reasonably well. Then, at age six, I started piano lessons. As I progressed to more demanding piano teachers, I learned that "faking it 'til you made it" just would not meet their standards. In fact, my best piano teacher, Mr. Green, taught me to practice very slowly *so there weren't any mistakes.* I found that if I practiced quickly, I practiced my mistakes right along with the rest of the piece.

Although his kind of practice was tedious, it was right. By using Mr. Green's method, I became a much better pianist, gaining a degree in piano performance. Too often, real estate agents practice the mistakes and end up with a sales system that is "more mistake than effective."

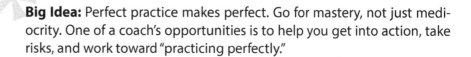

> **Big Idea:** Perfect practice makes perfect. Go for mastery, not just mediocrity. One of a coach's opportunities is to help you get into action, take risks, and work toward "practicing perfectly."

A Desire to Do It Again

If you have ever experienced the exhilaration of a fine performance, you know you want to run right out and do it again! Success is a great motivator. As we progress through Units 4–7 we will be discussing self-motivation. For now, suffice it to say that good performance is the best motivator—and, correspondingly, the best motivator for selling is selling. This is the greatest reason to get out into the real estate field, even before you are comfortable: to motivate yourself to continue your quest for a successful real estate career.

■ Summary

Week one activities have you jumping right into your career. After all, you want to make a sale fast, so we're starting you fast! In week one, you are making a total of 100 sales calls. You're likely to get

- two qualified buyer leads and two qualified seller leads,
- two buyer showings, and
- one listing presentation.

What a start to your career!

This is also the week that you'll want to get all of that housekeeping out of the way. Organize everything. Learn the office operations. Find out how to do those reactive activities, like floor time, if you have it. Start learning the technical aspects of the business, like finance, as assigned in your business-supporting activities. We've also started you in skill development—learning and practicing those sales calls and sales skills that will get you more business easier. Finally, you started using the time-management tools that ensure you get started like a future superstar.

Congratulate yourself for an action-packed, focused first week in the business.

Manager's Tip: Ask the agent to provide you the checklists from each week a day before your meeting about that week so you can review them and be ready to work with the agent. Have ready an example listing presentation and resources for your agent to use to assemble the presentation. Have ready an example buyer presentation and resources for your agent to use to assemble the presentation. See the References and Resources unit for more information.

Week Two Start-Up Plan

Welcome to week two of your four-week start-up plan. This week you will learn and put into action additional types of lead generation—one of the priorities in your *30 Days to Dollars* lead-generating plan. They are

- For-sale-by-owner or expired listings (you choose) and
- open houses.

Even though you may choose not to use some of the lead-generating methods introduced here long term, you are expanding your skills. You are developing a lead-generating repertoire so you'll have it when you need it. When I was in college, I worked my way through school playing piano in bars. (I learned more about human nature than I really wanted to know!) I found that the more tunes and styles I could play, the more tips I made. Hence, I developed a wide repertoire. I never knew when it would come in handy. Having several lead-generating skills available to you is your insurance plan against changing markets.

■ Week Two *Up and Running* Plan

Besides learning more sales skills in week two, you will start assembling your systems for managing the buyer and seller sales processes. By the end of this program, I want you to have complete systems in place so you can go faster, build better, and create your business on the strongest foundation possible. Here are your actions for this week.

Business Producing

Make 100 sales contacts using the following lead-generating methods:
- Make 25 contacts to people you know
- Circle prospect 50 people
- Call on at least 25 for-sale–by-owner or expired listings (see Units 8 and 10 for skill development)

Reactive lead-generating actions:

- Hold one public open house this weekend
- Do initial follow-up on online leads

To prepare and develop the best strategies, talk to three people in your office. Even though I've assigned only one open house in this series, if you are encouraged to do this in your company and you have traffic in these houses, assign yourself at least one open house per week.

Get these three results:

1. Secure two qualified buyer appointments.
2. Show homes to two qualified buyer groups.
3. Secure one appointment to do a listing presentation.

These assigned activities are already in your spreadsheets, your *30 Days to Dollars* lead-generating plan, and your *30 Days to Dollars* lead-generating results for your week two (in Unit 12). All you need to do is log your actuals.

Business Supporting

Do these regular actions:

- Create your weekly schedule in advance of the following week (a blank form is in Unit 12 for you).
- Add at least 50 contacts to your database.
- Write at least 15 follow-up notes.
- Implement your social media plan daily.
- Evaluate your buyers and sellers using the buyers and sellers evaluation sheets (in Unit 12).
- Do the activities in your marketing (follow-up) plan for this week.
- Practice the sales skills assigned for this week.
- Apply the sales skills that are assigned for this week in real life.
- Follow your technology planner.
- Add to your resource notebook.
- Add to your attitude notebook.
- Add to your office notebook.

Online Resources to Help You Assemble Your Comparative Market Analysis and Presentation

First, let's define terms. A comparative market analysis (CMA) shows home sellers how their home fits into the pricing in the market. It is not a full-listing presentation. It is only the pricing part of the listing presentation. See your manager first for suggestions on how to do a comparative market analysis and any tools recommended. Online resources for CMAs are www.cloudCMA.com, www.ToolkitCMA.com, and www.Property-Minder.com.

Listing Presentation Resources

Different strokes for different folks! Be careful of using a canned online listing presentation at all times. You want to be flexible. You want to communicate with that seller the way the seller wants to be communicated with. So, use your technological tools wisely. For a comprehensive training or presentation program on the listing process, see *Your Complete Power Listing System* (www.carlacross.com). One online listing presentation resource includes Top Producer®. In addition, there are many free online listing presentations available. Beware: These are too generic to be very useful to you. To make your listing presentation stand out, you must communicate your specific value.

Another tip about company listing presentations is to take the time to add your perspective. Unfortunately, most are written from the perspective of the company, not the agent. Remember, the seller wants to know what you—I mean you, the agent—will do for them, not just what the company will do or how big the company is. You are the focus; the company is the support. See Figure 5.1 for suggested materials for listing presentations.

You will see "marketing plan" in my listing presentation checklist. To assemble that marketing plan, refer to *Your Complete Power Listing System*. In addition, there are online marketing programs that work for you to provide your listing exposure to the market.

Resources You May Want to Use to Market Your Listings

- Virtual tours. help buyers visualize properties for sale and are important to include. Virtual tour programs include Obeo, RealBiz Media, and Paradym. TourFactory also includes many features involved in marketing the listing, including marketing pieces and reports. Check out all these programs to see what combinations you need.
- Single property websites—AgencyLogic, Listing Domains, and Listings Unlimited
- Interactive voice response (IVR) technology—iHOUSEweb and Proquest Technologies, Arch Telecom, and ArchAgent
- Marketing your listings and capturing leads—Listings-to-Leads

Note to managers:

Have listing presentation resources ready for your agent, including company or independent resources, so the agent doesn't have to start from scratch.

Please understand that I am not endorsing any of these. I'm just helping you get an idea of the dozens of programs you can use to sell real estate. Good overall resources for products are www.crs.com and REALTOR® Magazine Online, which have articles galore on technology and how to use it.

At the end of the week, measure your results using the four measurements below. Before your appointment with your manager, do these specific business-supporting activities:

1. Use the Daily Planner.
2. Evaluate your time management on your weekly schedule.
3. Check off your completed activities on your weekly accomplishments.
4. Complete the goals/actuals spreadsheets weekly.

FIGURE 5.1   Suggested Materials for Seller Listing Presentations

---

Materials can include the following (may be a hard copy or an online presentation, depending on your seller's needs):

1. How you publicize the property to other agents (show a list of agents and an example of an email you send them; target this email to agents specializing in properties of this type)

2. How you advertise the property (show examples of your company advertising)

3. Examples of your social media and showing how you use social media to market the property, including your Facebook business page and your blog

4. How you make a brochure for the property (show a sample of the brochure or flyer you use)

5. How you publicize the property on the company or your website (show a picture of one of your listings on the website and how you publicize it)

6. How you hold open houses (show a checklist of what you do to prepare for the open house; show pictures of you holding the home open)

7. Your checklist for after the listing is signed (to prove that you are organized and responsible)

8. What services your company provides (list all the services and why they are important to the seller)

9. The services you provide (such as circle prospecting, contacting other agents, etc.)

10. The differences about your company (list them)

11. How you are different as an agent (list and show them)

12. Pricing principles (and why overpricing is not in the seller's best interest)

13. Market trends

14. Marketing plan (in writing); include examples of how you use social media to promote a home (craigslist, your blog, ActiveRain, Facebook business page), plus realtor.com®, Trulia, and Zillow. Do you have a Google map of the home location? If so, take a screen shot and include it.

15. Marketing calendar (in writing)

16. Pictures of homes you've listed or sold

17. Testimonials of those you have worked with (should also be in your professional portfolio)

18. Stills of your virtual tours

Excerpted from *Your Complete Power Listing System*, www.carlacross.com.

Here are additional business-supporting assignments:

- Practice and apply sales skill 4 to master sales skills, Objection-Busting (see Unit 10).
- Start assembling listing presentation materials (talk to your manager for ideas and a possible company presentation, and see the References and Resources unit).
- Assemble your listing presentation materials by putting into a folder the information you want to share with sellers about your services. Figure 5.1 gives you suggestions about what can go into this presentation.
- Add one social media. This week is creating your Facebook business page and establishing a Twitter account (if you decide to add Twitter at this time). Inspect three agents' Facebook business pages to get ideas on effective pages. Read Facebook rules on posting so

you're sure to follow the rules. If you need it, find a graphic artist or webmaster to create your Facebook business page. See how agents are using Twitter. Do you want to add it now or add it your second or third month in the business?

Caveat: Do not spend hundreds of hours making your social media perfect right now. Just get your website or blog started, along with your Facebook business page. Keep working on them throughout your program and after. Remember, your main job is to proactively generate leads, not play on the computer with social media!

Tip: I do my two blogs at the beginning of each week and schedule them to be published throughout the week. I also schedule them to appear in Twitter. Most importantly, if you do a blog, you must be consistent!

After you have chosen the materials you want to include, put them in an order that makes it easy for you to present them. One sales tip is, as you assemble the materials, ask yourself, "Which objection does this particular visual counter?" See more about visuals to handle objections in Unit 10.

Review three agents' listing presentations and take notes. Integrate their ideas, with their permission, into your marketing presentation.

Interview three agents on the three most common objections sellers have to listing and how these agents handle the objections. Write their answers and practice the ones you like best.

Note to managers:

Have buyer presentation resources ready for your agents so they don't have to reinvent the wheel.

Buyer presentation. Assemble a buyer presentation, similar to a seller presentation but focused for buyers (see your manager and the References and Resources unit for ideas, as well as *Your Complete Buyer's Agent Toolkit* at www.carlacross.com). Figure 5.2 (hard copy and online, depending on the needs of the buyer) also gives you ideas about what you can put into a buyer presentation.

Tip: As with listing presentations, company buyer presentations spotlight company features, not yours. Use your company buyer presentation, but spotlight you. Why? You want to prove to a buyer that you are professional, prepared, organized, and fully dedicated to helping them find the right home for them.

Review three agents' buyer presentations and take notes. Integrate the ideas you like, with their permission, into your buyer presentation. By the way, you may find that few agents in your office use buyer presentations. However, with the majority of buyers being represented by buyer's agents, it's very important to treat buyers as though they are as important as sellers—because they are!

Interview three agents about the three most common objections buyers have to buying and how these agents handle these objections. Write their answers and practice the ones you think are best.

To gain technical skills. Write two purchase and sale agreements. Include one practice agreement for purchasing the property you currently own and one using a method to purchase other than conventional financing.

FIGURE 5.2   Suggestions for Buyer Presentations
(hard copy and online, depending on the needs of the buyer)

Materials can include the following:

1. The steps in purchasing a home
2. Time line for purchasing a home
3. Steps after you've purchased the home
4. Loan application checklist
5. Home inspection checklist
6. Offer preparation checklist
7. The parties involved in the purchasing process—and what they do
8. Market conditions
9. Describe your ideal home
10. Prioritize your home needs
11. How I work for you
12. How to choose the right agency relationship for you
13. Types of agency representation
14. Services of a buyer's agent
15. The buyer's agency agreement
16. Checklist for the buying experience
17. Advice to buyers
18. What is a REALTOR®?
19. Most used terms
20. If we work together
21. My commitment to you

Excerpted from *The Complete Buyer's Agent Toolkit*, www.carlacross.com.

■ Why Put All That Time into Creating Visual Systems?

The Benefits of Visuals

- Builds credibility
- Is self-teaching
- Helps organize
- Counters objections
- Builds confidence

This week, I've asked you to start organizing your seller and buyer visual presentations. Why? Because I want to give you every bit of support, guidance, and added edge that I can to ensure you convert leads to customers and clients. Creating visual systems does five things for you:

- It makes you look credible and professional—we believe what we see, not what we hear.
- It is a self-teaching tool—you'll learn how to counter those objections and how to present to buyers and sellers 100% faster with these tools than without them.
- You'll learn how to best organize your presentation to flow smoothly.
- You'll learn the visuals that best counter the common objections.
- It is a great confidence-building tool—you will never feel like you're out on a limb without the answers to sellers' and buyers' questions.

Trying to give a professional presentation without the visuals is like trying to play a Mozart sonata just by listening to it. Trust me—as a musician, it can't be done. Not only is it very difficult to remember what you wanted to say to a buyer or seller when you're under stress, it just isn't nearly as effective for you. I know because I've had agents do listing presentations in class for other agents with visuals and without them. The agents without visuals were voted worst presenters and not as credible as those with visuals!

You're Going to See and Hear the Good, the Bad, and the Ugly

When you talk to agents in your office about presentations and objections, you are going to be amazed. Some of the information you get will be good. Some will be outdated. Some will be outright wrong or bad. What may be stunning to you is the lack of substantiation for what agents tell you. Even though we've been teaching agents for years to "put your visuals where your mouth is," most agents just think they can talk people into anything!

Big Idea: Put your visuals where your mouth is.

Tell the truth attractively. We all know that overpriced listings don't sell. That's the truth. But when we tell sellers their overpriced listing won't sell, sellers just think we want a quick commission! So, we need to tell the truth "attractively." To do that, we need to show third-party endorsement. That is, we need to show the statistics credible organizations like the National Association of REALTORS® (see the References and Resources unit) and our multiple listing services (MLSs) provide us. We need to show articles on market trends and reports on these trends by survey agencies. That way, we don't sound like we're just selfish salespeople. Instead, it's clear that we know what we're talking about because we're substantiating it with credible information. Start thinking like that now, and you'll gain the trust and loyalty of many more buyers and sellers than you would by just talking!

Big Idea: Working hard now to provide credibility and substantiation for your claims gains you loyal customers and clients—for life.

Big Idea: Trust isn't gained by bluffing someone. It's gained by telling the truth attractively, by keeping your promises, and by putting the client ahead of yourself.

■ Stop Before You List That Property!

Here's some training advice. This advice is very blunt because you are going to see lots of practices and get some advice that is not in the best interest of sellers and buyers. And, because you're new, you're going to be confused about what are really "best practices." So, forgive my bluntness, but I feel that's what it takes here! I'm putting this in week two because you may already have a lead to list a property by this point. If you're like most new agents, you think any listing is better than none. After all, it's something to practice on. At least, that's what I thought. But as I gained a few more months in the business, I realized how listing overpriced properties hurt everyone—the seller, the office, and me. So don't list it yet. Before you do, ask yourself four questions:

1. Is this listing going to sell within normal market time? If not, why is it in a seller's best interest that I list this property? (Studies show that listings that don't sell quickly end up staying on the market much longer and ultimately sell for less than they are worth—the old shopworn principle.)
2. Am I listing this property just to get a listing? (If so, in my opinion, you're not practicing seller agency, you're practicing "agent agency." You just want sign and ad calls, or maybe you want to impress your broker.)
3. Is this listing going to make a better reputation for me or a worse one? (If it doesn't sell, you will get a poor reputation both with homeowners and other agents.)
4. Is this listing consistent with my values? (Do you feel that you put the best interest of the client first, or are you putting your best interests first?)

The simple reasons we list overpriced properties are that we
- want a listing so we can use it to snag ad and sign calls or impress our broker,
- don't know what to say to a seller to get it priced right, and
- don't realize we're costing the seller thousands of dollars and are adversely affecting the reputations of our office, other agents, and ourselves.

You'll find agents in your area (or even in your office) whose strategy is to list everything. I caution you against that strategy for the reasons above. I believe that listing properties that won't sell in normal market time is mostly the cause of the poor reputation we have earned with consumers. You can be a part of changing that reputation, or you can confirm it!

Big Idea: Listing overpriced properties is not a service to your office, your associates, the seller, or you. (Agents just think it is because they don't understand the concept of short-term gain, long-term pain.)

Resources to Set Standards of Practice

Note to managers:

Review those standards with your agents. Your ethics, culture, and vision for your company are at stake. Assure your agents you will show them how to win with high ethics, not expediency.

In Unit 9, I've given you four documents with which you can set your standards of practice for sellers and buyers. That way, you're not wasting your time or misleading your customers and clients. These are exceptional time-management tools. In addition, they will help you hold to the standards you said you wanted to practice before you went into this business. Remember, buyers and sellers are looking for that agent who will tell them the truth—in their best interests!

Big Idea: There are many ways to practice real estate. The really successful agents practice it in the best interests of sellers and buyers.

■ Final Thoughts for Week Two

If you have been lead generating consistently, you have probably found some buyers to qualify. It's hoped that you have even shown houses to a few buyers this week. On the listing side, you have found at least one homeowner who is interested in selling his home. You have made one listing presentation. As the list grows and opportunities increase, you begin to experience some time management challenges. To help you manage your time, try the following recommended solutions.

Continue Your Weekly Plan

It's amazing how many agents don't plan their week ahead of their week! In fact, from teaching sales skills workshops, I have found that less than 10% of experienced agents actually lay out a week's work in advance. When they look at what they have accomplished the prior month, they are stunned. From analyzing their prior month's activities, they discover that they have been nonproductive because they

- let non–income-producing activities dominate their schedule,
- allowed well-meaning people to steal their time, and
- placed too much emphasis on support activities.

They became their own assistants! However, with new insights, agents can get back on track and create a plan that helps them reach their goals. *Up and Running* teaches you, from the beginning, how to prioritize your activities so that you can avoid this common mistake. Take advantage of your manager's help in staying focused and on track.

Don't Stop Lead Generating

The good news is you are getting some results from your lead generating. The bad news is that you will be tempted to stop lead generating. After all, it's more fun working with people than finding them! However, your income directly depends on your lead-generating numbers. It isn't true that we can ever, no matter how long we're in the business, stop lead generating. Says my friend Bill Feldman, former real estate agent, owner, and head of business development for one of the largest regional companies in the United States, "When you stop pedaling the bicycle, you fall off." Pedaling the bicycle fast enough to stay on track simply means planning, executing, and measuring your business start-up plan to provide you with enough new leads to get the results that will meet your goals.

Big Idea: The best experienced agents never stop lead generating because they know it's the cornerstone of a productive business.

Are You Resisting Getting into Action?

I'll bet you didn't know how challenging real estate sales were until now. To cope with those challenges, your creative subconscious may be coming up with ways to convince you to avoid getting into action. You might even start believing your subconscious! One of the most common reasons is the old "I can't do that because I don't know enough." Or, maybe your subconscious has convinced you that you're not organized enough to get into action, or that you're not perfect enough.

Ned, an agent in my office, acted in a way that is an example of creative avoidance. In the business eight months, Ned had made only one sale. However, he was in the office regularly and appeared busy with paperwork. He attended law courses and was well-informed on financing. One day I saw Ned collating maps. I asked him what he was doing. He explained that he was putting together a series of maps for a buyer's tour. I thought that was exceptional; buyers would really want to know the whereabouts of the homes they were seeing. Unfortunately, Ned had used his strategy with only six buyers—all the buyers he had put in his car in the past eight months! He had spent his time on this nifty map system but had not talked to enough people to get them into the car—or have the opportunity to appreciate the map system! Which is more important to your goal attainment—talking to people, qualifying them, and showing them homes; or working diligently on a map system in case you find someone who wants you to show them homes?

How do you get into action? In a wonderful book, *The Conative Connection*, Kathy Kolbe explores the ways different personalities get into action—not how we learn, but how we get into action. Some people barge ahead and worry about the details later. We start badly, but because we're tenacious, we surprise people by how good we finally get. Unfortunately, our supervisors often remember only how bad we were when we started. We must be tough-minded and keep at it; we must retain an image of ourselves as finished products, because others will not see us that way. Other people observe the action for a long time. Finally, when we feel ready to perform well, we get into action. We start slowly but well. Because of our slow start, we don't get much positive reinforcement from our supervisors (or coach or manager), who note our lack of progress compared with others in the office. If slow starters are tenacious and believe in themselves, they become very good because they practice perfectly. Kolbe points out several "get into action" styles. This book will help you pinpoint your "get into action" style, as well as the barriers and challenges you face as you start your real estate career.

Go ahead—be embarrassed. There is no way to be experienced until you get experience. No agents like to take risks, be embarrassed, or have buyers and sellers guess that they are new in the business. But face it—everyone has been new in the business. Just go ahead and get those first few months over with. You will be embarrassed every day—many times. As a new agent, my most common statement to buyers or sellers was "I don't know, but I'll find out." In music, little could stump me—but in real estate anything could stump me! Still, I muddled through it, and you will, too.

Big Idea: Your ability to get into action and risk being embarrassed is one of the attributes of a successful new agent.

Why not take your time? I've interviewed prospective agents who told me they really didn't want to sell real estate right away. They wanted to learn everything they could. Then, after six or eight months, they would feel ready to sell real estate. It doesn't work that way! I wish I could tell you that you can successfully launch your real estate career by taking lots of time to "get ready." However, if you take all the time in the world, you will fail for three reasons:

1. Real estate is a performance art. It doesn't matter how much you know; it only matters how you interact with people, and that takes practice and performance. To remember and emulate good performance, we need to perform right after we have heard, seen, and practiced that performance. Learning something in a class and letting that skill lie dormant for months just guarantees poor skill—and high stress.

Big Idea: 99% of what we learn we learn by *doing*.

---

2. The only true motivator is a sale. Tell me you're in no hurry, that you have plenty of time to make your first sale. Tell me you're not concerned that you make a sale fast. I predict that within three months, you'll be mentally and emotionally out of real estate. Why? Because you'll see others around you making sales and getting listings. The agents in the office will be congratulating them.

You'll feel left out. Good agents in the office won't spend time with you, and you won't know why. After all, you have lots of questions you need answered, and you believe they should answer them. (I've never figured out why a new agent would think it's an experienced agent's duty to be an answer man.) You'll find it's tough to stay motivated without some positive reinforcement. The longer it takes you to make a sale, the more reasons you will find to leave the business.

Big Idea: If you want to motivate yourself, make a sale.

---

3. Your manager, coach, and experienced agents will lose interest in you. Because they don't see you taking meaningful action steps, your mentors will naturally become less motivated to help you. For you to stay motivated, you need the positive support of your mentors. From my experience, it takes about two months for managers and mentors to lose interest in a new agent. If an agent doesn't go to work fast, I, as a manager, may feel as if I've failed. No matter how motivating I've tried to be, nothing seems to be working. I feel like I'm expending a lot of energy for nothing. Then, I turn my attention to other agents who are creating activities. It not only makes me feel better, but it makes me feel as though my program works! (It also makes me feel appreciated. After all, we managers are human!) It's difficult and time-consuming to constantly think of new ways to motivate agents after they are deflated!

Big Idea: It's your job to motivate yourself. It's your manager's job to hold you accountable to the plan and appreciate your efforts. Cause your manager, coach, and agents to stay interested in you by taking the actions in *Up and Running* every day.

■ Straight Ahead and Strive for Tone

A drummer I worked with in a jazz musical trio used to tell me this as I hesitated on the stand about launching into a challenging jazz piece. I'd start to chicken out, and Doug would yell, "Straight ahead and strive for tone!" What that means is, quit agonizing and theorizing about it, and just do it! Do it the best you can—and you'll learn how to do it better. You'll also surprise yourself once in a while about how well you did. That will motivate you to do it again.

■ Summary

Congratulations! You've just contacted 100 more people; you've gotten some sales results from your efforts. You've continued honing your sales skills and sales packaging. You're starting to systematize your work with buyers and sellers. You're substantiating your claims with visuals. You're creating trust and confidence for long-term results and lifelong loyalty. You're on your way to a career that will truly be a business, not just an avocation! Now, on to week three.

Tip: Until you present your listing and buyer presentations to someone and get feedback, you don't know how you'll do "for real" (it's the difference between practicing piano alone and playing the piece for your teacher). So, this week, practice giving your listing and buyer presentations three times each to your manager or other agents and get feedback. You don't want to practice on your real client!

Week Three Start-Up Plan

This week you will add to your lead-generating and sales skill repertoire. To gain confidence in purchase and sale agreements, you will write some agreements using different methods of financing. To increase your credibility with buyers and sellers, make these exercises challenging.

Even though you are new in the business, now is the time to set yourself apart from the crowd, and you will have an exercise in this week's action plan to do just that.

■ Time to Assess Your Progress

Now you have enough lead-generating numbers to analyze your results and make adjustments. You'll see, in your week three plan, that you'll be asked to look at your numbers. Ask yourself these two questions:

1. What are my best sources of leads so far?
2. Am I getting the number of appointments I need to attain my goals?

If you're not getting the number of appointments you need to get sales and listings, increase your number of best lead-generating activities. Now you're in the world of self-management.

Manager's Tip: Help your agent analyze his conversion numbers—lead-generating opportunities to listing appointments and sales interviews. Does your agent need to increase his lead-generating opportunities?

One Method to Expand Your Lead-Generating Opportunities

I'm very aware of your budget considerations. In fact, I think it's fair to say that new agents have lots of time and little money! (At least that was true of me.) That's why I suggested you start with the lead-generating priorities here. But, let's say you aren't generating the number of leads you need. What should you do? Besides expanding your lead opportunities with the priorities of *Up and Running*, you may consider using a service that promotes your listings to deliver more leads to you. One I like is Listings-to-Leads (see more in the References and Resources unit). The reason I like it is twofold: I personally know and trust the founder, and I like the fact it integrates all social media and makes it very easy to promote your listing in the most effective methods. Caveat: You must be willing to follow up on those leads immediately and consistently! Remember, the potential client expects a response within two hours! (Successful agents will cut you some slack here and say that eight hours is a safe response time to retain the lead.)

■ Week Three *Up and Running* Plan

These activities are all listed in your week three accomplishments in Unit 12, Week Three forms.

Business Producing

Make 100 sales contacts using these leadgenerating methods:
- Make 25 calls to people you know.
- Circle prospect 25 people.
- Choose from other methods for another 50 proactive contacts.
- Hold one open house.
- Follow up on initial online leads—at least 25 (reactive opportunity).

Get these results:
- Secure two qualified buyer appointments.
- Show homes to two qualified buyer groups.
- Secure one appointment to do a listing presentation.
- List one marketable property.

Now it's time to stop and assess your ratios of lead generation to results. If you are not getting enough appointments, increase your lead generating. These assigned activities are already in your spreadsheets, your *30 Days to Dollars* lead-generating plan, and your *30 Days to Dollars* lead-generating results for week three (in Unit 12). All you need to do is log your actuals.

Business Supporting

Do these regular actions:
- Create your weekly schedule in advance of the following week (a blank form is in Unit 12 for you).

- Add at least 50 contacts to your database.
- Write at least 15 follow-up notes.
- Add one social network; this week it's LinkedIn.
- Do your social media plan.
- Recommunicate with at least 50 prior online leads, implementing the online lead communication plan in Unit 9.
- Evaluate your buyers and sellers using the buyers and sellers evaluation sheets (in Unit 12).
- Do the activities in your marketing (follow-up) plan for this week.
- Practice the sales skills assigned in this week.
- Apply the sales skills in real life that are assigned for this week.
- Follow your technology planner.
- Add to your resource notebook.
- Add to your attitude notebook.
- Add to your office notebook.

At the end of the week, measure your results using the four measurements below. Before your appointment with your manager,

1. use the daily planner,
2. evaluate your time management on your weekly schedule,
3. check off your completed activities on your weekly accomplishments, and
4. complete the goals/actuals spreadsheets weekly.

Additional business-supporting assignments include the following:

To master sales skills,
- practice and apply sales skill 5, the hum technique (see Unit 10),
- gain performance excellence with sales skill 5 (see Unit 10),
- practice your listing presentation three times (see your manager for presentations or see the References and Resources unit),
- practice your buyer presentation three times (see your manager for presentations or see the References and Resources unit),
- gather three visuals to counter sellers' objections (see your manager or the References and Resources unit), and
- gather three visuals to counter buyers' objections (see your manager or the References and Resources unit).

To gain technical knowledge,
- learn two methods of writing purchase and sale agreements using alternative methods of financing, including one offer contingent on the sale of the purchaser's home. See your manager for help with this.

To promote yourself and gain more business,
- start gathering the information you need to create a professional portfolio. See Unit 9 for more information. Also use this information to flesh out your profile in each of your social media.

■ Maintain That "Successful Agent" Job Description

You are learning good business habits that lead to creating a productive business. You are correctly prioritizing your activities in order to build the right job description. However, because you have many other "job description models" (agents who aren't productive) in your business, you may be tempted to drop your *Up and Running* plan. After all, it's not easy to complete all those lead-generating and business-supporting activities that fast!

Be careful who you model. John (not his real name) was an agent in the first office I managed. When I was still working as an agent, I admired John's depth of information about waterfront property. Everyone went to him to learn what waterfront listings were on the market at any given time. Since I never kept track of that information, I figured I would get it from him! John was happy to help me out. Later, when I became manager of the office, I discovered that John was completing only four transactions a year—in his third year in the business—not enough to continue to build his business or support our office image as full-time, committed professionals. Yet John, who had received positive reinforcement for his knowledge, was content. As we had established standards of excellence in our office (which included production minimums), it was my job as a manager to work with John to help him increase his production. Working together, John and I agreed that for him to stay with our office, he would have to change his job description from *waterfront expert* to *successful salesperson*. In fact, it proved impossible—John liked the comfort of collating and the importance accorded him as a waterfront expert more than the excitement of selling real estate.

Big Idea: Behavior that's rewarded is repeated.

■ Create the Future—Your Way

You have been in the business three weeks. Is your image of yourself different from the one you had when you started in this business? Successful performers have learned to create a completed picture of themselves as great performers—long before they are terrific performers. This helps them to predict the outcome of their efforts. If you don't know where you're going, you can't get there!

Lou Tice, the founder of Pacific Institute, calls this skill *self-efficacy*. It is the ability to create yourself as a finished product in your head and hold that image, even though no one in the outside world has a clue that you are going to end up that way. What a skill! This technique is practiced in karate. When our son, Chris, took karate lessons, he first watched great performers—black belts—performing the *katas* (fighting moves in a format) and *kumite* (actual fighting). Then he envisioned himself performing each part of these moves—just like they did. Finally, he performed the moves for his coach very slowly, *practicing perfectly.* His coach watched carefully to ensure that he was practicing perfectly. After he perfected each move in context, he practiced performing faster. This method of creating perfect performance paid off. He won many medals in national and international competition—even while experiencing great growth spurts. His developed skill of self-efficacy ensured that his mind would hold the picture of his perfect performance. This skill has proved to be invaluable throughout his life.

Big Idea: To become a master of whatever you want, hold your future picture of yourself more strongly than your present reality.

Develop the Professional "You"

Take a few minutes in a quiet place by yourself. Imagine yourself as the successful real estate agent you intend to be. What will you do? What kind of recognition and power will you gain? What affiliations will you make that reflect your ideal of yourself as a pro? Create a movie with you as the star, complete with the movement, color, dialogue, tastes, and smells. Make it fun, exciting, and rewarding. Play it over and over in your head 20 times a day for a month. Doing this will counteract your "growth spurts"—objections, barriers, negative self-talk, lost leads—as you start your career. You must develop some mental ammunition. Remember, people treat you as they see you. They can't see the new movie you have created until you start acting it out. Even then, they will try to put you back into your "old movie." It's human nature. Unwittingly, we help our friends fail by not becoming supporting players in their new picture. You must have a strong movie to move yourself in the direction you want to go so that others can get caught up in the new action and let go of the old.

Big Idea: Develop an ideal future "movie" of yourself, with color, sound, and feeling.

Show That You're the Professional of Choice

Recently, an agent who had been in the business about a year told me she couldn't get people who came to her open houses to appreciate her belief that she could help them. The reason she couldn't get them to appreciate her was that she didn't have time to engage them in conversation—to show them that she was knowledgeable and caring. Before she could talk to them, they were inching out the door. Her problem, stated in context of self-efficacy, was that she wasn't able to play her "movie as a pro" for people. But how could she? The public comes into open houses for three reasons:

1. To see the home
2. To get information
3. To avoid the salesperson (!)

What does the public think about real estate salespeople? Generally, that one is as good as another. In training courses, I ask agents how they are different from the public's general view of a real estate agent. The reply is usually, "I'm an honest, enthusiastic, service-oriented professional." Then I ask the students how they *demonstrate* these qualities. The reply is, "I demonstrate my qualities through the way I act with buyers and sellers." Here's the problem—people attending an open house want to avoid you, not get to know you. They will not give you the time to see you in the actions that prove your qualities. Unless you can *quickly* show them you are a cut above the generic agent, they will attempt an escape, just as they have with the other ten agents whose homes they have visited.

Project the Professional "You"

How do professionals in other fields demonstrate their professional selves? Envision your doctor's office. On the walls are diplomas that give you confidence about the doctor's qualifications. How do restaurants demonstrate—before you eat the food—that their food and service are good? Reviews from the newspaper and testimonials from customers are often displayed. You can inspire confidence in your services by adopting some of the same promotional strategies that successful professionals and businesses use. In this week's assignments, you were to start developing your professional portfolio. This serves two purposes:

1. It increases your confidence.
2. It shows buyers and sellers why they should choose you.

Screen Your Movie—Increase Your Confidence

Developing a portfolio provides an additional benefit. During the development process, you complete exercises that help you develop your unique approach to the business. You draw on your particular strengths, services, and business approaches that differentiate you from the generic agent. You then project these in a pictorial way to communicate added value to the potential client or customer. The result is an overall promotional strategy that will compete successfully in the marketplace. The best news for you, the new agent, is that this process helps develop your "movie" and greatly increases your confidence level.

■ Final Thoughts for Week Three

Remember, it's not the finished portfolio that is most important; it's the process of thinking through your strengths, challenges, and competitors. In the highly competitive world of real estate sales and management, you must have a clearly, precisely defined picture of you as a "cut above." To compete, you must create, define, refine, and promote yourself masterfully. The bonus to you is that you will have created your "movie!"

Big Idea: Create a scrapbook of the future you.

■ Summary

You're further along your journey to a sale. You're gaining the habits that ensure success. Don't let your regular activities get boring. They *should* be getting predictable. You are learning the lead-generating habits of successful real estate agents. You're also gaining time-management and lead-generating habits that will propel you to a much higher career over the long term. (You won't really know that until you see yourself outselling those who started in the business the same time you did.)

On the business-supporting side, you're adding sales skills and technical competencies, too. Keep practicing to get so competent you have mastery. In addition, keep working on all your systems and packaging. You should be working on them throughout your whole sales career.

Be sure to keep tracking and analyzing your contact ratios. Make adjustments quickly. Remember, your goal is a sale in your first four weeks.

Big Idea: Regularly doing lead-generating activities creates success habits for the long term.

Week Four Start-Up Plan

You are now approaching your final week in the *Up and Running* start-up plan. This week you will continue making the sales contacts to create early success. Because it's your last week in this plan, you get to choose the type of lead generating you will complete. You will refine your seller and buyer presentations. You will add to your professional portfolio. These systems should be on their way to being professional, polished, and practiced by now to ensure your success at every point of contact. (Note: As a pro, you will always be refining and tinkering with your systems. The objective in the first month is to get them to the point where you can use them as presentation guides.)

Manager's Tip: Review the agent's progress to date. Be ready to help that agent fill in any needed skills or systems, so that agent is up to speed for the next 60–90 days. Help your agent create that next 60-day plan using the principles of *Up and Running in 30 Days*. I've provided a template for this at the end of this unit.

■ Week Four *Up and Running* Plan

These activities are all listed in your week four accomplishments in Unit 12, Week Four forms.

Business Producing

Make 100 sales contacts using your favorite method or methods:
- Continue your online lead follow-up program (at least 25)
- Hold one public open house

Get these results:

- Secure two qualified buyer appointments
- Show homes to two qualified buyer groups
- Secure one appointment to do a listing presentation
- List one marketable property
- Sell one house

Time to stop and assess your ratios of lead generation to results. If you are not getting enough appointments, increase your lead generating.

These assigned activities are already in your spreadsheets, your *30 Days to Dollars* lead-generating plan, and your *30 Days to Dollars* leadgenerating results for week four (in Unit 12). All you need to do is log your actuals.

Business Supporting

Do these regular actions:

- Create your weekly schedule in advance of the following week (a blank form is in Unit 12 for you).
- Add at least 50 contacts to your database.
- Write at least 15 follow-up notes; answer all your emails within one day.
- Evaluate your buyers and sellers using the buyers and sellers evaluation sheets (in Unit 12).
- Do the activities in your marketing (follow-up) plan for this week.
- Do your social media planner assignments.
- Practice the sales skills assigned in this week.
- Apply the sales skills that are assigned for this week in real life.
- Follow your technology planner.
- Add to your resource notebook.
- Add to your attitude notebook.
- Add to your office notebook.

At the end of the week, measure your results using the four measurements below. Before your appointment with your manager,

1. use the Daily Planner,
2. evaluate your time management on your weekly schedule,
3. check off your completed activities on your weekly accomplishments, and
4. complete the goals/actuals spreadsheets weekly.

Here are additional business-supporting assignments:

- Practice and apply sales skills 6 and 7 (from Unit 10).
- Complete all listing process materials, including a market analysis package; include eight visuals to counter common listing objections.
- Review and complete your qualifying/interview package for buyers, including visuals for countering buyers' eight most common objections.

- Complete your personal promotional materials—a professional portfolio, your personal brochure, or both; polish and refine your biographical information on your social media pages.
- Add one social network—YouTube; investigate purchasing a camcorder or using your smartphone to record your message to your clients; inspect three agents' use of YouTube (What's effective? What's not?); sketch your video plan and do one test video. See the video marketing companies, too, in the References and Resources unit.
- Gain performance excellence in two new sales skills (choose from the seven critical sales skills).
- Add three more visuals to counter objections sellers give you (to your seller presentation).
- Add three more visuals to counter objections buyers give you (put in your buyer presentation).

■ Summary

In your last week of *Up and Running*, you've had more freedom to create your own plan. You've chosen the kind of lead-generating activities that seem to work best for you. Because you've been doing so many lead-generating activities, you're able to analyze which are your best sources of business. You've also analyzed your ratios of leads to appointments to sales. Now you're starting to self-manage. You've also refined your various packages and presentations. This is the week when you really have an opportunity to put it all together. If you've completed all the business-producing and business-supporting assignments during the program, you are far ahead of almost all new agents who've started careers in the last year!

■ What You've Accomplished in Your Four Weeks

Congratulations! You have completed your first four weeks in the business. Not only have you finished (you might say "conquered") this program, you have formed the habits of successful self-management.

In business-producing activities, you have

- completed consistent, high-number contacts for prospects,
- qualified prospects for time management and control of your career, and
- sold one home and listed one home.

You have organized the following support systems to the business to allow you to move faster:

- Listing process systems (including your market analysis)
- Technical knowledge: purchase and sale agreements, finance, market analysis
- System for qualifying and interviewing buyers
- Contact management system populated with all your contacts
- A budget and a time line for your professional management
- Resource notebook, office notebook, and attitude notebook for knowledge management

- Marketing plan
- Technology plan
- Social media plan
- Personal promotional tools and plan
- Orientation procedures
- Tools of the trade

You have practiced the following sales skills in the office and in the field:

- Seven critical sales skills
- Four major types of lead-generating scripts

You have gained exceptional measurement and time management skills using

- a weekly planner,
- a daily planner,
- weekly accomplishments, and
- a goals/actuals spreadsheet.

Evaluate Your Progress in this Program

How did you do in this program? As a new addition to this fifth edition of *Up and Running,* I'm providing you an evaluation to use to celebrate your wins and set up your plan for your next 60 days—and beyond. Share this evaluation with your manager or coach, and email it to me at carla@ carlacross.com to let me know what you found helpful—and what additional information or skills would have helped you launch your career.

Here's the evaluation (and it's at the end of Unit 12).

FIGURE 7.1   End-of-Program Evaluation of *Up and Running in 30 Days*

Name: _____   Email: _____

We hope you have had an awesome experience during *Up and Running in 30 Days* and that you've made real progress toward your goals. Please complete the evaluation to ensure we have helped you attain your goals in the best way possible—and to help you plan your next steps.

From Your Perspective

1. Have you seen progress from the beginning of this program to now?

    a.   In what ways?

2. Are you accomplishing what you intended to accomplish? Please explain.

3. What have been your biggest benefits from this program?

4. Has this program helped you launch your business, get into the business-producing stream, and start to make money? If so, how?

5. Are the resources included helpful to you, and in what ways?

6. What could we have done to make the resources more helpful to you?

7. What barriers, if any, have prevented you from attaining your goals and completing this program?

8. Your assessment of your progress in your lead generating plan:

9. Your assessment of your progress in the business support work:

10. Rate yourself on effort during the program (1 is low/10 is high): Why did you give yourself that rating?

Your Coach (if your manager or someone else is coaching you)

1. What has been the most helpful thing your coach has done to assist you?

2. How could your coach be more effective in helping you?

Take *Up and Running* with You as You Excel in Your Career

Although we have portrayed this as your four-week plan, the business-producing part of the plan is actually a solid business-producing plan for your entire career. Now that you've had the opportunity to find your best sources of business, keep working them and measuring your results. Keep refining your systems and sales skills to build long-term mastery for a high-producing real estate career.

Big Idea: The principles in the *Up and Running* plan are foundations for your entire career life.

Manager's Tip: Be ready to provide your agent with an additional 60-day plan of action. This would include best sources of lead generation, needed skill development, and needed systems implementation. I've provided a template for this plan in this unit, and in Unit 12, at the end of your fourth week plan.

FIGURE 7.2 *Up and Running* 60-Day Plan

You've completed the *Up and Running in 30 Days* program. Now, you're ready to plan your next 60 days. Also review your marketing budget planner, your technology planner, and your social media planner to further refine your next 60-day plan. Assess what you finished and what you still need to complete, and create dates for completion.

Goals for your 60-day plan:

Total lead generating activities: _____   Each month: _____   Each week: _____

Total buyer appointments: _____   Each month: _____   Each week: _____

Total sales: _____   Each month: _____   Each week: _____

Av. $ per sale: _____

Total income from sales closed: _____

Total seller appointments: _____   Each month: _____   Each week: _____

Total listings: _____   Each month: _____   Each week: _____

Total listings sold: _____   Each month: _____   Each week: _____

Av. $ per LS: _____

Total income from listings sold/closed: _____

Sales closed and listings sold = closed income next 60 days: _____

Planning Each Week and Keeping Track of Your "Actuals"

Use one planner per week, and write your goals in each column, breaking down your 60-day goals from above. Then, as you go through the week, write your 'actuals' in each column. Use the principles you've already learned and practiced in *Up and Running in 30 Days*.

FIGURE 7.3 Weekly Activities and Results

Name _____   Date _____

From Business Start-Up Plan	Leads	Appts.	Business-Producing Activities	Hours	Business/Personal Management	Hours
People You Know			Lead Generation		Personal Development Quiet Time	
Circle Prospecting			Leads Generated Listing Appts.		Workout Review of Life Plan	
Expired Listings			Listings Taken Listings Canceled or Expired		Review Business Plan Staff Meetings	
FSBO			Listings (Turned Down) Listings (I Didn't Get)		Family Time	
Re-call Current leads			Price Reductions Listings Sold			
Follow Up/Online Leads			Buyers Appts. Set Buyer Interviews		**Evaluation: Rate Yourself 1–4 (4 is high)**	
Reactive: Open House			Buyer Contracts Qualified Showing Offers Written		Lead generation	
Floor Time			Buyer Sales		Working with Clients	
Online Leads			Sales Fails		Closing	
Other			Listings Closed		Practicing Sales Skills	
			Buyers Closed		Packaging	
			Commissions Pd. Out		Other	

Compare your weekly results to your weekly goals. On a scale of 1–10, rate yourself: _____

Why did you give yourself that rating?
_____
_____

How could you raise it?
_____
_____
_____

Coaching Opportunities for You

According to the Inman Select survey of hundreds of brokers and agents, one of the most important attributes of new agent success was having a coach. Yet, few new agents take advantage of coaching opportunities. There are several reasons:

- They think it costs too much.
- They don't know who to choose as a coach.
- They believe their manager will coach them.
- They don't think they need a coach.

Yet, with failure rates for new agents so high, it is the savvy new agent who stacks the deck in her favor to succeed. Because of the reasons above, Carla Cross has created two coaching programs. The first, which is extremely affordable, is a completely online program based on the principles in this book. In eight weeks, the agent implements a proven start-up plan, gets needed training with 25+ videos, gets online coaching from Carla Cross, and enjoys a high level of support with over 50 checklists, processes, and systems—all included in the program. Cross has added a coaching component in her Coaches' Corner, so managers can become great coaches. See more at www.upandrunninginrealestate.com.

For those ready to take advantage of one-on-one coaching, Cross has Career Achievement. Her coaches are all real estate professionals, and clients receive a completely customized success program based on their goals and needs. See more at www.carla-cross.com/coaching/career achievement.

The Skills of Lead Generation

You've seen your four-week *Up and Running* plan. You're anxious about starting because you don't know how to make those sales calls. Units 8, 9, and 10 are the training components of *Up and Running*. Here, I'll give you the skills you need to get into action (and only the critical skills—remember this is not a training program!). In this unit, I'll teach you the four approaches and scripts you need to make contacts with your best sources of leads. In Unit 9, I'll show you how to keep it going to turn contacts into sales, how to qualify those leads so you know if they are good buyers or sellers, and how to create and implement a marketing plan to follow up with them until they buy or die. In Unit 10, I'll teach you the seven most important sales skills I know you'll need to get more leads and convert them to buyers and sellers. Is that all the training you'll ever need? Of course not. You'll keep refining your skills and gathering more information for your whole career—I hope.

Big Idea: The most successful people in life are *always* challenging themselves to get better at what they do.

Why these particular skills? The sales skills and systems I'm sharing with you here are the most important skills and systems you need right now to get those sales and listings you want in your first year in the business. As you learn these skills, you may say to yourself, "These seem so easy and basic. Every agent must know and use them." Not true. These skills do seem easy to grasp, but, in the heat of the moment and without lots of practice and coaching, these skills get lost, and we just revert back to what is natural. Unfortunately, what's natural may not be effective *sales communication*.

Your best source of leads and how to contact them. To get your business off to a quick start, you will want to go to the best sources for leads. In this unit, we'll discuss why I've chosen certain sources as best for you, along with the pros and cons of certain sources. I'll give you the training you'll need to jump right in. I'll show you how to make contacts with the four types of leads. I'll give you the scripts and letters you'll need to use. There's a lot of training in Unit 8.

■ First: How Our Lead Generating Is Constructed

To create an effective lead-generating plan, follow these five principles of real estate marketing:

1. Segment your markets.
2. Be proactive.
3. Work the best sources.
4. Work the numbers.
5. Be frequent and consistent in your marketing.

These are the principles we followed in creating your *30 Days to Dollars* lead-generating plan, a portion of the *Up and Running* plan.

Segment markets. The population explosion and information overload—these and other cultural developments make it impossible to promote yourself effectively to everyone. To be an effective lead generator today, you must *segment* and *prioritize* your potential markets. By segmenting your potential markets, you will discover certain best targets. A *target market* is a group of people defined through common demographics (i.e., age, income, real estate needs) and psychographics (i.e., lifestyle). To be an effective marketer, you need to clearly define your target markets and devise specific methods to sell to each. *30 Days to Dollars* segments markets and prioritizes them by best sources of business.

Further segmentation. In the trends unit at the beginning of this resource, I listed the segmentation of buying populations as a huge trend. As you keep creating and evolving your lead-generating sources, keep mini-segmenting those sources to specifically address their needs. Remember that the needs of first-time buyers are radically different than those of baby boomers.

Be proactive. To be successful in real estate today, you must get most of your business from proactive prospecting—you go out and meet people. *30 Days to Dollars* uses mainly proactive activities. There are two kinds of lead generation:

1. Proactive—you go out and find people
2. Reactive—you sit and wait for people

You can control the number of leads you can get (and the money you make) only through proactive methods.

Work the best sources. To be successful, you'll want to start with your best sources of business. *30 Days to Dollars* prioritizes these sources for you.

Proactive sources include the following:

1. Best—people you know
2. Good—circle prospecting
3. More challenging—for-sale-by-owner (FSBOs) and expired listings

These are the four lead-generating sources I'll teach you to contact in this unit, in that order.

Why have I named *people you know* and *circle prospecting* the best sources for new agents? Because they

1. are least expensive (you don't have the money to spend on high-cost lead generation);
2. are easy to work with and require few developed sales skills (you want results from your lead generating quickly—even before you develop sales skills);
3. are low rejection (new agents think they can take rejection, but are surprised and frustrated when they get dozens of nos);
4. have the biggest payoff for low cost and energy;
5. have little competition from other agents (people who already love you are more likely to work with you; when you go to a neighborhood to circle prospect, you're assured that very few other agents are willing to make the effort to meet potential customers face to face); and
6. build on the principles of correct lead-generating priorities, so you'll keep these principles for your long-term business forever (experienced agents' best source of business is, again, people who think they're wonderful—those past customers and referrals).

Why are FSBOs and expired listings more challenging? They require great sales skills, tenacity, and ability to handle rejection. Most new agents are not quite skilled enough and get so much rejection anyway that giving them more rejection their first month seems like cruel and unusual punishment!

Reactive sources include the following:

- Open houses
- Online leads
- Relo leads
- Floor time

Big Idea: All the sources listed here, with the exception of online leads, are known as traditional sources of leads. Remember to mix and match your sources with traditional and contemporary (e.g., online, social media, and so on).

As a new agent, you may be relying on various reactive methods to get leads. Be sure to track your contacts versus actuals in each of your sources using the goals/actuals spreadsheet so you'll know which are your best sources—and which are a waste of your time.

Big Idea: To increase your success rate with reactive leads, master your qualifying and closing sales skills.

■ The Eight-Point Strategy to Turn Online Leads into Sales

The Eight-Point Online Strategy

1. Rapid response
2. Capture the lead
3. Screen the lead
4. Interact with the lead
5. Humanize your communications
6. Go from key-board (cold) to voice communication (warm)
7. Develop sales skills
8. Stay in touch forever

Although online leads are strictly a reactive method to get business, I'm including them here because they have become so important. In the past few years, agents have become excited about online leads, only to be discouraged by them after they've gotten a few. Why? Because of the low conversion rates. Does that mean you shouldn't care about online leads? No. It means you must develop an online strategy to deal with these leads. Here's my eight-point strategy:

1. Have a rapid response method to any inquiry—according to a John L. Scott Real Estate survey, most inquirers want a response to an inquiry within two hours. Agents, on the other hand, took an average of 54 hours to respond, and only one half of the agents ever bothered to respond at all! If you're not interested in responding rapidly, don't count on capturing online leads.
2. Have a method to capture that lead's information immediately. You must use your database and contact management system diligently.
3. Have a method on your website that gives the potential client the information they want and lets them refine it.
4. Have the ability on your website to "require consumers to opt in (provide their contact information with you) in order to receive more information.
5. Develop the skill of using warm language in your email replies to portray yourself as an empathic human being. You need to humanize an otherwise cold medium. See the sample online reply note in Unit 13.
6. Develop a method to go from "online questions and answers" to verbal communication. Think in terms of picking up the phone earlier rather than later. The only way you will form a relationship is to use one or more of the communication senses—hearing, seeing, or feeling. These aren't communicated via email or text!
7. Develop the sales skills to turn that inquiry into a loyal client. (Don't just keep feeding them information. Ask good questions to find out their needs, then attach benefits. Ask them if those are the benefits they want. Finally, decide on their dominant buying motives and remind them of what they really want. See sales skills

2 and 7 in Unit 9 for much more information on these skills and how to apply them in any situation.)

8. Be ready to stay in touch with this would-be client for many months to years. Remember that inquirers may be only casually looking at the beginning of their house hunt. However, they did inquire so they have some level of interest! Create your system to stay in touch over a period of time. Often, it's the agent who is persistent and consistent who finally turns that lead into a client—and a sale or listing sold. Your mindset should be that you're in real estate for the long-term, not just a sale tomorrow.

Resources to help you capture and manage your online leads. There are many companies offering services to provide online lead management. They include Market Leader, Placester, and Top Producer®. See my expanded list in the References and Resources unit.

In addition, some real estate franchises offer branded management services. New agents should talk to their managers about which services they prefer.

The important point here is to use something! New agents generally don't capture their leads even in a database, so their hard work to find potential leads goes nowhere. Don't let that happen to you. By the second week in the business, you should be putting your leads into a CRM or at least a database or spreadsheet.

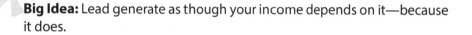

Big Idea: Spend most of your time and resources on your best sources.

Work the numbers. To be an effective marketer, you must make enough contacts to generate quality leads. *30 Days to Dollars* shows you which markets to target and how many calls you need to make—overall, 100 sales calls per week to ensure success—for one sale and one listing in your first 30 days in the business.

Big Idea: Lead generate as though your income depends on it—because it does.

But I'm Different

My main goal here is your success—your success in your first 30 days, not your first 30 years! So, if you don't have enough leads that week in the source I've assigned you in your *30 Days to Dollars*, go to another source. If you just despise contacting the source I assigned, substitute a source. If you find something doesn't work for you in your area, change the source. What you can't change is high numbers of contacts consistently. It surprises me how some agents and managers refuse to start the *Up and Running* plan because they believe in different source priorities. The bottom line is, if you're convinced your source priorities work best for you in your area, I'm happy for you! Just get it done.

Big Idea: Don't hide behind "I'm different" to avoid lead generating.

How to Make Contacts in Each of the Four Proactive Lead-Generating Sources

This unit shows you exactly how to make the sales call in each of the target markets in *30 Days to Dollars.* To make it easy for you to access, I've provided the scripts and letters for you to use, all saved in Unit 13.

There are literally thousands of ways to make sales contacts and to follow up. I've chosen four approaches here that are easy to implement and get you results, but the best way is the one that works for you. Start with one method, and then make adjustments for your style and market area.

Big Idea: The best method to make a contact is the method you prefer.

Practice makes perfect. Before you make a sales contact, craft your sales approach using the sales skills described in this unit and Unit 10. Before you actually apply the sales skill in person, practice with your manager; a fellow agent; or your spouse, friend, or child—they will provide valuable feedback to help you be more effective in your actual sales calls.

1. Best Source of Business: People You Know

Many new agents look forward to letting people know they are in the real estate business, but they don't know how to do it. I'd recommend you do a one-two punch: a letter followed by a phone call.

Figure 8.1 is a sample of the letter you can use to write to your best lead-generating sources. It's also saved in Unit 13 for you.

Big Idea: Increase your chances of a lead dramatically by following up any mailing with a phone call.

To *craft a sales call* (sales skill 1, to be applied in week one), use the following technique:

1.   Think of a particular person to call

2. Determine a potential real estate need and benefit (sales skill 2, to be applied in week one) to this person
3. Write three questions to ask the person to discover these needs
4. Determine your *call objective*
5. Write a *question to get a lead* (sales skill 3, to be applied in week one) or appointment
6. Write an opening statement

This method of crafting calls works for crafting any initial sales call. For example, Joe Smith is a family friend. A potential real estate need and benefit to Joe is a rental home, which will reduce his tax burden.

See Figure 8.2 for a worksheet to craft a call.

Here are three questions to ask Joe:

1. Is the equity in your present home enough to get a second mortgage to refinance for money to buy another home?
2. Have you thought about reducing your tax burden?
3. Have you looked into purchasing a home as a rental?

FIGURE 8.1   Letter: Introduction to People You Know

Dear _____,

I'm writing (or emailing) you this note to let you know I've just begun a new career. I'm now selling real estate with [*insert your company name*]. It's an exciting profession, and I've already found that my background in [*fill in your pertinent background*] has helped prepare me well for my new profession. In addition, I've had the benefit of attending a wonderful training program at our company, and I'm being coached by [*put in your manager or coach's name*] so I'm getting the guidance and advice agents need to really be of service to buyers and sellers.

With all this knowledge and training behind me, I'm excited to help buyers and sellers. If you know of someone who wants to buy or sell in our area, please let me know. I'll give them the very best service I can, backed by the great reputation of my company and the support of my manager.

If I can answer questions about the state of the market for you, I'd love to do that, too. I'm keeping abreast of the market trends and prices in your area.

My contact information:

[*Your name*
Office name
Office address

Phone
Fax
Email
Website and blog]

Sincerely,

[*your name*]

Optimize your opportunity. Write a thank-you note or an email within one day of your meeting, thanking them for their time and enclosing your card.

- The *call objective* is to get an appointment.
- The question to get the appointment is: "When can we explore this potential?"

- The opening statement is: "I have been thinking about you. I'm in real estate now, and I have been exploring how to help people ease financial burdens with real estate."

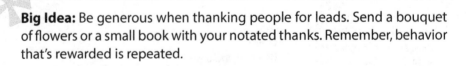

Big Idea: This process, crafting a sales call, works for any type of lead!

This script is also in Unit 13 for your quick reference.

FIGURE 8.2   Craft Your Own Sales Call to People You Know

Name of person: _____

Potential real estate need(s): _____

Benefit to the person of your service: _____

Three questions:

1. _____

2. _____

3. _____

Your call objective: _____

Question to get the order: _____

Opening statement: _____

Practice this sales call with a friend until you are comfortable.

After the call, immediately send that handwritten note of thanks for the lead (see more below), then put that information in your database.

Big Idea: Be generous when thanking people for leads. Send a bouquet of flowers or a small book with your notated thanks. Remember, behavior that's rewarded is repeated.

A common mistake agents make is only rewarding people for a lead that results in a closed sale. You want to reinforce leads and motivate people to give you more of them!

What no means. Did you know that, on average, people say no to a salesperson four times before they say yes? But 96% of salespeople give up after the third no! (They quit right before that customer is ready to say yes.) That's why tenacious agents always do so much better! I don't mean they are pushy (unless they have no sales communication skills at all!). I mean they understand it's human nature to say no. They also know when it's in the customer's best interest to continue forward on the sales process. (Have you ever said no to something you wish you had said yes to?) Your job as a salesperson is to find a gracious method to keep going. Armed with the statistics I shared above, you will expect the no, and have the next sentence ready.

FIGURE 8.3 A Script for Calling on People You Know

"Hi, Sally. I have been thinking about you. I'm in real estate now. Oh, you got my announcement postcard? Good. I've already learned to stay in contact frequently, since I guess agents aren't the best with that! Yes, I'm with ABC Realty, a wonderful firm in downtown Bellevue. Oh, you know that firm? Yes, I think I made a great decision. I wanted to call and let you know I'm working hard to do things right. I just got through my training school and, boy, is there a lot to learn! It was great, though, and I feel really prepared to help people now. Yes, I have two sales and three listings so far. Yes, that's really great for a new agent! Also, I work with George Snell, who is my manager and coach. So, for these first few months, I have a real expert looking over my shoulder every step, which I think helps my clients feel comfortable. It's kind of a 2-for-1 benefit. Do you know anyone who needs my help? Great. [*Take down the information. Ask who, when, where, can you use Sally's name.*] Well, thanks again and I'll talk with you soon."

Big Idea: No doesn't mean no forever. It just means no for now, or "I'm not ready," or "I don't trust you yet!"

A script to get referrals regularly. With people you know, ask: "Since I'm starting my real estate career, could I count on you to refer me to those who want to buy or sell? I'll touch base with you regularly."

A script to keep in touch. Find a reason to keep in touch. With people you know, ask: "Can I put you on my mailing list? We have a wonderful real estate newsletter (or e-newsletter) that keeps you updated on the market so that you will have the latest in specific real estate information."

The Personal Note: Optimize the Power of That Call

After every conversation, no matter the lead source, follow up with a personal note, thanking that person for her time and that you look forward to working with her in the future. See Unit 13 for a sample note.

Big Idea: A personal note humanizes you against that online cold communication. Use handwritten notes generously. (As an agent, I always wrote more notes than anyone else in my office—and I was the number one agent in the office.) You can use email for an immediate thank you, but always remember the added power of the hard-copy, handwritten note.

■ 2. How to Circle Prospect

You've seen how to contact your best source of business—people you know. Now we'll investigate your second source: homeowners in areas where you work. *Circle prospecting* means contacting homeowners in an area where you work—in person—to provide them with information about a property in their area. The object of circle prospecting is to get a lead.

You can circle prospect for the following reasons:

- A new listing
- A house sold
- A listing sold
- An open house
- A price reduction

Why do it? As soon as a sign goes up in someone's yard, the people all around that sign start thinking about selling. The For Sale sign triggers a subconscious desire in other homeowners. Seasoned agents will tell you this: a For Sale sign always begets another For Sale sign. Why not be the agent of choice for those potential sellers?

How to get circle prospecting opportunities. You have no listings or sales. How are you going to get opportunities to circle prospect? Don't worry. If you're in a real estate office of any size, you have literally 60 to 100 opportunities per month to circle prospect. How? Just go to the agent who was the listing or selling agent for the reasons above. Ask that agent if you can circle prospect the property. Why? Successful, seasoned agents are too busy to circle prospect—or they're too lazy!

Big Idea: Put your circle prospecting strategy in your listing presentation to impress sellers with the fact you will personally promote their property.

Why Circle Prospecting Works

Circle prospecting works for several reasons:

- Homeowners are curious about what is happening in their area.
- Because few agents will take advantage of this opportunity, you have no competition with other agents!
- Homeowners want to see an agent face-to-face and are impressed that you took the time and energy to contact them in person.

How to choose the best area. This area should be one that you like, one that is closest to where you live or where you work, and one that homeowners will identify with you and your office. It should be one where you have several opportunities over time to get to know the homeowners. Circle prospecting, when done at a mastery level, is like geographical farming (getting to know the homeowners in a particular area over time), except you are expanding your opportunities to several areas, and you have immediate reasons to call, so you'll get a lead faster.

When should you go? Find out the percentage of workers in your area. In many areas, both homeowners in the home work and are gone most of the day. Choose the time to go when they are home. Generally, after 5:00 pm or Saturday morning are the best times. Catching them doing yard work outside is great!

There are two important keys to success in circle prospecting:

1. Contact homeowners in person only—it's much more effective. Don't waste your money just sending a postcard! As a homeowner, I get postcards all the time about *just listed* and *just solds*. However, I've never seen a salesperson come to my door. Do you think I'd list my home with a postcard? No. You want a lead!
2. Visit the same homeowner three times within a short period for different reasons so the homeowner will get to know and trust you. (Three possible reasons include the following: the home is newly listed, there is an open house, the home sells.)

Big Idea: Repetition creates familiarity, which creates trust, which gets you a lead.

To prepare for circle prospecting, first decide on the reason why you are calling on the homeowner. Then create your materials and design your script using the *craft a sales call* (sales skill 1) method.

The Outline of Your Call

1. Introduce yourself, and tell the homeowner why you are there. Be sure to include a benefit (sales skill 2) to the homeowner.
2. Ask the homeowner about the subject property: "Have you seen the Smith listing?"
3. Ask for a lead (sales skill 3): "Do you know anyone who . . . ?" (indirect) "Are you thinking of . . . ?" (direct)

> Optimize your opportunity. Write a thank-you note or an email within one day of your meeting, thanking them for their time and enclosing your card.

Advanced technique. Design your script to have a second question ready to follow up the first no (see indirect and direct questions example above). Let's say that your first question is: "Do you know anyone who . . . ?" Your next question can be: "Are you thinking of . . . ?"

The Circle Prospecting Script

See Figure 8.4. This script is also in Unit 13 for your convenience.

FIGURE 8.4   Circle Prospecting Script

"Hi. I'm Carla Cross with ABC Realty. We just listed the Smith home down the street. Have you seen the property? No? I'm going to be holding it open this weekend, and I'd love to invite you over. I'll even have coffee and cookies. I'm sure you'll be interested to see how the Smiths have creatively remodeled that tri-level. The listing price is $347,500. Here's a flyer with all the information and the open house date and time. By the way, [*ask an indirect or direct question to get a lead*]:

   Indirect: Do you know anyone in the area who has thought of selling?

   Direct: I see your home is one of the largest in the area. Have you thought about downsizing?

Thanks for your time. I'll check back because I'll be letting you know when the property sells."

■ 3. How to Contact For-Sale-by-Owners

FSBO listings are an immediate source of business. After all, they let you know they are trying to sell their homes because they advertise and put up a sign! But they are also tough on salespeople. Why? They don't want to pay you a commission. They want to keep the money. They may see you as competitors. They may not trust real estate agents. They may have had a bad experience. And they're kind of sitting ducks for salespeople. So, after dozens of aggressive real estate agents with few sales skills get through telling FSBOs things like "You're foolish to try to sell it yourself," you can bet they have learned to avoid all real estate people—and they're ready to avoid you, too.

About FSBOs. According to the National Association of REALTORS® survey, less than 15% (the specific percent depends on the type of market) of all sellers sell their homes themselves (and about a quarter of those sales are to people they know). About half of the FSBOs said they wouldn't sell their own home again! So you have a majority opportunity, according to the statistics.

Note: Keep up to date with buyer and seller buying habits by purchasing the National Association of REALTORS® annual survey, *Profile of Home Buyers and Sellers*. See www.nar.realtor.org/research to order. This is a wonderful resource to use when educating buyers and sellers.

Note to managers:

Purchase these reports regularly. Use them to educate agents. Help them include these survey results in their listing and buyers' presentations.

Big Idea: We believe what others say, not what we say. Third-party substantiation is very important to increase trust today.

Wimps and wimpettes need not apply. Unfortunately, most agents who start making calls on FSBOs do it without developing the sales skills they need. They don't have a good method, and, after getting beaten up by a few FSBOs, just give up. This source is not for the wimpy! To contact and convert them to your listings, you must make this market a specialty and highly develop your sales skills over time. Because you're new, here's an approach that will work well for you because it's a low-rejection, low–sales skill approach. What it requires, though, is consistency and organization.

Big Idea: Calling on FSBOs successfully requires skill, tenacity, and consistency.

How to Find FSBOs

You don't have to do any research. Just watch for new FSBO signs in your area, buy a service that tells you the new FSBOs each week, or watch your local newspaper. See the References unit for a company that provides FSBO and expired leads—for a price, of course.

The recommended "drip" method. Surveys show that something happens with the FSBO property within six weeks: owners list their property, sell it themselves, or take it off the market. I've given you the process, along with what to say (the script) and the items to give, during this six-week time frame.

When doing this program, follow these rules:

- Make all sales calls in person. You want to form a relationship. You want to be their professional; you do not want to create an argument. You don't want to tell them they're stupid for trying to sell the home themselves!
- Go when the sign first goes up—the FSBO is still nice and eager to see anyone!

- Follow up consistently. You want to prove you are reliable; that you'll do what you say you will do. You will be one of the few agents who keep coming back!
- Give one new piece of information (not too much) each week. You want to show them you know your stuff. But you don't want to "give away the farm." Remember, the particular items aren't important. It's consistency that is important.

Here are some suggested items to bring when you call on an FSBO:
- Brochures from your title company (only one at a time)
- A list of tips to get your home ready for sale (can probably get from your title company or an inspection company)
- A list of what an inspector looks for (get from an inspection company)
- From a loan officer: items the purchaser will need to apply for a loan
- Two–three loan rate sheets from a mortgage company, to give the seller an idea of possible loans for buyers
- "How to Choose a Real Estate Agent" (complete with the help of your manager, or see the References and Resources unit)
- "What I've Learned Selling Homes" (a document created by the agent)
- "What Buyers Are Looking for Today" (an article from your local newspaper)
- Articles about the market in your area (get from your newspaper)
- Time line: from sales agreement to closing (create with the help of your manager, or see the References and Resources unit)

Figure 8.5 gives you a flowchart of this process.

Manager's Tip: Make an area of your office to keep these items. Ask your favorite mortgage provider, title company, escrow company, attorneys, inspectors, and so on to keep the area stocked. Now, your new agents don't have to stay in indecision to start this method!

As you give the item, ask if there is anything about the information you left the prior week that the seller needs help with. This is the excuse the sellers will give you when they are frustrated because they can't sell their own home. Now, make the appointment with both parties there.

On the appointment, answer questions and do your visual listing presentation.

Success rate. Using this program, studies show new agents can convert about one out of five sellers.

FIGURE 8.5   Converting FSBOs to Listings

Call/Time Frame	What to Say	What to Give
When sign first goes up	Introduce yourself: mention you saw sign; give materials to help you; I'll be back	One piece of buying/selling information (see list in this unit)
Week 2	Same as above; ask question about materials given*	Same
Week 3	Same	Same
Week 4	Same	Same
Week 5	Same	Same
Week 6	Same	Same

Objective: Make appointment to do listing presentation.

The FSBO Script

> Optimize your impression. Send a thank-you note or email within one day of your call or visit.

See Figure 8.6. This script is also in Unit 13.

Other FSBO methods. You may want to take a more aggressive approach that requires a mastery of several sales skills. If so, see your manager for other methods. Your manager may have created a resource book of various methods to make these lead-generating contacts. Or, see an agent in your office who calls on FSBOs successfully. Don't get hung up on criticizing a particular method. Get the method you refer, practice the sales skills, make the first contact, and be consistent. Those are the principles that are most important.

■ 4. Listings That Have Expired

FIGURE 8.6   FSBO Script

First visit: "Hi. I'm Carla Cross with ABC Realty. I noticed your sign just went up. Selling your home? Great. I'd like to give you some information to help you. Why? We need 'Sold' signs in the neighborhood to show buyers it's a very desirable place to live. Here's *[name the piece of information you're handing them]*. I know it will be useful to you because it*[fill in the benefits, using sales skill 2, explained in Unit 10]*. I'll check in next week to see how it's going. Thanks for your time."

Second week and subsequent weeks: "Hi, Carla Cross again with ABC Realty. How's it going?*[Seller will probably tell you it's going great.]* Good. Was the information helpful that I dropped off last week?*[Seller probably won't remember what it was, but will tell you it was helpful.]* Great. Here's another item that I've found really helpful to sellers.*[Give them the item.]* I'll check back with you later."

Around week five: "Hi, this is Carla (oh, you remember . . .). How's it going? Is there anything about the information I've given you that I can help you with? Questions?*[Seller will, at this point, be getting desperate and will use your question as a rationalization to invite you further.]* Okay. I'd love to answer that, but now is not a good time. I could come over tonight or tomorrow night. Which would be better for you and your spouse?*[You want both parties there.]* "

At the presentation: First, answer their questions. Then, go into your presentation. "I appreciate your time. Here's the answer . . . Let me show you how I work, so you'll have the benefit of choosing the right person should you decide to list your property. *[Now, do your listing presentation.]* " (See the References unit for presentation help.)

Do you know how to get a high customer satisfaction rating from a seller? (A high rating means you got done what the seller wanted done and she will refer you to many others.) No, it's not that you kept in touch. A huge survey from Consumer Reports showed sellers rated us high on customer satisfaction only when we *get the home sold fast for close to full price*.

That doesn't say "Get the home sold slow," or "Get the home sold way below listed price!" Expired listings are those listed by sellers who really wanted to sell at one time. But the agent took an overpriced listing. Now, that seller is a dissatisfied customer. And the seller whose home didn't sell within a short period of time isn't just mad at that particular agent and company—she's mad at all real estate companies! Your job, if you contact expired listings, is to turn around the perception of the seller and get that home listed at the right price.

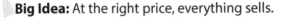

Big Idea: At the right price, everything sells.

How to Contact Expired Listings

Your multiple listing service (MLS) may give you expiration dates. If not, simply track the listings in the area you want to list. You'll want to target your efforts in areas where you can build your reputation as a person who gets homes sold.

Big Idea: Target FSBOs and expired listings in areas where you want to make a name for yourself. You need to build name recognition!

Contact right after the listing has expired. The best strategy is to contact the seller just after the listing has expired. If your MLS shows you expiration dates, preview the home before expiration so you have an idea of its condition. It is a violation of MLS rules to contact a homeowner to talk about listing his property during the term of the listing! But you can preview, and you should.

As a different strategy, you may also try contacting those homeowners who gave up trying to sell their homes weeks or months before. They may be willing to give it another try now.

Optimize your impression. Send a thank-you note or an email within one day of your call or visit.

The *Up and Running* expired listing strategy. This is an approach that works well for the new agent because it doesn't require aggressive sales skills and forms a good relationship with the seller. You are going to take the survey approach. You are going to contact the seller (either in person or by phone) and ask survey questions about the property. Your script is Figure 8.7, which is also in Unit 13. By asking these questions, you will discover the problem areas of the prior listing, the seller's motivation, and the seller's degree of cooperation with you.

■ After the Conversation: Send a Pre-List Package with Your Thank-You Note

---

FIGURE 8.7   The Expired Listing Script

Opening: "Hello. I'm Carla Cross of ABC Realty. Is your home still on the market? [*They may have re-listed and it isn't in your MLS yet.*] [*If no . . .*] Are you still interested in selling at some point? [*If yes, or maybe, or sometimes, even no*] I'll tell you why I ask. I work in this area and would like to stay abreast of the properties available. In case I get a buyer for your home, I'd like to be prepared so your property is represented properly. Do you have about three minutes? [*If yes, go ahead. If no, ask, "What time would be convenient for me to give you a call?"*]

Questions: "What do you feel are the biggest selling points of your home? That sounds like it should be attractive to many buyers! What kind of buyer do you feel would be attracted to your home? Why? Why do you feel it didn't sell? What do you feel was the best marketing the agent did? What would you have liked to see? If you were to list again, what would you be looking for in a listing agent? When and where are you moving?" [*Use the "feel" words. Don't criticize the other agent. Just get the information and hum in agreement.*] [*If you don't have an opportunity to ask these questions, or you feel it isn't appropriate to ask all the questions on the phone, save them to ask at the appointment. You need to qualify this seller!*]

Close: "It sounds as though you have a very sellable property if just a few adjustments are made. I'd love the opportunity to share my thoughts with you. [*If you have a successful track record, tell the seller now.*] I'm proud to say that I've helped [*or, our office has helped*] many sellers get their homes sold after they'd been unsuccessful with a different agent. Could I come over at [*time*] or [*alternate time*] when both of you would be home? It would take no more than 45 minutes, and you could tell me 'not interested' at any time! If you decide not to sell your home at this time, at least you will have a different perspective. And hopefully you'll think of me if you decide to sell in the future."

Immediately after hanging up, write a personal thank-you note and attach it to your pre-list package, which you will send that same day. Why? You want to prove to the seller that you are different: You follow up, you keep your word, and you actually communicate (the prior listing agent didn't, especially when the seller started calling because his listing wasn't selling . . .). This package can include the services you provide, your successful track record (or that of your office), how you work, your professional portfolio (see Unit 9), advice on selling their property, changing market trends, helpful hints to selling, and information on why now is the right time to buy. You can use many of the materials you have gathered to call on FSBOs. (For more information on creating a pre–first visit seller's package, see the References and Resources unit and see your manager.)

Presentation tip: Get the National Association of REALTORS® *Profile of Home Buyers and Sellers* published each year, and use pertinent statistics from it to prove your credibility and prepare the seller for reality.

At the home, ask any questions you didn't have an opportunity to ask. Then, do your listing presentation. Close for the listing.

Manager's Tip: Please review the processes here for calling on FSBOs and expired listings. Share with your agent other strategies you use in your office. There is no one right way. Lots of methods work. The one commonality is that agents must be practiced, tenacious, and willing to keep in contact with those potential clients.

Big Idea: Listing only homes that sell sets your professional standards high and ensures you create the success record FSBOs and expired listing sellers are seeking.

Resource: A "for pay" resource to find and work with several types of home sellers is www.theredx.com, a site that provides FSBOs, expired listings, and preforeclosure information to members. REDX also provides free educational teleseminars for its members.

■ Reactive Leads: Converting the Online Lead

A sample online lead capture and conversion system is shown in Figure 8.8.

Manager's Tip: Be ready to recommend to your agent an online lead capture or follow-up system or customer relationship management (CRM) software. Popular programs for agents include Top Producer™ and Wise Agent. Also check out Cross Coaching Toolbox—great for new agents because it's affordable, easy to use, and combines contact management, website, and marketing resources, all in one.

FIGURE 8.8   An Example of a System to Capture and Convert Leads

Lead Capture	Lead Conversion	Client Loyalty
Program to capture the lead/input to contact management with notes	One day after inquiry—pick up the phone	Ongoing communication through contact management
Fast follow-up	Each day—call	Training—communication skills
Training—best method to answer initial inquiry/ time frames for following up	Training—develop script	Goal: Communicate until they buy or die
Develop emails/scripts for emails	After one week—call once a week	
Goal: Prove dedicated professionalism	Training—develop script to interview/screen	
	Goal: Prove you deserve trust/ gain rapport	

■ Summary

We've just provided the training you need, along with specific scripts, to make the four major types of lead-generating contacts. First, we began with the *why* behind the prioritized best sources of leads in this program. I want you to take these principles into your self-management throughout your whole career.

It's extremely important to your success that you start with these prioritized sources and keep your own numbers so you know your best sources for your long-term success. Too many times, new agents do a little of this, a little of that, and never master any one type of lead generation. So, they never learn what works for them.

In addition, I've provided the specific skills and scripts required in making these four types of lead-generating contacts. But you've only read them. To master these skills, you need to practice. You also need to apply them in the field dozens of times. You'll find you naturally gravitate to certain types of contacts and certain types of scripts. Make them your own, and no market will ever conquer you. You'll conquer it!

> **Big Idea:** Practicing and applying these sales skills dozens of times in the field makes the difference between low and high payoffs for your efforts. Get an agent partner and get blazingly good at telling the truth attractively!

In the next unit, we'll look longer term at your business and discuss some of the business-supporting systems you'll want to put into place now:

1. An evaluation system for your leads—so you choose to work with the right people (a great time management tool)
2. A marketing plan—your system to keep in touch until they buy or die
3. Your professional portfolio, the most important piece of self-promotion you'll need right now (to gain the confidence of buyers and sellers)

Must-Haves in Your Sales Arsenal: Qualifying Procedures, Marketing Plans, and Your Personal Promotional Tool

You've seen the four-week plan. You're starting the plan. You have the scripts for lead generating. Now, you need three other systems to turn those leads into sales:

1. A qualifying system for your leads—so you choose to work with the right people (a great time-management tool)
2. A marketing plan with a social media component—your system to keep in touch until they buy or die
3. A self-promotion tool—your professional portfolio (to gain the confidence of buyers and sellers)

In the last unit, I gave you an online inquiry and follow-up plan. This is another one of your systems to ensure no one falls through the cracks!

Manager's Tip: Have a sample prelisting and prebuyer package made up to show your agent. Provide your agent with your preferred buyer and seller qualifying questionnaires. If you don't have access to these things, see the References unit here.

◼ Qualifying Buyers and Sellers for Effective Time Management

According to new agents, the most difficult challenge to master is *time management.* For many, problems with time management stem from agents not qualifying buyers and sellers. Not everyone should be put in your car and shown homes! Before you ever put a buyer in your car or go to a listing presentation, ask yourself, "Is doing this in my best interest?"

Usually the new agent's motto is, "I'll work with anyone." Unfortunately, adopting that attitude leads to bad habits, wasted effort, and disappointment over those buyers and sellers who refuse to close. To help you get off on the right foot, create the kind of judgments great agents make, and spend your time effectively, I have created four tools. Following them will force you to look before you leap. These qualifiers teach you where to draw the line. I call these your *professional standards*; that is, what you will and won't put up with!

Professional standards. Here are some examples of situations in which you need to have these standards in place:

- Would you put a buyer in your car who wouldn't meet with you for an hour first?
- Would you work with a buyer who wouldn't be loyal?
- Would you work with a buyer who wouldn't be honest with you?
- Would you list an overpriced home?
- Would you do a buyer or seller presentation without all parties present?

You will see many more areas in my evaluators that help you think through these situations and decide where to draw the line so you don't waste your time and money—or get taken advantage of. By the way, everyone has professional standards, even if they didn't have the benefits of thinking through them like you do here. Their standards are simply what they allow!

Big Idea: Lack of professional standards leads you to work with anyone, wasting your precious resources, causing disappointment, and leading to depression. Your professional standards spring from deciding where to draw the line.

Your tools for buyers:

1. Tracking Qualified Buyers (you should integrate your tracking system into your CRM)
2. Qualified Buyer Evaluator

Your tools for sellers:

1. Listing Presentation Qualifier
2. Marketable Listing Evaluator

The Two-Step Process

Many times we're so happy to snag a buyer or seller that we forget to take it one step at a time. Here's the model I want you to use to qualify buyers and sellers. Think of the job interview process. The interviewer asks lots of questions to the interviewee. If the interviewee's answers warrant, the interviewer then sells the interviewee. It's no different in the process of working with buyers and sellers (you are the interviewer):

- Interview first (use the questionnaires in this unit)
- Sell second

Big Idea: The biggest mistake agents make in working with buyers and sellers is to flip the order of the presentation and end up with little information and no credibility.

Figure 9.1 is a graphic representation of how to arrange your presentation.

In this unit, we're going to explore the first part of the process: the interview.

Buyers First

Ask questions and make judgments with your professional standards. New agents work with more buyers than sellers as a rule, so we'll tackle qualifying buyers first. How do you avoid working with those you really don't want to work with? Qualify them. What does that mean? Ask questions first before you put buyers in the car or meet them at a property. Listen to how these buyers answer and compare those answers to your professional standards. I'll share with you some qualifying questions you should ask and show you how to use the evaluators for buyers.

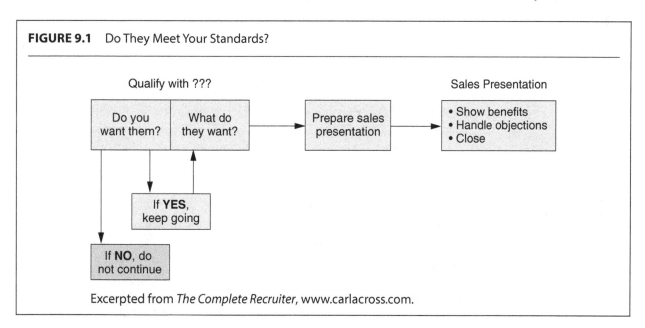

FIGURE 9.1 Do They Meet Your Standards?

Excerpted from *The Complete Recruiter*, www.carlacross.com.

Using the quick questionnaire. You will meet buyers on the fly, such as in open houses, an incoming call, or perhaps an online lead. (You will have to develop a rapport with your online leads before qualifying them.

That's why picking up the phone as soon as possible is so important.) You need to have your quick qualifying questions ready.

Figure 9.2 is a short questionnaire you can use when you need it. Have it with you at all times so you won't forget to ask these questions—and save yourself time and money so you don't pick people who aren't motivated or who already have an agent!

FIGURE 9.2   Quick Qualifying Questionnaire for Buyers

- How long have you been looking for a home?
- What attracted you to this home?
- When do you want or need to move?
- Have you been prequalified by a lender?
- Are you working with a real estate agent?

Qualify the buyer first for these things:

- Motivation
- Needs
- Ability to be loyal to you

The buyer consultative session.   You aren't going to be able to do a credible job unless you take the time to sit down with the prospective buyer and do a consultative session using a comprehensive buyer questionnaire. The consultative session is a meeting, about an hour long, during which you educate the buyer on buying today and ask qualifying questions. Here are two essential components of the process:

1. To appear professional, have a buyer's questionnaire ready for every buyer so you can get all the answers you need before showing homes. See the References and Resources unit for a comprehensive program for working with buyers, and see your manager. She may have a comprehensive program or questionnaire already.
2. Use your buyer presentation to stay on track during your consultative session. It will contain the same kinds of things as your seller presentation. See your manager for company materials and suggestions about what can go into your buyer presentation.

I told you *Up and Running* is not a training manual, and this is one topic that can't be taught adequately here. To become a competent buyer's agent, you need to take a real in-depth course on buyer representation and gather the professional materials to represent buyers professionally.

Tracking Qualified Buyers

Figure 9.3 is a tracking tool so you can be sure you are working with enough qualified buyers. It's also in Unit 12 because you're going to use it weekly for effective time management.

As a new agent, your job is to gather as many qualified buyers as quickly as you can. This tracking tool helps you see how you're doing. Every time you qualify buyers, add them to your sheet. Check off that you used the questionnaire and that they were both at the session. Keep track of the number of showings (the number of times you take them to look at homes, not the number of homes shown). Estimate when they will buy so you have a sense of your potential income. Finally, log when you sold them. Share this information with your manager in your weekly coaching meeting.

The reason you are using this hard-copy tool is to teach yourself how to work with only qualified prospects. Not doing so is a huge time waster, and time management is an agent's biggest challenge.

FIGURE 9.3   Tracking Qualified Buyers

Record and qualify your buyer leads

Date of Qualifying Meeting	Name	Address	Question-naire Used?	Both at Qualifying Session?	# Showings	Sales

Excerpted from *The Complete Buyer's Agent Toolkit*, www.carlacross.com.

Using the Buyer's Potential Evaluator

Figure 9.4 is a tool you'll be using every week for effective time management. It's in Unit 12 for your weekly use.

I love this tool because it forces agents to evaluate the worth of that particular buyer to them. Take a look at the areas I've listed. These are the areas where you need to set boundaries. Take the evaluator and decide your own boundaries. Add other boundaries that are important to you. Now, add to my questionnaire the questions you would need to ask to find out whether buyers meet your professional criteria. Don't be afraid you won't get any business. It's human nature to want the very best. You are choosing them, as they are choosing you!

FIGURE 9.4   Buyer's Potential Evaluator

Rate on a scale of 1–4 (4 is the highest)

	1	2	3	4
1. Buyer answered all qualifying questions.	1	2	3	4
2. Buyer is motivated to purchase. (Rate each spouse/partner separately.)	1	2	3	4
3. Buyer is realistic about price range expectations.	1	2	3	4
4. Buyer is open and cooperative	1	2	3	4
5. Buyer will purchase in a timely manner.	1	2	3	4
6. Buyer is a referral source and will provide referrals.	1	2	3	4
7. Buyer has agreed that you will be his or her exclusive agent.	1	2	3	4
8. Buyer has signed a buyer agency agreement.	1	2	3	4
9. Buyer will meet with loan officer to be pre-approved.	1	2	3	4
10. Buyer answered financial questions openly.	1	2	3	4
11. Buyer has no other agent obligations.	1	2	3	4
12. If buyer has home to sell, he or she is realistic about price.	1	2	3	4
13. Buyer will devote sufficient time to purchasing process.	1	2	3	4
14. Both spouses/partners will be available to look for home.	1	2	3	4
15. This buyer is worthy of my time, energy, and expertise.	1	2	3	4

Use this evaluator with each buyer to ensure you are working within your standards to achieve effective time management and referrals.

Excerpted from The Complete Buyer's Agent Toolkit, www.carlacross.com.

What happens without standards? Many agents think that they will get tough later. Bob (not his real name), an agent in my office, refused to qualify buyers. He simply tried to talk to them between showing homes while driving them around. He told me he intended to start doing a better job of qualifying them when he was more successful. Bob lasted in the business only a few months. He felt people took advantage of him. He had trouble closing; he kept trying to find the magic words to make buyers do what he wanted. He thought memorizing closing techniques would solve his buyer problems. In truth, though, great qualifying makes those old-style, manipulative closing techniques worthless (and, good riddance!). Bob's refusal to set professional standards and lack of results led to depression and lowered self-esteem until he shrank out of the business.

Big Idea: Become a great qualifier, and your troubles with closing will disappear.

But, I'm afraid I won't have anyone to work with... Yes, you will, if you increase your lead generating. Start right—prospect for hundreds of potentially qualified prospects. Then, be tough when you qualify them.

Big Idea: The cure for not closing prospects is more lead generating, not more closing skills—plus great qualifying questions.

Qualifying Sellers

The following is a common scenario for new agents (even some experienced agents still fall into this trap): A prospective client calls during your floor time and requests a market analysis on his home. You're so excited that you make an appointment without asking any qualifying questions. You inspect the home and do all the work required to complete a market analysis. You return to the home and give the prospective client your complete, full-color, 20-page market analysis. You don't hear from him. You call and find out that he wanted the market analysis to give to his niece, who just entered the real estate field, for an assignment in her training school. You feel used. However, the prospective client feels, because you provided the market analysis service without qualifying him, he got what he wanted. And he assumes that you got what you wanted. *Was* it what you wanted? Don't think so.

Big Idea: As a professional, it's your job to teach the seller how you work.

The two-step qualifying process. To list a property, use a two-step process, just like the process for qualifying buyers:

1. Qualify the seller and the property for salability.
2. Present your marketing plan, including pricing, to the seller.

Remember that flowchart, Figure 9.1, excerpted from *The Complete Recruiter*? All real estate professionals, from agents to managers, need to use the same process—in the same order—to qualify candidates. Apply this flowchart to qualifying sellers as you did with buyers.

Start Qualifying on the First Phone Call

Qualifying starts during the first phone conversation with the seller. I've collected these questions into a questionnaire for you (Figure 9.5) so you can have it ready on the fly. Be ready *not* to go on that appointment if they don't meet your standards!

Big Idea: Prepare your knockout factors—those answers sellers give you that cause you to not want to go further. Those knockout factors become your professional standards.

FIGURE 9.5 Quick Qualifying Questionnaire for Sellers

- When do you want or need to move?
- Where are you moving?
- Have you ever sold a home before?
- What are you looking for in a listing agent?
- When can I come over and preview the home and visit with you?

After the phone call and before the appointment. Stand out from the crowd! Send a thank-you note along with your pre-list package (see the References and Resources unit or ask your manager for ideas about what can go in the package). This is one of those comprehensive areas that can't be adequately covered in *Up and Running*. However, there are fine training programs on listing practice and excellent listing process packages.

Before you go to the appointment. Enter your potential clients in your Listing Presentation Qualifier (Figure 9.6) and start evaluating the sellers. Track each of the sellers with this checklist and share it with your manager during your weekly coaching meeting. Use it, too, to hold to your professional standards. This is in Unit 12 because you'll be using it each week for time management.

FIGURE 9.6 Listing Presentation Qualifier

Date of Presentation	Name	Address	Want to Sell?	Both Home?	2 Hours Pre-Scheduled?	How Much $ Want?	Marketing Presentation Completed?	Results

Excerpted from *Your Complete Power Listing System,* www.carlacross.com.

The Consultative Meeting at the Sellers' Home

What should you do first as you meet the seller at his home? Qualify him! Why walk around the home if the seller isn't going to meet your professional standards? To prepare the seller for how you're going to work, explain the process. Here's your script: "So I can get to know you, Mr. Seller, I have some questions to ask you. Then, I'll walk through the home with you so you can show me your home's features."

The comprehensive client questionnaire. You will need to develop a much more comprehensive client questionnaire. See your manager or the References and Resources unit.

How a top agent works. Let's look at an agent who's made a tough, professional, personal boundary of not listing properties she has determined will not sell in normal market time. This agent will not list properties that are more than 3% over her analysis of what that property will actually sell for. Why this personal boundary? This pro wants to establish a name for herself as a REALTOR® who only lists properties that sell. Her reputation depends on "sold" signs on properties. Obviously, this reputation will attract only serious sellers who appreciate her professional attitude. During the first appointment, if she determines that the sellers want more money for their home than her initial professional opinion indicates, she will not make the next appointment. Why should she waste her time and ruin her reputation? Or, if after the second appointment the sellers want more money for their home than her expert opinion warrants, she won't list the home.

Recently, I saw how this strategy works. An agent in my office prepared a marketing plan for a seller. However, because the competition priced the property $50,000 higher than our agent, the seller chose to list with the competition. Unfortunately, the competition did not work in our area and used the wrong homes to diagnose the home's selling challenges.

Initially, the seller was pleased with the listing agent because he listed the home at such a high price. Of course, the seller expected selling agents to bring customers. However, agents who wanted to create trust and loyalty with their buyers would not show the overpriced home to their buyers. So the seller saw few potential buyers.

After three months of lost marketing time, the disillusioned seller listed with our agent at the right price. However, irreparable damage had been done to all parties involved. National surveys show that this added time on the market costs the seller thousands of dollars. Homes that are on the market a long time sell for less than if they were listed at the right price and sold quickly. (Remember Charles Revson's marketing truism: Create demand. When buyers compete, the price goes up.) Because the first listing agent did not create a satisfied customer, he will not get any return business. Unfortunately, the agent who lists the home the second time around won't have as satisfied a customer as if he had been able to list the home first—at the right price.

> **Big Idea:** Overpricing properties causes negative results for sellers and a negative perception of our industry.

Using the Marketable Listing Evaluator. Figure 9.7 is an evaluator to ensure you are qualifying sellers to your standards. It's also in Unit 12 because you'll be using it each week for effective time management.

Sellers qualify agents. And good agents carefully qualify sellers. How confident would you feel if your doctor did not ask you any questions but simply prescribed aspirin every time you came to the office?

Sellers' confidence in an agent is raised when they know that the agent has established certain criteria for marketing property. Why waste sellers' time—and money—if the property won't sell? Answering the questions on the Marketable Listing Evaluator with each potential listing ensures you establish your professional boundaries.

> **Big Idea:** Deciding that you'll list only homes that will sell within normal market time is the most important professional standard you'll uphold.

■ Building Your Marketing Plan

It's not over after your first contact! We discussed the fact that buyers take longer than ever from that first inquiry to their buying decision. That means you must stay in touch—until they buy or die—and you must create a marketing plan for those you have met. You must become "top of the mind" to them so, when they are ready to make a buying decision, they work with you.

Frequency and Consistency Are Key

Here are two truisms from the world of marketing you need to grasp to design a good marketing plan:

1. Frequency is more important than reach.
2. Consistency is everything.

> **Big Idea:** frequency + consistency = success

FIGURE 9.7 Marketable Listing Evaluator

1. Property listed at competitive price	Yes_____	No_____
2. Full-term listing agreement	Yes_____	No_____
3. Seller to complete obvious repairs/cleaning before showing	Yes_____	No_____
4. Easy access (e.g., key, phone for showing)	Yes_____	No_____
5. Yard sign	Yes_____	No_____
6. Immediate possession	Yes_____	No_____
7. Extras included (e.g., appliances)	Yes_____	No_____
8. Available for first tour	Yes_____	No_____
9. FHA/VA terms available if appropriate	Yes_____	No_____
10. If short sale or foreclosure, I am qualified to be the representative	Yes_____	No_____
11. If short sale or foreclosure, forecast for successful closing is good	Yes_____	No_____
12. Below market interest rate if seller financed	Yes_____	No_____
13. Post-dated price reduction	Yes_____	No_____
14. My desired commission	Yes_____	No_____
15. In my evaluation, this property will sell within listed market range, in normal market time for this area.	Yes_____	No_____
16. I will receive referrals from the sellers.	Yes_____	No_____

Use this evaluator with each of your potential listings to ensure sellers meet your standards.

Excerpted from *Your Complete Power Listing System,* www.carlacross.com.

The first truism means that it's much more effective to contact fewer people frequently than to contact many people just a few times, so don't spend money mailing one card once to a thousand strangers. Don't spend thousands of dollars once to put an ad in your Sunday newspaper saying you are the greatest. Instead, contact those who already know you or hear of you frequently and consistently.

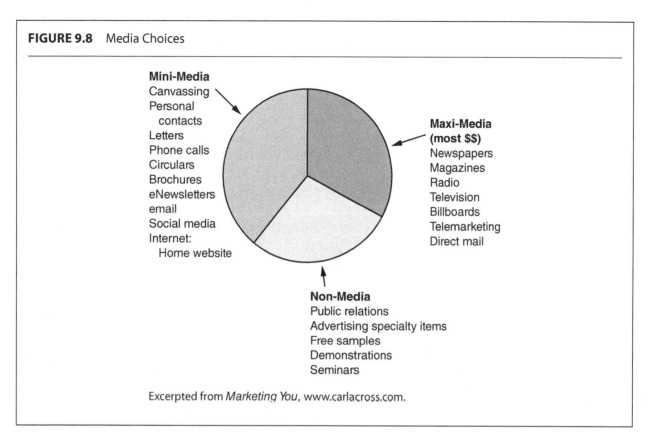

FIGURE 9.8   Media Choices

Mini-Media
Canvassing
Personal
   contacts
Letters
Phone calls
Circulars
Brochures
eNewsletters
email
Social media
Internet:
   Home website

**Maxi-Media
(most $$)**
Newspapers
Magazines
Radio
Television
Billboards
Telemarketing
Direct mail

Non-Media
Public relations
Advertising specialty items
Free samples
Demonstrations
Seminars

Excerpted from *Marketing You*, www.carlacross.com.

Consistency is key. One of the mistakes agents make in their marketing plans is that they send a great big newsletter to their contact list once a year. That's not consistency. Consistency means communicating with them at least monthly. Some marketing experts suggest communicating with them weekly for the first few weeks. Then go to monthly. Why? It takes frequent, consistent communication for the potential client to recognize and remember you.

Designing Your Marketing Plan

Sit down now and write how you will communicate with those you already know frequently and consistently. That may include the following:

- Postcards
- Letters
- Newsletters or e-Newsletters
- Emails
- Personal visits
- Gifts
- Telephone calls
- Parties

Your Media Choices

The previous figure gives you an easy way to look at some choices. Which category do you think is lowest cost? Non-media and mini-media. Start there. Why? You have time but no money! Also, you are in a personal-service, relationship business. Use the marketing strategies that get you in front of people to reinforce the qualities you want them to recognize about you.

Don't waste your money! A study by Baylor University showed agents spent the most money on their worst sources of business: website, postcards, and ads. Just because someone else is doing it, doesn't mean you should do it. However, you must implement a marketing plan. Be sure your website also performs the function you want it to perform—bringing you leads (more about that later in this unit).

Proving you made the transition to real estate sales. How will you prove to people who know you as a musician, for example, that you are now a capable real estate professional? Remind them over and over that you are successfully selling real estate. Mailings to these people are easy. They are the same mailings you are doing to promote properties. Each time you have a brochure or flyer on a property you or someone in your office has listed, merely drop that flyer in the mail with a note: "Just wanted you to know the latest in property values," "Just wanted to keep you abreast of the market," "Thought this property would fit some of our friends," or "Please pass on this information to someone you know." By sending the flyer, you are teaching your friend that you are actively engaged in selling real estate. You are also showing your friend that, over time, you are accountable for keeping in touch in a professional way.

Marketing Campaigns

Technically, marketing campaigns are spaced repetition drips on a specific target market (homeowners in a specific area, past clients, first-time home buyers, etc.) for a specific amount of time. Many real estate–specific CRMs contain pre-set drip campaigns, along with scripts and templates. They follow the principle of consistent, long-term marketing. That's all good. However, don't think you can get away with merely sending emails or cards on a regular basis to create raving clients for life!

That's why I prefer to call what you do in marketing a marketing plan. I want you to pick and choose your communication vehicles carefully, and mix them up. Remember, we're selling homes to human beings. We need to be more than automated in our marketing.

Your Complete Marketing Plan

You're not done with your marketing plan until you've decided the what, who, how, and how much—for a year. For example, at the end of the year, as part of my business plan for my speaking, coaching, and product businesses, I design a marketing plan that consists of mailings, newsletters, emails, personal calls, and gifts. Then, I attach a budget and assign names to carry out the plan. I schedule each of these events in my Goldmine (my contact management program). Now I don't have to scramble every month to decide how I'm going to keep in contact with my best sources of business. It's all planned for the whole year. My team and I work on the monthly marketing tactics so we stay in touch with you . . . forever!

After you've designed your plan, put your activities in your contact management system so they will drive you.

Remember our agent advice, too, about not spending your marketing dollars on promises of leads given to you.

See your manager after you've made a draft of your plan. Your manager knows what works and will give you guidance in best marketing choices (plus company marketing opportunities or endorsements that will save you money).

Social Media Marketing: Planning Your Social Media with the Social Media Planner

Because there are so many choices in social media, I'm providing a social media planner as shown in Figure 9.9 from my friend and tech guru John Mayfield. I've included John's contact information in the References and Resources unit.

How to Start with Social Media

Start now! I'm assigning you a new social network each week of the four-week plan, so you can take it step by step. By the end of four weeks, you will have each social network in place and will have started your social media plan with John's social media planner. Once you get up and running, you may choose to integrate your social media plan into your overall marketing plan because, as I've said before, social media is a group of marketing media available to you, just like the other traditional media.

Social Media Experts

Need some guidance or coaching with social media? In the References and Resources unit, I've included social media experts and courses. Ask your manager, though, for a recommendation that he thinks is best for you. There are proprietary schools, REALTOR® associations, and community colleges in your area that offer tech courses and courses in social media.

A Worksheet Marketing Planner for You

Figure 9.10 is an example plan I created so you can plan your ongoing marketing. I've provided you a blank marketing planner in Unit 12 so you can create your own plan. After you create your plan, set a date on which to have each of your marketing materials and scripts ready to use. Finally, put each of these dates in your contact management system so you'll remember to do it!

Big Idea: Schedule implementation of your marketing plan.

FIGURE 9.9   Social Media Planner

Social Media Planner							
Activities Use this chart to keep track of your social networking activities each week. Remember, the more activities you can perform each week, the more exposure you'll receive, which leads to more potential for business.	Sunday	Monday	Tuesday	Wednesday	Thursday	Friday	Saturday
Status Updates and Comments							
Provide your status update before 9 am (LinkedIn, Facebook, Twitter)							
Provide another status update after lunch (Facebook, Twitter)							
Provide final status update before going to bed (Facebook, Twitter)							
Create and post __ links to news articles found online per __							
Comment on at least __ people's status updates on Facebook per __							
Comment on at least __ people's posts on a LinkedIn group per __							
Bookmark __ websites and blog posts on Delicious or StumbleUpon per __							
Videos and Photos							
Upload __ videos to YouTube per __							
Upload photos to Instagram per __							
Upload __ videos to Flickr per __							
Blogging							
Write __ blog(s) per __							
Post __ blog(s) to ActiveRain per __							
Read and comment on at least __ blogs on ActiveRain per __							
Network Building							
Add __ friends on Facebook per __							
Add __ connections on LinkedIn per __							
Add at least __ friends on Plaxo per __							
Follow __ people on Twitter per __							
Follow people on Instagram per __							

This Social Media Planner is provided compliments of John Mayfield, www.RealEstateTechGuy.com, social media and technology expert.

Companies That Have Ready-to-Use Marketing Plans and Materials

As a new agent, I urge you to use some premade materials and plans, such as those available from The Personal Marketing Company, ProspectsPLUS!, Sendsations, Top Producer®, Michael Lewis, and Cross Coaching Toolbox. Blue Mountain and SendOutCards are other programs you can use to send and personalize cards. A resource I use for postcards and other hard-copy marketing materials is Expresscopy. Your company may have marketing pieces and copies you can use, too. See your manager for recommendations.

FIGURE 9.10   Your Marketing Plan—A Sample

1.   Name your target market (who you're marketing to).
2.   Put your actions in order of the dates to be accomplished.
3.   Assign work to be accomplished in each tactic. Add your budget figure.
4.   Tally your total budget from this target market.

Target Market: _____

Action	Assigned To	To Be Done By	Budget
Introduction	agent	1st month (Jan)	200 people @ 50 cents = $100
Implement social media plan	agent	each day	$0–$100/month; depends on services/programs purchased
Phone calls (ask for referrals)	agent	2nd month (Feb)	200 people @ 25 cents = $50
E-Newsletter (one page)	agent	1st–2nd month (Feb)	200 people @ 25 cents = $50
"Spring Ahead" postcard	agent	3rd month (Mar)	200 people @ 30 cents = $60
Personal visit—seeds for spring plants	agent	4th month (April)	200 people @ 50 cents = $100
E-Newsletter (one page)	agent	5th month (May)	200 people @ 25 cents = $50
"Just Listed" postcard	agent	6th month (June)	200 people @ 30 cents = $60
Phone calls (ask for referrals)	agent	7th month (July)	200 people @ 25 cents = $50
E-Newsletter (one page)	agent	8th month (Aug)	200 people @ 25 cents = $50
"Just Sold" postcard	agent	9th month (Sept)	200 people @ 30 cents = $60
Personal visit—pumpkins	agent	10th month (Oct)	200 people @ $1 = $200
E-Newsletter (one page)	agent	11th month (Nov)	200 people @ 25 cents = $50
Holiday card	agent	12th month (Dec)	200 people @ 50 cents = $100

Notes:
E-Newsletter four times per year; preprinted postcards three times per year
Regularly send anniversary cards to each person you sold a home to
Take housewarming gift within two weeks after closing (to both buyers and sellers) (most important!)
Increase your postcards (just listed or just sold) as you can, to prove you are a successful agent
You also need to expand this to after-the-sale tactics:
- Deliver a present to the new homeowner within 10 days of move-in
- Send an after-sale survey to all buyers and sellers

Excerpted from *Beyond the Basics of Business Planning*, the online business planning site for real estate professionals, www.carlacross.com.

Remember, your job is to get your face and name in front of those who already know something about you, over and over again. Your job is not to spend lots of money in low-payoff items!

Big Idea: Heroes aren't those who make their own marketing plan. Heroes are those who implement a plan and get results.

Expanding Your Marketing Plan to Include New Homeowners

It's stunning but true. A survey showed that only 40% of agents ever went back to the new homeowner they just sold—after closing! That means the client thinks the agent took the money and ran! Don't be one of those secret agents. Expand your marketing plan to include a closing gift, hand-delivered. What should it be? That's not nearly as important as the fact that you cared enough to show up after you got your check! In addition, send after-sale surveys to ensure you did a great job. You'll get testimonials, and those survey results will make your confidence in your business abilities soar. You can use a survey company like SurveyGizmo or SurveyMonkey, or see your manager for suggestions on surveys and company strategies.

Big Idea: It's not what you do, it's that you do something consistently and frequently. How frequent and consistent is your marketing?

■ Marketing *You*

You've found out how to set your professional standards. You have the information and forms to qualify buyers and sellers for effective time management. You know now how to build a marketing plan. You're almost done with your people management systems. The last thing you need to do is develop your professional portfolio. You need a method to stand out from the crowd. You need a method to build your confidence and self-esteem so you can better build your business.

What the Portfolio Is For

Experienced agents have a track record of success. They can tell buyers and sellers about how they listed properties that sold, how they sold 50 homes the prior year, and so on. Because you're new, you don't have that track record. Can you compete? Yes. How? By showing the prospective buyer your lifelong successes, talents, skills, and values.

What is a professional portfolio? It's a pictorial of you, your background, your skills, your hobbies, and your talents, with letters of recommendation from those who know and trust you. It's like a movie of you! Only, it's not expensive to produce like a movie.

Big Idea: The portfolio speaks volumes for you so you don't have to brag.

Why a Portfolio Works

As a new agent, I had no successes. I hadn't even been in a field closely related to real estate! So, what did I have? At first, I was actually bereft. I didn't feel I had anything to offer. But as I thought about it, I realized I had taken with me into real estate my lifelong achievements. What I knew about myself was that I had to have been dutiful, responsible, and accountable to have practiced piano regularly all through college and held a job requiring 12 hours of work a week while still finding time to study. I knew I could handle several things at once—a skill certainly required in real estate. Also, I knew I had become a pretty good negotiator from having to negotiate fees for music jobs. What I needed to do was to demonstrate those same skills to my friends in a new business. That's how I came up with the idea of the portfolio.

Big Idea: Your professional portfolio builds trust and confidence in buyers and sellers.

What a Portfolio Looks Like

Picture a top-of-the-line three-ring binder. Inside, you'll have stationery dividers—title pages that introduce you. Inside each of those sections, you'll include pictures, letters, diplomas, testimonials—the list is almost endless of the evidence you can use to show people who don't know you and what you bring to real estate that benefits them. The cost is less than $20 per portfolio. The value is unbeatable!

How to Create Your Portfolio Contents

Complete the portfolio exercise in Figure 9.11. Ask yourself, "What skills do I bring from my former career, business, avocation, and so forth? What are the benefits of these skills to buyers and sellers? How can I show it?"

After you've brainstormed this information, start throwing all kinds of evidence in folders with your divider page names. (See the References and Resources unit for a complete guide, *Marketing You*, www.carlacross.com.)

FIGURE 9.11   Portfolio Exercise

List Your Skills	Benefits to Buyers/Sellers	Show It—Evidence

Excerpted from *Marketing You*, www.carlacross.com.

How to Use the Portfolio

Make several portfolios because you're going to need them. You'll be so busy! Use them in the following situations:

1. Open houses—have one open on the counter
2. Pre–first visit buyer package—include it and pick it up when you do your qualifying and presentation
3. Pre–first visit seller package—include it and pick it up when you do your qualifying and presentation

Is Your Profile on Every Website, Blog, and Social Media Site You Use?

I am constantly amazed at how little agents believe they are in competition with other agents for the consumers' business. If you don't put a complete profile in each social network you use (your Facebook business page, LinkedIn, and so on), you are missing the opportunity to let others know you and the scope of your expertise. Use the material you've created by doing the portfolio as a springboard to populate your social media sites. You'll be ahead of 90% of agents! Remember, consumers are looking increasingly online to choose a real estate professional. Don't be left out.

Tip: Pick five agents in your office and area at random. Check out their biographies on various websites. What did you find? If you were a potential client, how would you judge those agents? How do you want to be portrayed?

Author Stefan Swanepoel suggests that you decide your motivation and your purpose before launching into any social network. Doing the exercises for your professional portfolio will help you immensely with the professional projection you'll want to accomplish with social media.

Testimonials—The Best Thing for Your Portfolio

We believe what others say about us, not what we say about us. You know that's true, and you'll want those testimonials for your portfolio. On the other hand, because you're new to real estate, you're probably wondering how you are going to get testimonials. You're going to get testimonials first from those you worked with in another business or a charity. Those testimonials will prove your character and your work qualities. To gather those testimonials, you can use a survey site like www.zoomerang.com or www.surveymonkey.com. Start using those now because you're going to be sending after-sale surveys every time your listing sells or you sell a home. You want to gather as many testimonials as possible, as fast as possible.

Check Out What Consumers Are Saying About Agents

As I told you in the trends unit, consumers are looking online to see what others are saying about their prospective agents and to give feedback on their experiences. See Zillow, Yelp, www.incredibleagents.com, and www.realestateratingz.com. Online agent reviews are a continuing trend, and you'll see more and more websites with client feedback about agents.

Other Benefits

Sometimes we need to be reminded of our value. That's the time to read your own portfolio. It raises our self-confidence and fights those negative feelings we get when we are rejected time after time. It forms the basis for other promotional pieces, like brochures. It gives you a wealth of information from which to draw your marketing strategies. It absolutely allows you to compete with the "big guys" successfully. (I know. All my top first-year agents created portfolios and used them to get listings and buyers against multi-million-dollar producers!)

■ Summary

You've learned the following three tools you need to build the rest of your career strategy:

1. A qualifying system for your leads—so you choose to work with the right people (a great time-management tool)
2. A marketing plan that includes social media—your system to keep in touch until they buy or die
3. A self-promotion tool—your professional portfolio (to gain the confidence of buyers and sellers)

Armed with these systems, you'll be able to include social media and populate that social media with your purpose and profile. You've gotten the forms and checklists that are really built-in self-management training tools (and you didn't even know I was training your mind!). You're building your systems so you can go fast and do well. Next are the seven critical sales skills you need to master to lead generate, qualify, handle objections, and sell.

Seven Critical Sales Skills for Success

Yes, you can sell homes to people without having effective sales skills, but it will take you much more time and much more money to do it than if you had mastered sales communication.

Also, here's a warning about online leads: They don't just turn themselves in to you! In fact, several online lead-generating companies have failed in the last few years because they made an assumption that an online lead required no sales skills from an agent! If you've been in sales for more than three nanoseconds, you know how untrue this is! So pay particular attention to these sales skills and apply them to all your lead opportunities. Your ability to make money is dependent on two things: (1) generating leads in large numbers and (2) developing the skills to take those leads from cold communication to warm relationship.

In this unit, I'll show you how to communicate with your potential buyers and sellers so you sell more homes more often. But there's one ingredient I can't provide in this resource: practice.

It's great you're reading about these sales skills, but reading about them doesn't mean you can do them. In each week of the four-week plan, you'll see I've assigned you practice for each of these sales skill areas. I've also suggested specific practices for you in each of the seven sales skills explained here. Why? Without practice, you'll just be able to say, "I heard that before." I've heard lots of piano concertos before, too, but that doesn't mean I can play them! So, read each of these, and take seriously my assignment of practicing each of these skills until you are an *unconscious competent*. That means when you are in a situation that requires using one or more of these skills, you unconsciously use the one you need at the time.

✓ **Manager's Tip:** In this unit, I've provided you a sample practice session for each of the seven critical sales skills. Teach one per sales meeting and get your agents practicing each one that week. Now you have expanded *Up and Running* into training.

■ Why These Particular Skills?

Because they are the most critical to your early success. I picked them from dozens of sales skills because you need these particular skills right now! These are the skills taught in every sales skills development program throughout the world of business. I know, because I've spent thousands of dollars learning them! They are also the skills that few real estate salespeople develop. Why?

1. Most real estate salespeople get focused on learning everything they can about finance, law, inspection, and so on—the technical points. That's because they are afraid of not knowing everything. In addition, most training programs in real estate companies are heavy on these technical subjects and contain very little or no sales training. New agents think memorizing facts and laws assure their success. Yes, knowing how to fill in the blanks on purchase and sale agreements is important. But we're working with *people*. Making money in our business depends 95% on our sales communication skills with people. We must develop great sales communication skills if we want to be successful—and help buyers and sellers make good buying decisions.

2. If these sales skills are covered in training programs, it's usually just a mention. Or, the only person doing the skill is the trainer. Agents don't have an opportunity to practice in class until they are skilled at them.

---

* **Big Idea:** Master these seven critical sales skills to increase your income and lessen your time and effort.

The Scripts

In this edition, I've added a unit just for the scripts you've seen. See Unit 13, which also has several sales letters and sales forms. These are training bonuses for you!

Using These Skills for Reactive Leads

As I explain each of these skills, I'll be showing you how to apply them with reactive leads: open houses, floor time, and online leads, for example. These skills work in all sales situations!

Big Idea: Learn each sales skill and relate it in context to all your selling situations, not just one (e.g., the hum technique works as you meet people in all lead-generating situations).

■ The Seven Critical Sales Skills

Here are the major sales skills you need to master right now to get a sale quickly. Each of these skills is introduced during your four weeks, and you have an assignment to practice them as they are introduced.

1. Craft a sales call script. This works to craft any type of sales call—the one to people you know, the one to the FSBO, or the one to the expired listing. This sales skill is to be applied with your first lead-generating source—people you know—in week one.

Big Idea: Plan what you're going to say and how you're going to say it before you make the contact.

---

2. Attach benefits. Show customers that there is something in it for them. Too often, salespeople only think of what a sale will do for them, not what it will provide for the buyers of their services! This sales skill is practiced and applied in week one.

Big Idea: Decide "what's in it for them" and verbalize that at every opportunity so you remind yourself it's not about you!

---

3. Ask a question to get the order. This skill is used in every situation where you want to get a lead. It seems simplistic, but too often salespeople fail to ask for the order. To ensure that you get a lead, craft and apply this simple yet critical sales skill in all sales situations. This sale skill is introduced in week one.

Big Idea: If you don't ask, you don't get.

---

4. Use the AAA method of objection-busting. This method of crafting a process to counter, defuse, or anticipate objections is critical to each sales situation. In truth, all salespeople encounter objections and rejections with each sales call. With the AAA method, you learn to craft a whole process to take objections from an adversary relationship to a discussion. Use this method, introduced in week two, to qualify buyers and sellers, and throughout the entire sales cycle. For more skill building in answering objections, see the References and Resources unit.

Big Idea: Answering an objection without skill is creating an argument.

5. Use the hum technique. This technique is a simplified version of asking questions that encourage the buyer of your services to open up (in sales, these are called *open-ended questions*). In addition, the hum technique couples asking open-ended questions with the "probe" sales skill. Probing means to ask more questions about a certain topic to get the inside story. Use this technique, introduced in week three.

Big Idea: Asking a lot of questions and getting simple answers doesn't reveal what you need to know to help a buyer or seller.

6. Tie down your benefit statement. Sometimes agents get enamored with the sound of their own sales voices. The "tie-down" brings the buyer of your services back into the conversation and allows you to check that you are still on track. This sales skill is introduced in week four. Use it throughout the sales cycle to ensure that the buyer of your services is still buying what you have to sell.

Big Idea: Check every so often to see whether what you think is a priority is true for your buyer or seller.

7. Discover the motive that drives the buyers' decisions. People make decisions based on feelings and rationalize these decisions with facts. However, few agents ever figure this out! They think people buy a particular home because it has three bedrooms! So they just keep showing three-bedroom homes in subdivisions until the buyer goes to another agent and buys a four-bedroom home on an acre—because it satisfies the buyer's emotional need for personal space. But people don't share their dominant buying motives easily, especially when they don't know us. So, as salespeople, we are easily misled!

Let's say your friend buys a Mercedes. Does he say that he bought it because he wants status? No. He says he bought it because studies show the car will actually cost less in the long run because it will hold its value. While this may be true, your friend's desire for *status* (the emotional motivational driver) prompted his decision. Why else do you think people keep getting married for the fourth or fifth time? Because the facts tell them it's the right thing to do? Dream on!

This sales skill, discovering the buyer's driving motivator, is introduced in week four.

Big Idea: People make buying decisions based on emotions and rationalize them with the facts.

How These Sales Skills Work Together

As you can see from my explanations, each of these sales skills has a relationship to the other. That's why I picked these seven. That's why I want you to master each of them, so you become seamless in your sales communications with buyers of your services.

I Don't Want to Be Manipulative

I don't want you to be one of those manipulative salespeople, either! It would be manipulative if you used these skills with bad intent. But you are going to use these skills with good intent. That is, when you are asking questions and probing using the hum technique, you are going to find out whether it is in the best interest of the buyer to go ahead. You are going to tell him the truth attractively! Why? I want you to create a long-term referral/relationship business. The only way you will do that is to keep the customer's best interests in mind.

If you have good intent, the worst thing you can do is stop someone from making the buying decision he wants to make because you lack the sales skills to guide him through the process.

Big Idea: Keeping the customer's best interests in mind while you use sales communication skills ensures you do the right thing and build the right kind of business.

■ Sales Skill 1: Craft a Sales Call Script

The following method of crafting calls works for crafting any initial sales call. Because you needed this skill to start lead generating with your best source—people you know—you have already investigated it in context of that lead-generating source. Use the worksheet in Figure 10.1. It is very similar to the one in Unit 8, which I've changed a bit here to be generic.

Here's the process:

1. Think of a particular person to call—or, if you're cold-calling, decide on the area you're calling and why.
2. Determine potential real estate needs and benefits to this person that you can provide.
3. Write three questions to ask this person to discover these needs.
4. Determine your call objective.
5. Write a question to get a lead or appointment—meet your objective.
6. Write an opening statement.

Example—Crafting a Cold Call

The cold call is a call you make to someone you know very little about. However, if you're calling a homeowner, you know the area in which the homeowner lives, and you can guess the homeowner may have one or more of several common needs. Let's say you are making cold calls in an area of large homes. One need may be that the couple's children have grown, and they are looking to downsize.

FIGURE 10.1 Craft a Sales Call to Any Type of Contact

Name of person: _____

Potential real estate need(s): _____

Benefit to the person of your service: _____

Three questions:

1. _____

2. _____

3. _____

Your call objective: _____

Question to get the order: _____

Opening statement: _____

Practice this sales call with a friend until you are comfortable.

Questions to ask include the following:

1. Have you considered downsizing?
2. Do you know the value of your home?
3. Have you looked into freeing some of the equity in your home to purchase a rental home as an investment?

The call objective is to get an appointment. The question to get an appointment is, "When can we explore this potential?" The opening statement is, "I'm calling today to explore with homeowners in your area some possible real estate opportunities."

In Figure 10.2, I've written a possible script for you to use in a downsizing situation. Notice that I start with an attention-getting phrase. I follow with a statement that may be a need for them. I couple it with a statement about our company and mention that we work the area and have young buyers, so the seller knows I'm reputable. I ask questions to find out if they have a need. I follow the questions with a close for an appointment, adding benefits to the seller of that appointment.

Big Idea: The more focused the call on that particular potential client's needs, the more opportunity you will have of getting an appointment.

FIGURE 10.2   A Script for Cold-Calling

"Hello. This is Carla Cross with ABC Realty. I'll just take a minute of your time. I'm calling today to explore with homeowners in your area some possible real estate opportunities [*the attention-getting phrase*]. We specialize in your area, and we have young buyers with small children looking for homes there. Your area seems perfect for a young family, is that right? [*Yes.*] Have you thought of downsizing? [*Address their need.*] [*Yes.*] Do you know what your home is worth? [*No.*] In just a few minutes I can show you the market trends and how your home compares with what's selling today, so, if you do want to take an opportunity to downsize, you'll know the equity you have available [*feature and benefit to the seller*]. I have some time Wednesday or Thursday evening. Would that work for you? [*close*] Here's my name and phone number again, just for your records [*give them that information*]. Thank you. I look forward to meeting you."

Immediately after the call, write a thank-you note and confirm your appointment. Put them in your database along with your appointment.

Applying this Skill to Online Situations

Let's say you get an online inquiry. As soon as possible, turn that cold inquiry into a warm relationship. Stop using email to respond and pick up the phone. One of the most successful online lead-generating agents has a standard for his team members: pick up the phone within one day of the online inquiry (after his team members have answered the initial online inquiry).

Craft a sales call to the inquirer, using the process I just outlined. The key here is to pick something the person asked you about that helps you get to know the person's lifestyle. For example, this particular inquirer is looking at homes with acreage. What do you need to know about his lifestyle that would start to form a relationship? After all, there are lots of reasons someone wants acreage. So, as you pick up the phone, one of your questions should be, "What will having acreage do for you?" Now you're starting to zero in on his lifestyle and his needs. To have a great call with this inquirer, you'll want to use the features and benefits, the hum technique, the tie-down, and then ask a question to get the order sales skills. They all work together.

Big Idea: All these sales skills apply to every sales situation, proactive or reactive.

Practice, Practice, Practice

Have your friend or your manager give you a lead-generating situation (e.g., responding to an online lead). Create a sales call that helps you form a relationship, find out the needs, and close with a call to action. Role play at least five different situations with your partner until you have mastered the process.

■ Sales Skill 2: Attach Benefits

A benefit is what a particular feature will do for the buyer of the feature. For example, this home has a fireplace. The fireplace is a feature, or fact. But what good is a fireplace if you don't need one for something? One benefit of a fireplace is that, when the electricity goes out, you can cook a meal in it! That may not be *your* primary benefit of having a fireplace in your home, but when our electricity was out for six days, it was a prioritized benefit to me! Buyers will be looking for the benefits of all the features you describe when you tell them about a particular property (see Figure 10.3).

Big Idea: There are many benefits for every feature, and each buyer has a specific benefit in mind.

FIGURE 10.3   What's in It for Me?

The amateur salesperson's mistake. Too often a salesperson recites the facts (called *features* in sales) thinking that facts will sell the home. A great example of this is agents who answer floor inquiries. Wanting to provide all the information, they recite all the features of a home. Then, when the buyer hears a feature he doesn't want, he hangs up! Unless you attach a benefit to each feature, the buyer doesn't even know why something should be important to him! What is important and interesting to the buyer is how he can use these features. A three-car garage is a benefit to the person who owns three cars (or lots of things). It's merely an unwanted expense to a single person with one car!

Note on Answering Those Online Lead Inquiries

Be careful to answer the questions from the inquirer, but do not regurgitate a features list. You need to develop skills to engage the inquirer, to turn that cold inquiry into a warmer lead. That's done by employing warmer methods of communication than email. What do I mean? We communicate by sight, sound, and feeling. Picking up the phone starts that warmer communication process. No matter how you're communicating, though, remember to attach benefits.

Big Idea: Finding an excuse to pick up the phone is a step toward becoming a professional salesperson.

Two ways to attach benefits. How do you discover what is important to a buyer?

1. One way is to ask a question about a feature. When a buyer requests a specific feature or need (e.g., a large family room), ask *why* or, a more graceful way to ask is, "What will having that do for you?" This tells you the benefit the buyer wants. Then, when you show a home with a large family room, remind the buyer that it provides plenty of space for that growing family. In this way, the buyer sees the relevance of the large family room.

Big Idea: Buyers make buying decisions based on the benefits of what that property will do for them.

2. Make a statement and attach a benefit. Then ask if that's the benefit the person wanted. "This home has a two-car garage (feature), so that you can park your two full-sized cars there (benefit)." Benefits answer the buyer's question: so what? To attach benefits to features, state the feature first. Then bridge to the benefit with the words "so that . . . "

Practice, Practice, Practice

Practice attaching benefits to the following features:

Feature	Bridge	Benefit
Family room . . .	so that	
Fireplace . . .	so that	
Low house payments . . .	so that	

Referrals to the agent are a benefit to the referring source because . . .

Listing with me is a benefit to you, the seller, because . . .

Working with me to find a home is a benefit to you, the buyer, because . . .

Add benefits to features in at least 20 situations until adding benefits becomes second nature to you. This sales communication sounds so simple, but companies and salespeople constantly violate the rule (just read most recruiting brochures or real estate ads!).

Manager's Tip: Do a short training session during your sales meeting in which you first define features and benefits, give an example, and then let agents throw features at each other and attach benefits.

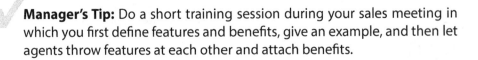

Big Idea: When you're talking, you're not learning anything! Asking questions and listening to your potential client's concerns moves you into the real world of sales.

■ Sales Skill 3: Ask a Question to Get the Order

An "order" is a "yes" of any type. For example, you ask George if he wants to purchase that home. He says yes. You just asked for the order—and got an affirmative answer! Otherwise, you could be showing homes to George, find one he tells you he likes, and . . . nothing. George just doesn't know he's supposed to "turn himself in" and tell you he wants you to sell him that home. Most of the time, your buyer will not ask *you* to sell him a home! (That's not the buyer's job.) Our rule is to get an order, you must ask a question. Do buyers give salespeople a yes without being asked? Once in a while. But, if you're the salesperson, you shouldn't expect the buyer to take the sales pro's role, should you?

Big Idea: Successful salespeople always ask, but less successful salespeople are afraid to ask—and will miss golden opportunities to increase their businesses.

Practice, Practice, Practice

I know. This seems like such a simple skill, but about 50% of the agents who enter real estate sales each year are not "order askers." They have the habit of *not* asking for the order—in every part of their lives. If you're one of that 50%, you'll have to retrain your brain to ask for the order—if you want to make money in real estate.

To get in the habit, put 15 pennies in one pocket. Every time you ask for the order each day, put a penny in the other pocket. Get rid of all the pennies every day—for a month. Now, you have a new habit.

Also, when you're assigned this skill, ask a question to every person you talk to for a week. That will get you into the habit of asking questions.

Getting Leads When Knocking on Doors

When knocking on doors, you can phrase a question two ways:

1. Choose a direct question: Are you thinking of selling or buying?
2. Ask an indirect question: Do you know of anyone who is thinking of buying or selling?

■ Sales Skill 4: Use the AAA Method of Objection-Busting

An objection is a statement from a buyer that expresses his concern. It may be something like, "There is no formal dining room" or "I just want to wait until rates come down" or "I already have an agent." Just think of objections as one of the several nos that you need to accept from your buyer to get to yes. Buyers give objections for lots of reasons:

- They want to slow down the sales process because they're afraid to make a buying decision.
- They have free-floating anxiety about making a buying decision, so they come up with reasons why they don't want to take a particular step forward.
- They don't trust the salesperson.
- They have a real concern.

Even though the first three reasons are smoke screens put up to take the salesperson off course, even those must be handled with care to maintain a good relationship with the buyer.

Here's an easy way to learn how to handle objections, and it works. Use the method I created, which I call the "AAA" method:

1. Agree
2. Ask
3. Answer

When the objection comes from the buyer (the buyer of your services, whether a purchaser or seller), *agree* that she has an important point (the first A). You're not agreeing that the buyer is right. You're agreeing with her right to have a concern. After all, it's important to the buyer! Instead of telling her how she's wrong and jumping in with the right answer, slow down a minute. Execute the second A: *ask* more questions to discover just exactly what the buyer is talking about. Finally, after you've really probed as to the real concern, execute the third A: *answer* the objection with new information. Then, close!

The wrong way to handle objections. There's a wrong and a right way to handle those objections. Unfortunately, few real estate agents have been trained in answering objections effectively. Instead of focusing on the process, they focus on the answers. Their fear is that they won't have snappy answers to every objection. To lower their anxiety, they try to memorize all the answers—scripts they think will solve their problems. Armed with these scripts, they wait for an objection and pounce with the "right" answer! That just creates an adversarial relationship—and starts an argument!

The Script

The dialogue would go something like this:

Buyer: I want to wait to purchase. (objection)

You *agree*: I understand your concern. Buying is a big decision.

You *ask*: To help me understand exactly what you're thinking about, do you mind if I ask you a few questions?

You probe and ask more: Tell me more about waiting to purchase.

You provide an *answer*: There's some information that could help you make the best decision. Let me show you . . . Do you have any questions? Let's go ahead.

Big Idea: Cushioning your answer with the first two As keeps the relationship intact.

Use the worksheet in Figure 10.4 to create an objection-buster for each of the objections you are working on in *Up and Running*.

Tip: To get dozens of sample scripts, hear role plays of objection busters, and learn the AAA method, see *Objection-Busters for Buyers and Sellers*, www.carlacross.com.

Gary Richter knows the importance of practice with handling objections. He advises: "Study the most common objections and learn quick and natural responses to those objections."

I would add that knowing how to *construct* an objection-buster is your best power tool. Why? Because you can construct it using your own style and words so it is really natural.

Using Visuals to Substantiate Your Objection Answers

We believe what we see, not what we hear. Yet, most of the time, agents fail to use visuals to substantiate the claims they make in answering objections. You can be much more credible if you use visuals—*evidence* that what you say is true. You have several assignments to create visuals to counter objections during your four-week *Up and Running* plan. It's not as difficult as you think. For instance, you know overpriced homes don't sell. But how can you prove it? There are several ways:

1. Show a comparison analysis. Find in your multiple listing service (MLS) figures for three-bedroom homes in a specific area that sold in the last 30 days. Find three-bedroom homes in that same price range and area that didn't sell. You will find that the sold homes were priced lower than the unsold ones.

2. As you inspect inventory, you will see a "right-priced" home that sells right away. You will also see a very similar home that is overpriced and doesn't sell. Take pictures of each, along with their MLS listing information, and put the two homes side by side in a comparison document. Show sellers that overpriced homes don't sell, while right-priced ones do.

FIGURE 10.4   Crafting an Objection-Buster

Objection

You **Agree** _____

You **Ask** _____

More Probing Questions

(Tell me more.) _____

(Please explain.) _____

(Then what happened?) _____

(How, what, when, why, how much?) _____

_____

You **Answer**

(Use visuals.) _____

_____

_____

Close

_____

_____

Excerpted from *Objection Busters for Buyers and Sellers*, www.carlacross.com.

Manager's Tip: Prepare several examples of these visuals so agents get an idea of how to find and construct these visuals.

See the References and Resources Unit for More Resources

See the References and Resources unit for two more resources with processes, scripts, and role plays, plus two resources with dozens of ideas for substantiating your claims with visuals so you are believable. Also, see the National Association of REALTORS® studies, listed in the References and Resources unit, which offer wonderful and credible statistics to use, including FSBO outcomes, market trends, and number of homes buyers viewed.

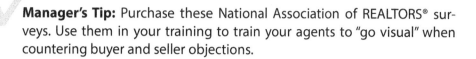

Manager's Tip: Purchase these National Association of REALTORS® surveys. Use them in your training to train your agents to "go visual" when countering buyer and seller objections.

■ Sales Skill 5: Use the "Hum" Technique

"I want a deal." Hearing that sentence strikes fear in the heart of a real estate agent! Why? Because we think we have to find the buy of the century. You assume you know what *deal* means to the buyer, and you show him homes that are overpriced by $20,000 so he can make an offer and get a deal. Later, you find out that all he meant was that he wanted to pay $1,000 less than the list price! When we jump to conclusions about what someone means, we can go off in the wrong direction. "Deal" can mean many things: the best buy in the area, a fixer-upper, lots of money off the list price, special terms, and so on. To find out what the buyer means, we need a sales communication technique—the hum technique. This skill, a simplified version of the ask-a-question-to-get-the-order sales skill, is fun to use. It provides lots of information about what the buyer really wants and encourages the buyer to keep talking (while it forces you to keep listening!).

Big Idea: The person who listens best sells the most homes.

Here's the technique:

1. Ask an open-ended question (one that requires more of an answer than yes or no). Here's a hint: open-ended questions are those that start with who, what, when, where, how much, or why.
2. Listen to the answer, pick out a core word, and repeat the word back to the talker, using a questioning upswing to your word. This will encourage your questioner to tell you more.
3. As your talker talks, simply hum. This, too, will encourage the buyer to continue talking. You'll discover lots of information and show that you are a skilled, attentive listener.

There is a musical rhythm to the hum technique: use a core word as a question, followed by hums at appropriate places.

Big Idea: Open-ended questions start with who, what, when, where, how much, or why; they provide much more of an answer than just a yes or no.

The Script

Buyer: I want a deal.

You: Deal? [*Choose the main subject of the sentence and repeat it.*]

Buyer: Yes. I want to buy at a fair price. I don't want to pay too much.

You: Hmmmmmmm. [*This encourages the buyer to give you more information. Alternate saying key words with hums.*]

When to Use This Sales Skill

Use this skill all the time. Successful salespeople aren't good talkers; they're good listeners. See how long you can continue a conversation without actually saying a whole sentence. When you can talk with someone for three minutes and let him do all the talking, you're on your way to becoming an effective salesperson.

Practice, Practice, Practice

Practice this technique on your spouse or a friend for three days in a row. When you see this person in the evening, ask him how his day went. Listen. Pick on key words. Say them back with a questioning tone. Keep him talking with a "hmmmmm." See how long you can sustain this dialogue (it's really more of a monologue) without saying a full sentence.

■ Sales Skill 6: Tie Down Your Benefit Statement

This is another simple sales skill, but one that's very important for creating rapport and agreement, and serves to move the sales process closer to a close. To use this technique, attach a question to your benefit statement. This cements the benefit in your customer's mind. Also, if you ask the buyer to agree with you on a particular benefit, and the buyer doesn't agree, you know he's after a different benefit for that feature. Now you know where to go in your sales communication.

Feature → Benefit → Tie-Down

The Script

Agent: "This home has a three-car garage (*feature*), which allows you to keep your antique cars at home so that (*bridge between feature and benefit*) you save rent (*benefit*). That is what you want, isn't it?" (*tie-down*)

Practice, Practice, Practice

Use Figure 10.5 to stay on track. Work in twos. One agent is the agent. The other agent is the buyer. Buyer: Give a feature to your sales partner, the agent. ("I want a home with a large fenced yard.") Agent: State the feature, attach a benefit with a bridge, and add a tie-down. ("This home has a large yard, so that your three children can play safely.") Do the exercise three times. Buyer: Sometimes, agree with the tie-down. Sometimes, disagree and let the agent change course. Now, reverse roles.

Manager's Tip: Use the above exercise as a training exercise in your new-agent training or in your office meeting.

Big Idea: Tie-downs increase the motivation and clarity of purchase in the buyer.

FIGURE 10.5 Practice Tie-Downs

Feature	Bridge	Benefit	Tie-down question
Large lot Private setting Quiet street Low down payment	so that . . .	you can have . . .	That's what you want, isn't it?

■ Sales Skill 7: Discover the Motive That Drives the Buyers' Decisions

Of all the seven critical sales skills, I think this is the most important because using it ensures we can help a person make the right buying decision for him. What are motives? They are emotional *reasons* people take actions. People buy homes to fill emotional needs—motives. Homes with three bathrooms are not very motivating; however, providing personal space for your growing family is.

Big Idea: People make buying decisions to fill emotional needs.

Example: the buyer says, "I want six bedrooms." You ask, "Why?" Buyer answers, "To provide enough space so my five kids each have their own bedroom. I never had that growing up, and, as a kid, I vowed when I grew up, my family would have the privacy I wish I'd had." Wow—what a strong motivator to purchase the home he subjectively feels provides his family that personal space!

As a salesperson, you need to go way past the desired features and discover the motives. Develop an attitude like Detective Columbo. Always wearing an old raincoat, Columbo spent his time trying to discover people's motives for the crimes he investigated. Without identifying a motive, Columbo couldn't figure out who did it. But he was very clever to probe and probe until he found out who had the best motive, and he investigated until his suppositions proved him right. I'm going to show you how to investigate until you discover the motive, too.

Following the Evidence to Discover Dominant Buying Motives

In sales, we call these motives dominant buying motives (DBMs). They are the drivers that compel buyers to make buying decisions. These are the emotional needs the buyer is seeking to satisfy in every buying decision. We uncover a particular buyer's dominant buying motives by following the evidence. First, we gather the features. We do that every time we ask the buyer what he wants in a home. We ask the seller why he wants to sell, or where he's moving. These are the facts. (Most agents stop finding out what the buyer wants once he has gotten the facts. The agent runs out and shows homes to the buyer. He finds one he thinks the buyer should purchase, but the buyers won't make a buying decision. That's because facts aren't compelling. Emotions are. We'll take action to satisfy these strong emotional needs.)

> **Big Idea:** Most buyers don't know their own dominant buying motives. Through expert questioning, we must help reveal them to the buyers and remind the buyers of these DBMs when they find the home that would fulfill them.

Dominant Buying Motives

- Personal space
- Prestige
- Security
- Family security

Question more deeply. We need to question much more deeply than just asking for the facts. To get to the emotions, we attach benefits and check with the buyer or seller to see if those are the benefits she wants. Finally, we uncover the DBMs—those motives that are revealed by the benefits the buyer wants. We usually can't ask directly if the buyer wants to fulfill these needs. So, after we attach benefits, we need to listen for the strongest motive. Although buyers may want to fulfill several DBMs, there is always one that takes priority over the others. (Think of the buyer who wants a view home in a prestigious area but gives it up when he finds there's no yard where his children can play. In this scenario, The DBM prestige fought with the DBM family security, and family security won!)

> **Big Idea:** Facts aren't compelling. Emotional needs are.

Here are the main DBMs, and an example of each:

- *Personal space* (whatever a person feels gives him adequate personal space; this is not physical space, and could be 1,000 square feet for some and 10,000 square feet for others)
- *Prestige* (they want to live among famous people or in a prestigious area)
- *Security* (they want a gated community or a condominium with security)
- *Family security* (they want the best schools or a safe area for their children)

One motive always dominates the others. People often do not know their own dominant buying motives, but they can express their needs in terms of features. They can agree on benefits. You need to help them translate their physical needs to emotional needs.

Big Idea: People don't buy homes because it will be a "good investment." They're all good investments! What will the good investment do for you? Provide you *security*. There's the DBM.

Practice, Practice, Practice

Your exercise. Why did you buy your last home? Follow the evidence from the features to the benefits and uncover that DBM. You probably didn't know until you did this exercise!

Another exercise. Using Figure 10.6, pick three buyers you are working with or you just sold to. What were their DBMs? If you don't have a clue, go back to the information you gathered when you interviewed them. Attach benefits. See which categories of DBMs the benefits fall into. Which was their high priority? That is their DBM. Wouldn't it be a powerful, clarifying tool if you could help buyers uncover these DBMs?

Manager's Tip: Use Figure 10.6 with the exercise above in your sales meeting to teach agents how to discover dominant buying motives.

Big Idea: In your interview process with buyers or sellers, make it a practice to uncover their DBMs. Arrange your questions so you start with features and then ask about benefits, so you can deduce their probable DBMs.

> **Big Idea:** Don't focus on any particular delivery method for these skills. Even though I've been referring to face-to-face and phone dialogues, you must also use these skills in written dialogue—emails for online inquiries. One of the big mistakes agents make in online inquiry answers is to run on about the features of a property. No sale, no contact, and no interest is generated!

FIGURE 10.6 Dominant Buying Motives

Features They Want	Benefits to Them	Dominant Buying Motive

■ Summary

Mastering the seven critical sales skills is the magic, the added ingredient you must develop to ensure you get the biggest payoff from your lead-generating efforts. Developing these skills is the second most important thing you'll do. Of course, the most important thing you'll do is lead generate. Coupling your lead generation with your sales skills development gives you the most powerful one-two punch a new agent can have. So, get to work now in practicing these seven critical sales skills in your office—and in the field. You'll get much better payoffs, and a huge boost in your confidence level, too.

> **Big Idea:** When it's time for buyers to make a buying decision, remind them of their DBM. You'll close every time because you're helping these buyers uncover their own needs and motivate themselves.

The Completed *Up and Running* Start-Up Plan

Sample *Up and Running* Weekly Schedule for Week One

Week: _____ One _____   Name: _____ Joan Smith _____

Time	Monday	Tuesday	Wednesday	Thursday	Friday	Saturday	Sunday
7–8	Organize desk		Day off	Write 40 follow-up cards			
8–9	Office meeting	Paperwork			Meet w/ mgr	Paperwork	
9–10	Office tour	Call 20 people I know		Call 10 people to ask for leads	Call 20 people to ask for leads	Show homes	
10–11							Show homes
11–12	Lunch	Floor time		Paperwork	Inspect		
12–1	Office orient.	Lunch		Lunch	Lunch	Lunch	Lunch
1–2	Inspect inventory	Start market analysis		Inspect inventory	Inspect	Floor time	Follow up
2–3					Bus. support work		In-person visits to five people
3–4	Call 20 people I know	Follow up		Follow up		Inspect inventory	
4–5	List 100 people to ask for leads	Inspect inventory		Meet with loan officer	Circle prospect 25 homes	Circle prospect 25 homes	
5–6							
6–7							
7–8							Do listing presentation
8–9							

Your *30 Days to Dollars* Lead-Generating Plan

Set your goals and track your results ("actuals")

Month: _____

	Week 1 G	Week 1 A	Week 2 G	Week 2 A	Week 3 G	Week 3 A	Week 4 G	Week 4 A	Totals G	Totals A
Proactive Activities										
People you know/meet [50/week]	(50)	50	(25)	25	(25)	25	25	25	125	125
Circle prospect [25/week]	(50)	50	50	50	(25)	25	25	25	150	150
FSBOs [25/week]	0	0	0	0	(25)	25	25	25	75	75
Expireds [25/week]	0	0			25*	(25)	25*	25	50	50
Reactive Activities										
Open houses [1 minimum]	0	0	(1)	1	(1)	1	(1)	1	3	3
Online leads	25	25	25	25	25	25	25	25	100	100

G=Goals
A=Actuals

Circled are the numbers of lead-generating activities from each source–in the specific week they are assigned in your *Up and Running* plan.
*By Week 3, you get to choose your favorite methods among those listed.

Your *30 Days to Dollars* Lead-Generating Results

Month: _____

Buyer Activities

	Week 1 G	Week 1 A	Week 2 G	Week 2 A	Week 3 G	Week 3 A	Week 4 G	Week 4 A	Totals G	Totals A
Qualifying interviews w/buyers	2	2	2	2	2	2	2	2	8	8
Qualified buyer showings	2	2	2	2	2	2	2	2	8	8
# sales							1	1	1	1

Listing Activities

	Week 1 G	Week 1 A	Week 2 G	Week 2 A	Week 3 G	Week 3 A	Week 4 G	Week 4 A	Totals G	Totals A
Qualified listing appointments	1	1	1	1	1	1	1	1	4	4
Marketable listings secured	0	0	0	0	0	0	1	1	1	1
# of listings sold	0	0	0	0	0	0	0	0	0	0*

G=Goals   A=Actuals

Note the results projected through time. These results are in your four-week *Up and Running* plan.

*Depends on your normal market time.

Yearly Goals and Monthly Activities

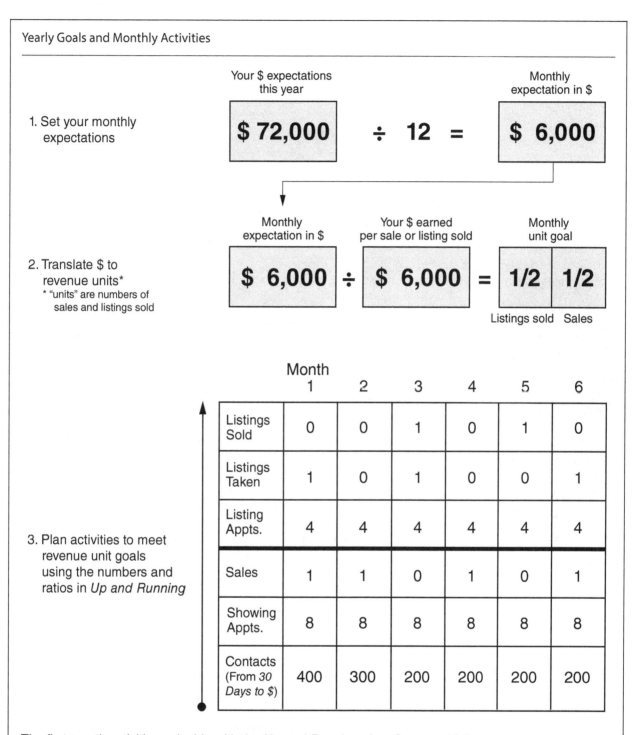

1. Set your monthly expectations

Your $ expectations this year

$ 72,000   ÷   12   = $ 6,000

Monthly expectation in $

2. Translate $ to revenue units*
   * "units" are numbers of sales and listings sold

Monthly expectation in $ Your $ earned per sale or listing sold   Monthly unit goal

$ 6,000   ÷ $ 6,000   =   1/2 | 1/2

Listings sold   Sales

3. Plan activities to meet revenue unit goals using the numbers and ratios in *Up and Running*

	Month 1	2	3	4	5	6
Listings Sold	0	0	1	0	1	0
Listings Taken	1	0	1	0	0	1
Listing Appts.	4	4	4	4	4	4
Sales	1	1	0	1	0	1
Showing Appts.	8	8	8	8	8	8
Contacts (From *30 Days to $*)	400	300	200	200	200	200

The first month activities coincide with the *Up and Running* plan. Our agent follows the same contact plan she used for her third month onward to schedule her contacts and business results for the remainder of the year.

Sample Budget for the New Agent

Sample Real Estate Budget
Real Estate Operating Expenses

Projections: 6 sales this year

                        6 listings sold this year

                        8 listings taken this year

Check with your manager for the average expenses in your area as you make your real estate budget.

	YEARLY ($)	MONTHLY ($)
Total marketing budget ($400 per listing or sale—includes postcards, online marketing, sphere marketing, after-sale present)	4,800	400
Professional fees (REALTOR® association dues, MLS)	1,000	83
Business car expenses (gas, oil, tools, repair)	2,400	200
Communication expenses (smartphone, data plan)	2,000	166
Labor/mechanical (unless you have an assistant)	1,200	100
Professional development	600	50
Supplies	1,200	100
Business insurance (L and I)	300	25
Legal fees/E&O	300	25
Licenses, permits	300	25
Other (website, blog, IDX technology, software, and so on)	1,200	100
TOTAL	15,300	1,275

Sample Budget Forecast for Year One

Month	1	2	3	4	5	6	7	8	9	10	11	12
Sales	1	1		1		1			1			1
Listings Sold			1		1		1		1		1	1
Income (closings)		6,000*	6,000	6,000	6,000	6,000	6,000	6,000	6,000	6,000	6,000	6,000
Expenses Out ($)	1,275	1,275	1,275	1,275	1,275	1,275	1,275	1,275	1,275	1,275	1,275	1,275
Profit ($)	(1,275)	4,725	4,725	4,725	4,725	4,725	4,725	4,725	4,725	4,725	4,725	4,725

Total income: $66,000

Total expenses: − $15,300

Profit: $50,700

*Note: If you make a sale in month one, that sale will be in month two, when the home closes. There is also a month lag from a sold listing to a closing.

Your Marketing Plan—A Sample

1. Name your target market (who you're marketing to).
2. Put your actions in order of the dates to be accomplished.
3. Assign work to be accomplished in each tactic. Add your budget figure.
4. Tally your total budget from this target market.

Target Market: _____

Action	Assigned To	To Be Done By	Budget
Introduction	agent	1st month (Jan)	200 people @ 50 cents = $100
Implement social media plan	agent	each day	$0–$100/month; depends on services/programs purchased
Phone calls (ask for referrals)	agent	2nd month (Feb)	200 people @ 25 cents = $50
E-Newsletter (one page)	agent	1st–2nd month (Feb)	200 people @ 25 cents = $50
"Spring Ahead" postcard	agent	3rd month (Mar)	200 people @ 30 cents = $60
Personal visit—seeds for spring plants	agent	4th month (April)	200 people @ 50 cents = $100
E-Newsletter (one page)	agent	5th month (May)	200 people @ 25 cents = $50
"Just Listed" postcard	agent	6th month (June)	200 people @ 30 cents = $60
Phone calls (ask for referrals)	agent	7th month (July)	200 people @ 25 cents = $50
E-Newsletter (one page)	agent	8th month (Aug)	200 people @ 25 cents = $50
"Just Sold" postcard	agent	9th month (Sept)	200 people @ 30 cents = $60
Personal visit—pumpkins	agent	10th month (Oct)	200 people @ $1 = $200
E-Newsletter (one page)	agent	11th month (Nov)	200 people @ 25 cents = $50
Holiday card	agent	12th month (Dec)	200 people @ 50 cents = $100

Notes:
E-Newsletter four times per year; preprinted postcards three times per year
Regularly send anniversary cards to each person you sold a home to
Take housewarming gift within two weeks after closing (to both buyers and sellers) (most important!)
Increase your postcards (just listed or just sold) as you can, to prove you are a successful agent
You also need to expand this to after-the-sale tactics:

- Deliver a present to the new homeowner within 10 days of move-in
- Send an after-sale survey to all buyers and sellers

Excerpted from *Beyond the Basics of Business Planning*, the online business planning site for real estate professionals, www.carlacross.com.

UNIT 12

Blank Forms for Your *Up and Running* Plan

These forms will be used either at the beginning of your program or throughout your four weeks.

■ Part One: Accountability and Planning Forms

To Complete as You Begin Your Program:
- Agreement to Ensure You're *Up and Running*
- Get Ready: Gather the Tools of the Trade and Get Ready to Sell
- Yearly Goals and Monthly Activities
- Budget for the New Agent
- Budget Forecast
- Your Marketing Plan
- Portfolio Exercise
- Technology Budget and Planner
- Your Social Media Planner for your Social Networking

To Complete Each Week:
- Your *30 Days to Dollars* Lead-Generating Plan (spreadsheet)
- Your *30 Days to Dollars* Lead-Generating Results (spreadsheet)
- Tracking Qualified Buyers
- Buyer's Potential Evaluator
- Listing Presentation Qualifier
- Marketable Listing Evaluator

Agreement to Ensure You're *Up and Running*

I, _____, agree to complete all the business-producing and business-supporting work in the *Up and Running in 30 Days* start-up plan. I understand each aspect of the plan and that it is constructed to help me get a fast start.

I want support from my manager, so I agree to make an appointment with my manager weekly. During that appointment, I will review the work completed for that week and my plan for the next week. I agree to do the following:

1. Keep each appointment
2. Be on time
3. Be prepared

To ensure that I get the most from my plan, I expect my manager to do the following:

- Meet with me weekly for at least one-half hour
- Help me keep my activities prioritized correctly
- Provide assistance in my development of specific business methods
- Provide me any resources necessary to complete the work in this program
- Provide the support and encouragement necessary to begin a successful career

I understand it's my business, and I agree to manage it according to the principles in *Up and Running in 30 Days*.

Agent _____ Manager _____

Date of this agreement: _____ End of program: _____

Get Ready: Gather the Tools of the Trade and Get Ready to Sell

Briefcase

Smartphone

Pen

Pencil

Colored pen or pencil

Calendar (or on your smartphone)

Highlighter

Scratch pad

Post-it notes

Daily planner

Access to your MLS

Street map

Paper clips

Tape measure (100 ft or 30.5 m)

Staple gun

Laptop computer

Handheld calculator

Digital camera

Other Materials

Attitude notebook*

Office notebook*

Resource notebook*

Car

Sold signs

Tape measure

Mallet and nails

Screwdriver

Flashlight

Coveralls

Overshoes

First aid kit

Forms**

Purchase and sale agreements

Wording for contract forms

Other contract addenda

Listing agreements

Other forms pertaining to listing

Be Sure You Have

Adequate car insurance (check your agency contract)

A method to keep tax records (see your accountant before you become an independent contractor)

Joined your REALTOR® organization

Completed your manager's orientation

Chosen a database or contact management program

*These notebooks are assignments in *Up and Running* to ensure you are tracking your attitude, your office resources, and other resources.

**Many of the forms you need are available online. Be sure to have your laptop with you everywhere and be able to access the internet.

Yearly Goals and Monthly Activities

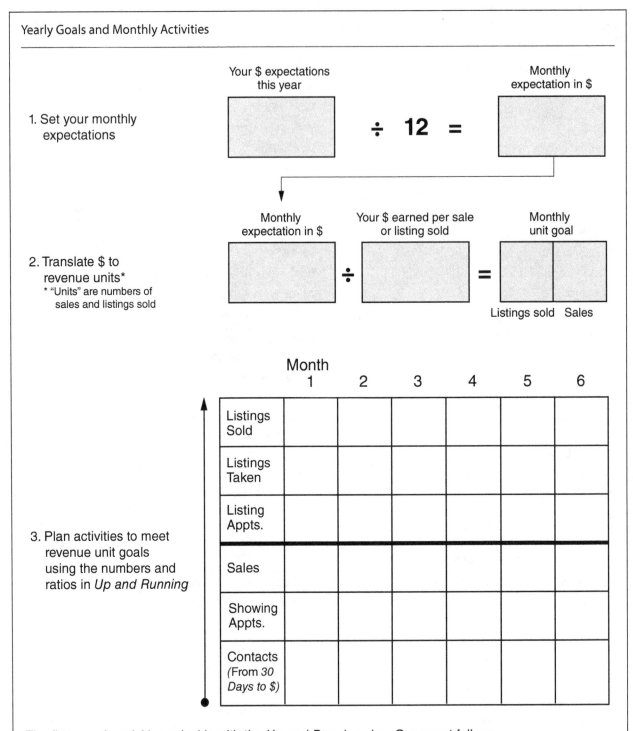

1. Set your monthly expectations

   Your $ expectations this year ÷ **12** = Monthly expectation in $

2. Translate $ to revenue units*

   * "Units" are numbers of sales and listings sold

   Monthly expectation in $ ÷ Your $ earned per sale or listing sold = Monthly unit goal

   Listings sold   Sales

3. Plan activities to meet revenue unit goals using the numbers and ratios in *Up and Running*

   Month

	1	2	3	4	5	6
Listings Sold						
Listings Taken						
Listing Appts.						
Sales						
Showing Appts.						
Contacts (From *30 Days to $*)						

The first month activities coincide with the *Up and Running* plan. Our agent follows the same contact plan she used for her third month onward to schedule her contacts and business results for the remainder of the year.

Budget for the New Agent

Your Real Estate Budget
Real Estate Operating Expenses

Projections: _____ sales this year

                      _____ listings sold this year

                      _____ listings taken this year

	YEARLY ($)	MONTHLY ($)
Total marketing budget ($400 per listing or sale—includes post-cards, online marketing, sphere marketing, after-sale present)		
Professional fees (REALTOR® association dues, MLS)		
Business car expenses (gas, oil, tools, repair)		
Communication expenses (smartphone, data plan)		
Labor/mechanical (unless you have an assistant)		
Professional development		
Supplies		
Business insurance (L and I)		
Legal fees/E&O		
Licenses, permits		
Other (website, blog, IDX technology, software, and so on)		
TOTAL		

Budget Forecast

Month	1	2	3	4	5	6	7	8	9	10	11	12
Sales												
Listings Sold												

Income (closings)												
Expenses Out ($)												
Profit ($)												

Net Profit:

Your Marketing Plan

1. Name your target market (who you're marketing to).
2. Put your actions in order of the dates to be accomplished.
3. Assign work to be accomplished in each tactic. Add your budget figure.
4. Tally your total budget from this target market.

Target Market: _____

Action	Assigned To	To Be Done By	Budget
Introduction			
Implement social media plan			
Phone calls (ask for referrals)			
E-Newsletter (one page)			
"Spring Ahead" postcard			
Personal visit—seeds for spring plants			
E-Newsletter (one page)			
"Just Listed" postcard			
Phone calls (ask for referrals)			
E-Newsletter (one page)			
"Just Sold" postcard			
Personal visit—pumpkins			
E-Newsletter (one page)			
Holiday card			

Notes:
E-Newsletter four times per year; preprinted postcards three times per year
Regularly send anniversary cards to each person you sold a home to
Take housewarming gift within two weeks after closing (to both buyers and sellers) (most important!)
Increase your postcards (just listed or just sold) as you can, to prove you are a successful agent
You also need to expand this to after-the-sale tactics:
- Deliver a present to the new homeowner within 10 days of move-in
- Send an after-sale survey to all buyers and sellers

Excerpted from *Beyond the Basics of Business Planning*, the online business planning site for real estate professionals, www.carlacross.com.

Social Media Planner

Social Media Planner							
Activities Use this chart to keep track of your social networking activities each week. Remember, the more activities you can perform each week, the more exposure you'll receive, which leads to more potential for business.	Sunday	Monday	Tuesday	Wednesday	Thursday	Friday	Saturday
Status Updates and Comments							
Provide your status update before 9 am (LinkedIn, Facebook, Twitter)							
Provide another status update after lunch (Facebook, Twitter)							
Provide final status update before going to bed (Facebook, Twitter)							
Create and post __ links to news articles found online per __							
Comment on at least __ people's status updates on Facebook per __							
Comment on at least __ people's posts on a LinkedIn group per __							
Bookmark __ websites and blog posts on Delicious or StumbleUpon per __							
Videos and Photos							
Upload __ videos to YouTube per __							
Upload photos to Instagram per __							
Upload __ videos to Flickr per __							
Blogging							
Write __ blog(s) per __							
Post __ blog(s) to ActiveRain per __							
Read and comment on at least __ blogs on ActiveRain per __							
Network Building							
Add __ friends on Facebook per __							
Add __ connections on LinkedIn per __							
Add at least __ friends on Plaxo per __							
Follow __ people on Twitter per __							
Follow people on Instagram per __							

This Social Media Planner is provided compliments of John Mayfield, www.RealEstateTechGuy.com, social media and technology expert.

Portfolio Exercise

List Your Skills	Benefits to Buyers/Sellers	Show It—Evidence

Excerpted from *Marketing You*, www.carlacross.com.

Technology Budget and Planner

Use this planner to create an action plan to purchase and implement the technology you feel will support your career best during your first few months in the business. Put a date to acquire each item. Put a price beside each item so you'll have a technology budget. Add up your costs so you can allocate a portion of your funds each month to technology. Check off as you achieve your technology goals.

	Priority	Date to Acquire	Cost	Achieved
A laptop computer, so you can work from anywhere				
Database for your prospects, clients, and affiliates				
Contact management program to run your marketing plan				
Capture and follow up on your online leads				
Measure your progress toward your goals software/service				
Smartphone to keep in contact with your customers				
Personal website and blog				
Digital camera				
Camcorder				
Financial management software				

Your *30 Days to Dollars* Lead-Generating Plan

Set your goals and track your results ("actuals")

Month: _____

Proactive Activities	Week 1		Week 2		Week 3		Week 4		Totals	
	G	A	G	A	G	A	G	A	G	A
People you know/meet [50/week]										
Circle prospect [25/week]										
FSBOs [25/week]										
Expireds [25/week]										

Reactive Activities	Week 1		Week 2		Week 3		Week 4		Totals	
	G	A	G	A	G	A	G	A	G	A
Open houses [1 minimum]										
Online leads										

G=Goals
A=Actuals

Circled are the numbers of lead-generating activities from each source in the specific week they are assigned in your *Up and Running* plan.

Your *30 Days to Dollars* Lead-Generating Results

Month: _____

Buyer Activities

	Week 1		Week 2		Week 3		Week 4		Totals	
	G	A	G	A	G	A	G	A	G	A
Qualifying interviews w/buyers										
Qualified buyer showings										
# sales										

Listing Activities

	Week 1		Week 2		Week 3		Week 4		Totals	
	G	A	G	A	G	A	G	A	G	A
Qualified listing appointments										
Marketable listings secured										
# of listings sold										

G=Goals   A=Actuals

Note the results projected through time. These results are in your four-week *Up and Running* plan.

*Depends on your normal market time.

Tracking Qualified Buyers

Record and qualify your buyer leads

Date of Qualifying Meeting	Name	Address	Question-naire Used?	Both at Qualifying Session?	# Showings	Sales

Excerpted from *The Complete Buyer's Agent Toolkit,* www.carlacross.com.

Buyer's Potential Evaluator

Rate on a scale of 1–4 (4 is the highest)

	1	2	3	4
1. Buyer answered all qualifying questions.	1	2	3	4
2. Buyer is motivated to purchase. (Rate each spouse/partner separately.)	1	2	3	4
3. Buyer is realistic about price range expectations.	1	2	3	4
4. Buyer is open and cooperative	1	2	3	4
5. Buyer will purchase in a timely manner.	1	2	3	4
6. Buyer is a referral source and will provide referrals.	1	2	3	4
7. Buyer has agreed that you will be his or her exclusive agent.	1	2	3	4
8. Buyer has signed a buyer agency agreement.	1	2	3	4
9. Buyer will meet with loan officer to be pre-approved.	1	2	3	4
10. Buyer answered financial questions openly.	1	2	3	4
11. Buyer has no other agent obligations.	1	2	3	4
12. If buyer has home to sell, he or she is realistic about price.	1	2	3	4
13. Buyer will devote sufficient time to purchasing process.	1	2	3	4
14. Both spouses/partners will be available to look for home.	1	2	3	4
15. This buyer is worthy of my time, energy, and expertise.	1	2	3	4

Use this evaluator with each buyer to ensure you are working within your standards to achieve effective time management and referrals.

Listing Presentation Qualifier

Date of Presentation	Name	Address	Want to Sell?	Both Home?	2 Hours Pre-Scheduled?	How Much $ Want?	Marketing Presentation Completed?	Results

Excerpted from *Your Complete Power Listing System*, www.carlacross.com.

Marketable Listing Evaluator

1. Property listed at competitive price   Yes_____   No_____

2. Full-term listing agreement   Yes_____   No_____

3. Seller to complete obvious repairs/cleaning before showing   Yes_____   No_____

4. Easy access (e.g., key, phone for showing)   Yes_____   No_____

5. Yard sign   Yes_____   No_____

6. Immediate possession   Yes_____   No_____

7. Extras included (e.g., appliances)   Yes_____   No_____

8. Available for first tour   Yes_____   No_____

9. FHA/VA terms available if appropriate   Yes_____   No_____

10. If short sale or foreclosure, I am qualified to be the representative   Yes_____   No_____

11. If short sale or foreclosure, forecast for successful closing is good   Yes_____   No_____

12. Below market interest rate if seller financed   Yes_____   No_____

13. Post-dated price reduction   Yes_____   No_____

14. My desired commission   Yes_____   No_____

15. In my evaluation, this property will sell within listed market range,   Yes_____   No_____
    in normal market time for this area.

16. I will receive referrals from the sellers.   Yes_____   No_____

Use this evaluator with each of your potential listings to ensure sellers meet your standards.

Excerpted from *Your Complete Power Listing System,* www.carlacross.com.

■ **Part Two: Planning and Tracking Documents for Each of the Four Weeks of** *Up and Running*

WEEK ONE

- Your Weekly Schedule for Week One
- Your Daily Planner (This is your master sheet. Make one copy per day for this week.)
- Your Start-Up Plan and Accomplishments for Week One

Up and Running Weekly Schedule for Week One

Week: _____   Name: _____

Time	Monday	Tuesday	Wednesday	Thursday	Friday	Saturday	Sunday
7–8							
8–9							
9–10							
10–11							
11–12							
12–1							
1–2							
2–3							
3–4							
4–5							
5–6							
6–7							
7–8							
8–9							

Suggested Hours Weekly:

Lead generating

Qualifying buyers/sellers

Show properties/listing properties

Purchase/sale agreements

How could you improve your schedule?

What You Did

10 _____ hours

5 _____ hours

5 _____ hours

5 _____ hours

Evaluate Your Weekly Schedule

Rate yourself on the effectiveness of your weekly schedule: _____

1–10 (10 is high)

Daily Planner

Date: _____

Priorities:		**Accomplished**	**Notes:**
1. _____		☐	_____
2. _____		☐	_____
3. _____		☐	_____
4. _____		☐	_____
5. _____		☐	_____
6. _____		☐	_____
7. _____		☐	_____
8. _____		☐	_____
9. _____		☐	_____
10. _____		☐	_____

	Lead Generating	Qualified Leads	Listing Appointments	Home Showings
Activity				
Hours Spent				

	Listings Obtained	Sales	Listings Sold	
Results				

Rate your efforts on a scale of 1–10 _____

How can you improve your rating? _____
_____

At the end of the week, transfer your numbers of activities to your spreadsheets in Unit 12.

Note: Make six copies of this sheet per week.

Your Start-Up Plan and Accomplishments for Week One

Check Off When Completed   Manager's Comments

Business Producing

Implement Your *30 Days to Dollars* Lead-Generating Plan

- Lead generate: Contact at least 100 people using these methods:
    - Call or contact 50 people you know (see Unit 8 for a script)
    - Circle prospect 50 people (see Unit 8 for definition and operation)
    - Follow up on initial online inquirers (reactive)
    - Other: _____
- Get two qualified seller leads
- Get two qualified buyer leads
- Show homes to two qualified buyer groups
- Go to at least one listing appointment

Business Supporting

Regular weekly/daily actions:

- Create your weekly schedule in advance of the following week
- Create your daily schedules each day using Daily Planner
- Add at least 50 contacts to your database (very important!)
- Write at least 15 follow-up notes
- Evaluate your buyers and sellers using the buyers and sellers evaluation sheets
- Do the activities in your marketing plan
- Do the activities in your social media planner
- Do the activities in your technology planner
- Practice the sales skills assigned in this week
- Apply the sales skills that are assigned for this week in real life
- Add to your resource notebook
- Add to your attitude notebook
- Add to your office notebook

Measure Your Results

- Daily Planner—evaluate your actions each day
- Weekly schedule—evaluate at end of week
- Weekly accomplishments—check off actions
- Goals/actuals spreadsheets—compare your results with the *Up and Running* plan

Your Start-Up Plan and Accomplishments for Week One (continued)

Check Off When Completed   Manager's Comments

Additional Business-Supporting Activities for Week One

Sales Skills

- Using sales skill 1, craft a sales script to call on people you know (see Unit 8)

- Using sales skill 3, ask for a lead (see Unit 10)

- Create three visuals to counter seller's objections to pricing

Sales Opportunities

- If you're going to hold open house or take floor time, get information from your manager on how to do each of these reactive lead-generating activities.

- Observe two public open houses this weekend. Interview the agents who hold them open about their methods.

- Observe at least one hour of floor time this week (or, if you don't have floor time, observe three agents handling incoming calls).

- Interview the agent who takes floor time about their methods.

Technical Information

- Orientation: Complete all your office orientation duties (get your business cards, etc.). Put all the information in your office notebook.

- Meet with a loan officer to learn the basics of financing (get a loan officer referral from your manager). Put all that information in your resource notebook.

- Ask three experienced agents to see their comparative market analyses (CMAs). Take notes so you can compile your own. Then, complete a market analysis on your own home. Practice presenting it to a "seller," so you'll be comfortable with the format and information. Need a model for a market analysis or software? See the References and Resources unit.

Planning

- Use the Your Real Estate Budget form to complete your budget

- Use the Technology Budget and Planner to make your technology plan

- Use Your Marketing Plan to create your marketing plan (see Unit 9 for how to create your plan and for a sample plan). Need some resources for marketing? See the References and Resources unit.

Social Networking

- Establish your website and blog

WEEK TWO

- Your Weekly Schedule for Week Two
- Your Daily Planner
- Your Start-Up Plan and Accomplishments for Week Two

Up and Running Weekly Schedule for Week Two

Week: _____   Name: _____

Time	Monday	Tuesday	Wednesday	Thursday	Friday	Saturday	Sunday
7–8							
8–9							
9–10							
10–11							
11–12							
12–1							
1–2							
2–3							
3–4							
4–5							
5–6							
6–7							
7–8							
8–9							

Suggested Hours Weekly:

Lead generating

Qualifying buyers/sellers

Show properties/listing properties

Purchase/sale agreements

How could you improve your schedule?

What You Did

10 _____ hours

5 _____ hours

5 _____ hours

5 _____ hours

Evaluate Your Weekly Schedule

Rate yourself in the effectiveness of your weekly schedule: _____

1–10 (10 is high)

Daily Planner

Date: _____

Priorities: **Accomplished**   **Notes:**

1. _____   ☐   _____

2. _____   ☐   _____

3. _____   ☐   _____

4. _____   ☐   _____

5. _____   ☐   _____

6. _____   ☐   _____

7. _____   ☐   _____

8. _____   ☐   _____

9. _____   ☐   _____

10. _____   ☐   _____

	Lead Generating	Qualified Leads	Listing Appointments	Home Showings
Activity				
Hours Spent				

	Listings Obtained	Sales	Listings Sold
Results			

Rate your efforts on a scale of 1–10 _____

How can you improve your rating? _____

_____

At the end of the week, transfer your numbers of activities to your spreadsheets in Unit 12.

Note: Make six copies of this sheet per week.

Your Start-Up Plan and Accomplishments for Week Two

Check Off When Completed   Manager's Comments

Business Producing

***30 Days to Dollars* Lead-Generating Plan**

- Lead generation: Contact at least 100 people using these methods:

    - Call or contact 25 people you know (see Unit 8 for a script)

    - Circle prospect 50 people (see Unit 8 for definition and operation)

    - Call on at least 25 for-sale-by-owners or expired listings (see Units 8 and 9 for skill development)

    - Hold one open house

    - Follow up on initial online leads (at least 25)

- Get two qualified seller leads

- Get two qualified buyer leads

- Show homes to two qualified buyer groups

- Go to at least one listing appointment

Transfer these numbers to your goals/actuals spreadsheets for week two so you can track your progress through time.

Business Supporting

Regular weekly/daily actions:

- Create your weekly schedule in advance of the following week

- Create your daily schedules each day using the daily planner

- Add at least 50 contacts to your database (very important!)

- Write at least 15 follow-up notes

- Evaluate your buyers and sellers using the buyers and sellers evaluation sheets in Unit 12

- Do the activities in your marketing plan for that second week (see the References and Resources unit for more information)

- Do the activities in your technology plan

- Do the activities in your social media planner

- Practice the sales skills assigned for this week

- Apply the sales skills that are assigned for this week in real life

- Add to your resource notebook

- Add to your attitude notebook

- Add to your office notebook

Your Start-Up Plan and Accomplishments for Week Two (continued)

Check Off When Completed   Manager's Comments

Measure Your Results

Daily Planner—evaluate your actions each day

Weekly schedule—evaluate at end of week

Weekly accomplishments—check off actions

Goals/actuals spreadsheets—compare your results with the *Up and Running* plan

Additional Business-Supporting Activities for Week Two

Practice New Sales Skills

- Sales skill 4: Objection-busting (refer to Unit 10 for more information)
- Apply the sales skills that are assigned for this week in real life
- Assemble listing presentation materials
- Interview three agents in your office about listing presentations
- Interview three agents in your office about three common objections and how they handle them
- Assemble buyer presentation materials
- Interview three agents in your office about buyer presentations
- Interview three agents in your office about three common buyer objections and how they handle them
- Write two purchase and sale agreements

Social Networking/Social Media Planner

- Add one social network: this week, it's a Facebook business page or Twitter

WEEK THREE

- Your Weekly Schedule for Week Three
- Your Daily Planner
- Your Start-Up Plan and Accomplishments for Week Three

Up and Running Weekly Schedule for Week Three

Week: _____   Name: _____

Time	Monday	Tuesday	Wednesday	Thursday	Friday	Saturday	Sunday
7–8							
8–9							
9–10							
10–11							
11–12							
12–1							
1–2							
2–3							
3–4							
4–5							
5–6							
6–7							
7–8							
8–9							

Suggested Hours Weekly:

Lead generating

Qualifying buyers/sellers

Show properties/listing properties

Purchase/sale agreements

How could you improve your schedule?

What You Did

10 _____ hours

5 _____ hours

5 _____ hours

5 _____ hours

Evaluate Your Weekly Schedule

Rate yourself in the effectiveness of your weekly schedule: _____

1–10 (10 is high)

Daily Planner

Date: _____

Priorities:	Accomplished	Notes:
1. _____	☐	_____
2. _____	☐	_____
3. _____	☐	_____
4. _____	☐	_____
5. _____	☐	_____
6. _____	☐	_____
7. _____	☐	_____
8. _____	☐	_____
9. _____	☐	_____
10. _____	☐	_____

	Lead Generating	Qualified Leads	Listing Appointments	Home Showings
Activity				
Hours Spent				

	Listings Obtained	Sales	Listings Sold
Results			

Rate your efforts on a scale of 1–10 _____

How can you improve your rating? _____
_____

At the end of the week, transfer your numbers of activities to your spreadsheets in Unit 12.

Note: Make six copies of this sheet per week.

Your Start-Up Plan and Accomplishments for Week Three

Check Off When Completed   Manager's Comments

Business Producing

***30 Days to Dollars* Lead-Generating Plan**

- Lead generation: Make 100 sales calls:

    - 25 to people you know

    - Circle prospect 25

    - Choose from other methods for another 50 proactive contacts

    - What you chose: _____

    - Hold one open house (reactive)

    - Follow up on initial online leads (at least 25)

- Secure two qualified buyer appointments

- Show homes to two qualified buyer groups

- Secure one appointment to do a listing presentation

Caveat: If you are not getting enough appointments, increase your lead generating.

Transfer these numbers to your goals/actuals spreadsheets for week three so you can track your progress through time.

Business Supporting

Regular weekly/daily actions:

- Create your weekly schedule in advance of the following week

- Create your daily schedules each day using the daily planner

- Add at least 50 contacts to your database (very important!)

- Write at least 15 follow-up notes

- Evaluate your buyers and sellers using the buyers and sellers evaluation sheets

- Do the activities in your marketing plan for that third week

- Do the activities in your technology plan

- Do the activities in your social media planner

- Practice the sales skills assigned for this week

- Apply the sales skills that are assigned for this week in real life

- Add to your resource notebook

- Add to your attitude notebook

- Add to your office notebook

Your Start-Up Plan and Accomplishments for Week Three (continued)

Check Off When Completed   Manager's Comments

Measure Your Results

- Daily Planner—evaluate your actions each day

- Weekly schedule—evaluate at end of week

- Weekly accomplishments—check off actions

- Goals/actuals spreadsheets—compare your results with the *Up and Running* plan

Additional Business-Supporting Activities for Week Three

- Apply sales skill 5, the hum technique (see Unit 10)

- Gain performance excellence with sales skill 5 (see Unit 10)

- Create 10 reasons why potential clients should choose you

- Write two purchase and sale agreements

- Practice your listing presentation three times (see your manager for a presentation or see the References and Resources unit)

- Practice your buyer presentation three times (see your manager for a presentation or see the References and Resources unit)

- Gather three visuals to counter seller's objections (see your manager or the references unit)

- Gather three visuals to counter buyer's objections (see your manager or the References and Resources unit)

Social Media/Social Networking

- Add one social network: this week, it's LinkedIn

WEEK FOUR

- Your Weekly Schedule for Week Four
- Your Daily Planner
- Your Start-Up Plan and Accomplishments for Week Four

Up and Running Weekly Schedule for Week Four

Week: _____   Name: _____

Time	Monday	Tuesday	Wednesday	Thursday	Friday	Saturday	Sunday
7–8							
8–9							
9–10							
10–11							
11–12							
12–1							
1–2							
2–3							
3–4							
4–5							
5–6							
6–7							
7–8							
8–9							

Suggested Hours Weekly:

Lead generating

Qualifying buyers/sellers

Show properties/listing properties

Purchase/sale agreements

How could you improve your schedule?

What You Did

10 _____ hours

5 _____ hours

5 _____ hours

5 _____ hours

Evaluate Your Weekly Schedule

Rate yourself in the effectiveness of your weekly schedule: _____

1–10 (10 is high)

Daily Planner
_____

Date: _____

Priorities: **Accomplished**   **Notes:**

1. _____   ☐   _____
2. _____   ☐   _____
3. _____   ☐   _____
4. _____   ☐   _____
5. _____   ☐   _____
6. _____   ☐   _____
7. _____   ☐   _____
8. _____   ☐   _____
9. _____   ☐   _____
10. _____   ☐   _____

	Lead Generating	Qualified Leads	Listing Appointments	Home Showings
Activity				
Hours Spent				

	Listings Obtained	Sales	Listings Sold
Results			

Rate your efforts on a scale of 1–10 _____

How can you improve your rating? _____
_____

At the end of the week, transfer your numbers of activities to your spreadsheets in Unit 12.

Note: Make six copies of this sheet per week.

Your Start-Up Plan and Accomplishments for Week Four

Check Off When Completed   Manager's Comments

Business Producing

***30 Days to Dollars* Lead-Generating Plan**

- Lead generation: Make 100 sales calls—you choose type
    - What you chose: _____
- Hold one open house (reactive)
- Follow up on initial online leads (at least 25)
- Secure two qualified buyer appointments
- Show homes to two qualified buyer groups
- Secure one appointment to do a listing presentation
- List one marketable property
- Sell one home

Caveat: If you are not getting enough appointments, increase your lead generating.

Transfer these numbers to your goals/actuals spreadsheets for week four so you can track your progress through time.

Business Supporting

Regular weekly/daily actions:

- Create your weekly schedule in advance of the following week
- Create your daily schedules each day using your Daily Planner
- Add at least 50 contacts to your database
- Write at least 15 follow-up notes
- Evaluate your buyers and sellers using the buyers and sellers evaluation sheets
- Do the activities in your marketing plan
- Do the activities in your technology plan
- Do the activities in your social media planner
- Practice the sales skills assigned in that particular week
- Apply the sales skills that are assigned for this week in real life
- Add to your resource notebook
- Add to your attitude notebook
- Add to your office notebook

Your Start-Up Plan and Accomplishments for Week Four (continued)

Check Off When Completed   Manager's Comments

Measure Your Results

- Daily Planner—evaluate your actions each day

- Weekly schedule—evaluate at end of week

- Weekly accomplishments—check off actions

- Goals/actuals spreadsheets—compare your results with the *Up and Running* plan

Additional Business-Supporting Activities for Week Four

- Practice and apply sales skills 6 and 7 (see Unit 10)

- Complete the listing process materials, including a market analysis package

- Review and complete your qualifying/interview package for buyers

- Complete your personal promotional materials—a professional portfolio and your personal brochure

- Gain performance excellence in two new sales skills (you choose from the seven critical sales skills)

- Add three more visuals to counter objections sellers give you (to your seller presentation)

- Add three more visuals to counter objections buyers give you (put in your buyer presentation)

Social Media/Social Networking

- Add one more social media strategy: this week, it's YouTube

■ Part Three: End of Program Evaluator and 60-Day Business Planner

On the next pages are two documents for you to complete to evaluate your progress and create your next 60-day plan.

End-of-Program Evaluation of *Up and Running in 30 Days*

Name: _____   Email: _____

We hope you have had an awesome experience during *Up and Running in 30 Days* and that you've made real progress toward your goals. Please complete the evaluation to ensure we have helped you attain your goals in the best way possible—and to help you plan your next steps.

From Your Perspective

1. Have you seen progress from the beginning of this program to now?

   a.   In what ways?

2. Are you accomplishing what you intended to accomplish? Please explain.

3. What have been your biggest benefits from this program?

4. Has this program helped you launch your business, get into the business-producing stream, and start to make money? If so, how?

5. Are the resources included helpful to you, and in what ways?

6. What could we have done to make the resources more helpful to you?

7. What barriers, if any, have prevented you from attaining your goals and completing this program?

8. Your assessment of your progress in your lead generating plan:

9. Your assessment of your progress in the business support work:

10. Rate yourself on effort during the program (1 is low/10 is high): Why did you give yourself that rating?

Your Coach (if your manager or someone else is coaching you)

1. What has been the most helpful thing your coach has done to assist you?

2. How could your coach be more effective in helping you?

Up and Running 60-Day Plan

You've completed the *Up and Running in 30 Days* program. Now, you're ready to plan your next 60 days. Also review your marketing budget planner, your technology planner, and your social media planner to further refine your next 60-day plan. Assess what you finished and what you still need to complete, and create dates for completion.

Goals for your 60-day plan:

Total lead generating activities: _____   Each month: _____   Each week: _____

Total buyer appointments: _____   Each month: _____   Each week: _____

Total sales: _____   Each month: _____   Each week: _____

Av. $ per sale: _____

Total income from sales closed: _____

Total seller appointments: _____   Each month: _____   Each week: _____

Total listings: _____   Each month: _____   Each week: _____

Total listings sold: _____   Each month: _____   Each week: _____

Av. $ per LS: _____

Total income from listings sold/closed: _____

Sales closed and listings sold = closed income next 60 days: _____

Planning Each Week and Keeping Track of Your "Actuals"

Use one planner per week, and write your goals in each column, breaking down your 60-day goals from above. Then, as you go through the week, write your 'actuals' in each column. Use the principles you've already learned and practiced in *Up and Running in 30 Days*.

Weekly Activities and Results

Name _____   Date _____

From Business Start-Up Plan	Leads	Appts.	Business-Producing Activities	Hours	Business/Personal Management	Hours
People You Know			Lead Generation		Personal Development Quiet Time	
Circle Prospecting			Leads Generated Listing Appts.		Workout Review of Life Plan	
Expired Listings			Listings Taken Listings Canceled or Expired		Review Business Plan Staff Meetings	
FSBO			Listings (Turned Down) Listings (I Didn't Get)		Family Time	
Re-call Current Leads			Price Reductions Listings Sold			
Follow Up/Online Leads			Buyers Appts. Set Buyer Interviews		**Evaluation: Rate Yourself 1–4 (4 is high)**	
Reactive: Open House			Buyer Contracts Qualified Showing Offers Written		Lead Generation	
Floor Time			Buyer Sales		Working with Clients	
Online Leads			Sales Fails		Closing	
Other			Listings Closed		Practicing Sales Skills	
			Buyers Closed		Packaging	
			Commissions Pd. Out		Other	

Compare your weekly results to your weekly goals. On a scale of 1–10, rate yourself: _____

Why did you give yourself that rating?
_____
_____

How could you raise it?
_____
_____
_____

UNIT | 13

Sample Scripts, Letters, and Processes

■ A Script for Calling on People You Know

"Hi, Sally. I have been thinking about you. I'm in real estate now. Oh, you got my announcement postcard? Good. I've already learned to stay in contact frequently, since I guess agents aren't the best with that! Yes, I'm with ABC Realty, a wonderful firm in downtown Bellevue. Oh, you know that firm? Yes, I think I made a great decision. I wanted to call and let you know I'm working hard to do things right. I just got through my training school, and, boy, is there a lot to learn! It was great, though, and I feel really prepared to help people now. Yes, I have two sales and three listings so far. Yes, that's really great for a new agent! Also, I work with George Snell, who is my manager and coach. So, for these first few months, I have a real expert looking over my shoulder every step, which I think helps my clients feel comfortable. It's kind of a 2-for-1 benefit. Do you know anyone who needs my help? Great. [*Take down the information. Ask who, when, where, can you use Sally's name.*] Well, thanks again and I'll talk with you soon."

Immediately after the call,
- send that handwritten note of thanks for the lead, and
- put that information in your database.

■ A Script for Cold-Calling

"Hello. This is Carla Cross with ABC Realty. I'll just take a minute of your time. I'm calling today to explore with homeowners in your area some possible real estate opportunities [*the attention-getting phrase*]. We specialize in your area, and we have young buyers with small children looking for homes there. Your area seems perfect for a young family, is that right? [*Yes.*] Have you thought of downsizing? [*Address their need.*] [*Yes.*] Do you know what your home is worth? [*No.*] In just a few minutes, I can show

233

you the market trends and how your homes compare with what's selling today, so if you do want to take an opportunity to downsize, you'll know the equity you have available [*feature and benefit to the seller*]. I have some time Wednesday or Thursday evening. Would that work for you?" [*Close*] Here's my name and phone number again, just for your records. [*Give them that information.*] Thank you. I look forward to meeting you."

Immediately after the call, (1) write a thank-you note and confirm your appointment and (2) update your database along with your appointment.

■ A Script for Converting the FSBO

First visit: "Hi. I'm Carla Cross with ABC Realty. I noticed your sign just went up. Selling your home? Great. I'd like to give you some information to help you. Why? We need 'sold' signs in the neighborhood to show buyers it's a very desirable place to live. Here's [*name the piece of information you're handing them*]. I know it will be useful to you because it [*fill in the benefits, using sales skill 2, explained in Unit 10*]. I'll check in next week to see how it's going. Thanks for your time."

Second week and subsequent weeks: "Hi, Carla Cross again with ABC Realty. How's it going? [*Seller will probably tell you it's going great.*] Good. Was the information helpful that I dropped off last week? [*Seller probably won't remember what it was but will tell you it was helpful.*] Great. Here's another item that I've found really helpful to sellers. [*Give them the item.*] I'll check back with you later."

Around week five: "Hi, this is Carla (oh, you remember . . .). How's it going? Is there anything about the information I've given you that I can help you with? Questions? [*Seller will, at this point, be getting desperate. He will use your question as a rationalization to invite you further.*] Okay. I'd love to answer that, but now is not a good time. I could come over tonight or tomorrow night. Which would be better for you?" [*If the individual has a partner ask what time works for both—you want both parties there.*]

At the presentation: First, answer their questions. Then, go into your presentation. "I appreciate your time. Here's the answer. . . . Let me show you how I work, so you'll have the benefit of choosing the right person should you decide to list your property." [*Now, do your listing presentation.*]

■ The Expired Listing Script

Opening: "Hello. I'm Carla Cross of ABC Realty. Is your home still on the market? [*They may have re-listed and it isn't in your MLS yet.*] [*If no . . .*] Are you still interested in selling at some point? [*If yes, or maybe, or sometimes, even no*] I'll tell you why I ask. I work in this area and would like to stay abreast of the properties available. In case I get a buyer for your home, I'd like to be prepared so your property is represented properly. Do you have about three minutes? [*If yes, go ahead. If no, ask*] What time would be convenient for me to give you a call?"

Survey questions: What do you feel are the biggest selling points of your home? That sounds like it should be attractive to many buyers! What kind of buyer do you feel would be attracted to your home? Why? Why do you feel it didn't sell? What do you feel was the best marketing the agent did? What would you have liked to see? If you were to list again, what would you be looking for in a listing agent? When and where are you moving? [*Use the "feel" words. Don't criticize the other agent. Just get the information and hum in agreement.*] [*If you don't have an opportunity to ask these questions, or you feel it isn't appropriate to ask all the questions on the phone, save them to ask at the appointment. You need to qualify this seller!*]

Close: "It sounds as though you have a very sellable property if just a few adjustments are made. I'd love the opportunity to share my thoughts with you. [*If you have a successful track record, tell the seller now.*] I'm proud to say that I've helped [*or, our office has helped*] many sellers get their homes sold after they'd been unsuccessful with a different agent. Could I come over at [*time*] or [*alternate time*] when both of you would be home? It would take no more than 45 minutes, and you could tell me 'not interested' at any time! If you decide not to sell your home at this time, at least you will have a different perspective. And hopefully you'll think of me if you decide to sell in the future."

Immediately after the call: Optimize your impression. Send a thank-you note within one day of your call or visit.

■ The Circle Prospecting Script

"Hi. I'm Carla Cross with ABC Realty. We just listed the Smith home down the street. Have you seen the property? No? I'm going to be holding it open this weekend, and I'd love to invite you over. I'll even have coffee and cookies. I'm sure you'll be interested to see how the Smiths have creatively remodeled that trilevel. The listing price is $347,500. Here's a flyer with all the information and the open house date and time. By the way, [*ask an indirect or direct question to get a lead*]:

Indirect: Do you know anyone in the area who has thought of selling?

Direct: I see your home is one of the largest in the area. Have you thought about downsizing?

Thanks for your time. I'll check back because I'll be letting you know when the property sells."

Immediately after the call, optimize your opportunity. Write a thank-you note within one day of your meeting, thanking them for their time and enclosing your card.

■ Script: Quick Qualifying Questionnaire for Buyers

- How long have you been looking for a home?
- What attracted you to this home?
- When do you want or need to move?
- Have you been prequalified by a lender?
- Are you working with a real estate agent?

■ Quick Seller Qualifier

- When do you want or need to move?
- Where are you moving?
- Have you ever sold a home before?
- What are you looking for in a listing agent?
- When can I come over and preview the home and visit with you?

■ Letter: Introduction to Your Career in Real Estate to People You Know

Dear _____,

I'm writing you this note to let you know I've just begun a new career. I'm now selling real estate with _____ [*insert your company name*]. It's an exciting profession, and I've already found that my background in _____ [*fill in your pertinent background*] has helped prepare me well for my new profession. In addition, I've had the benefit of attending a wonderful training program at our company, and I'm being coached by _____ [*put in your manager or coach's name*] so I'm getting the guidance and advice agents need to really be of service to buyers and sellers.

With all this knowledge and training behind me, I'm excited to help buyers and sellers. If you know of someone who wants to buy or sell in our area, please let me know. I'll give them the very best service I can, backed by the great reputation of my company and the support of my manager.

If I can answer questions about the state of the market for you, I'd love to do that, too. I'm keeping abreast of the market trends and prices in your area.

My contact information:

[*Your name*
Office name
Office address

Phone
Fax
Email]

Sincerely,
[*your name*]

To optimize this, write a short, handwritten note at the bottom of each of your letters.

■ Online Reply Note

Dear _____,

Thank you for inquiring about homes in our area. I have lived here for 15 years and love it, and would welcome an opportunity to show you why when you visit. It looks to me as though you need four bedrooms. Do you have children? Or, do you need a space for an office? If you'll let me know your needs for bedrooms, offices, and so on, I'll help you narrow your scope to preview the right properties for you. I know it can be overwhelming to see all those properties without some filters.

My contact information:

[*Your name*
Office name
Office address

Phone
Fax
Email]

Sincerely,
[*your name*]

■ Capturing and Following Online Leads

FIGURE 13.1   An Example of a System to Capture and Convert Leads

Lead Capture	Lead Conversion	Client Loyalty
Program to capture the lead/ input to contact management with notes	One day after inquiry—pick up the phone	Ongoing communication through contact management
Fast follow-up	Each day—call	Training—communication skills
Training—best method to answer initial inquiry/ time frames for follow up	Training—develop script	Goal: Communicate until they buy or die
Develop emails/scripts for emails	After one week—call once a week	
Goal: Prove dedicated professionalism	Training—develop script to interview/screen	
	Goal: Prove you deserve trust/ gain rapport	

UNIT 14

References and Resources

Here are training, marketing, and systems references for you to use as you start your business.

■ Training Resources

These sales and management resources are available from Carla Cross Seminars, Inc. and Carla Cross Coaching at www.carlacross.com. Carla's resources have been reviewed and are recommended by the Real Estate Brokerage Managers' Council (CRB) and the Council of Residential Specialists (CRS), the two highest designations available to real estate professionals, than any other training provider. More programs by Carla Cross are recommended and endorsed by these prestigious entities than any other trainer's.

Coaching for New Agents: *Up and Running in Real Estate*

From Carla Cross Coaching, this program puts *Up and Running* on steroids with automated online accountability forms and training videos from Carla—all online. These videos teach the agent the sales skills in *Up and Running*, plus providing coaching, motivation, and inspiration—at a very affordable price. Carla created this program to take the burden from the manager to coach the agent in *Up and Running*. Yet, Carla has created a unique method of keeping the broker in the loop, too. Coaches' Corner allows those coaching their agents in the program to see the agents' work and provides dozens of coaching tips on how to get the best from the program. See www.upandrunninginrealestate.com.

One-on-One Coaching: Career Achievement Coaching

Your next step after *Up and Running* is one-on-one coaching from Carla Cross Coaching. This is for real estate agents looking to take their careers to the next level. This coaching program builds further than the principles of *Up and Running*. In this program, you'll speak with your coach once a week for the first month (45 minutes), then twice a month for the next five months (30-minute calls). This program includes a client manual to set your goals and track your results, two complimentary CDs, an in-depth behavioral profile to let you know your strengths and sales challenges, and *The Business Planning System for the Real Estate Professional*, your complete business planning guide. See www.carlacross.com for more information.

One-On-One Coaching for Leadership: Leadership Mastery

Carla Cross personally coaches a select number of owners and managers in her unique one-on-one program, designed to increase profits and productivity. Carla analyzes the needs of each of her clients, and, together, they design a program to recruit, select, train, and coach agents to exceptional success. See www.carlacross.com for more information.

To Market Yourself

Marketing You from www.carlacross.com explains how to market yourself to get client loyalty and highest commissions. Use this resource to raise confidence and increase competitive advantage. All of the following are online for immediate access: 100-page resource, 1 audio, plus 11 bonus forms.

■ In-Depth Resources to Train and Coach Your Agents

For Long-Term, Detailed Business Planning

Beyond the Basics of Business Planning from www.carlacross.com offers training and all the forms to write an effective business plan—a complete tutorial with training videos. Online for immediate access. One program is available for agents, and one program is available for leadership.

For Prospective Agents and Those New to Real Estate

What They Don't Teach You in Pre-License School from www.carlacross.com gives you the rest of the information you need to start your career right. A 240-page ebook with budgets, time lines, and job descriptions for new agents. Makes a great recruiting tool for managers, too. Includes new agent expectations survey and real estate trends, plus 77 interview questions new agents should ask—and managers should be prepared for. Included is a detailed action plan to use during pre-license class, *Hit the Ground Running*.

To Create an Effective Sellers' Process—The Complete System

Your Complete Power Listing System from www.carlacross.com is a complete online tutorial on working with sellers, plus all the forms and presentations an agent needs. This resource covers from the first phone call to after closing. Two hundred eighty pages with 35 checklists, processes, and systems. Twenty visuals to anticipate and counter objections. Gain loyalty, confidence, and get sold listings. Includes a PowerPoint presentation, ready to customize.

To Create an Effective Buyers' Process—The Complete System

Your Complete Buyer's Agent Toolkit from www.carlacross.com is a complete tutorial, along with all the systems and forms for a buyer's agent needed to sell more homes to buyers faster and create lifelong loyalty. Inside the Toolkit, there are three buyers packages: *The Pre-Appointment Package*, *Your Guide to Purchasing a Home*, and the *Home Buyer's System*. Over 235 pages of detailed information along with over 25 checklists and processes to manage the buying process. This is truly an at-home study program for professional buyer agency.

Quality tested and recommended by CRS.

Objection Busters

Never be stumped by an objection again! Learn how to bust any objection with Carla's AAA method. The method is carefully spelled out, so you can apply it to any objection. You'll be in control of all situations! Colorful flash cards help you learn fast and easily. Hear role plays of the most common objections. Most common objections are role-played on the accompanying CD.

- *Buyer Series (Objections Buyers Give)*: 8 common objections and 16 answers; role-play dialogue and written scripts
- *Seller Series (Objections Sellers Give)*: 6 common objections and 18 answers; role-play dialogue and written scripts
- *Recruiting Series (Objections Recruits Give)*: 6 common objections and 14 answers; role-play dialogue and written scripts

Technology/Social Networking Trainers/Training

- *e-PRO® certification program,* www.epronar.com; this is a 2-day comprehensive course on social media marketing.
- www.realestatetechguy.com, John Mayfield (573-756-0077); order his Technology Boot Camp CD. John is a successful salesperson and owner, national instructor, and great mentor. He has many illustrious credits, including past president of CRB (Certified Real Estate Broker) Council; he consults to companies in France and lives there part of the year. We highly recommend John as a tech expert.
- *Internet Marketing Specialist Designation (IMSD),* www.retechnology.com
- GRI (Graduate, REALTOR® Institute) www.nar.realtor/designations-and-certifications/gri-designation

- CRS (Certified Residential Specialist), www.crs.com
- ABR® (Accredited Buyer's Representative), www.rebac.net

Marketing, Technical, and Training Resources

These resources are listed solely for your convenience. Carla Cross does not endorse any of these. See your manager for specific recommendations.

Marketing

ProspectsPLUS!	www.prospectsplus.com
The Personal Marketing Company	www.tpmco.com
SendOutCards	www.sendoutcards.com
QuantumDigital	www.quantumdigital.com
Sendsations	www.sendsations.com
Cross Coaching Toolbox	www.crosscoachingtoolbox.com
Blue Mountain Cards	www.bluemountaincards.com
Market Leader	www.marketleader.com
Expresscopy	www.expresscopy.com

Many of these companies offer client follow-up programs, as do most CRMs.

Website Design and Other Web Services (May Include IDX)

MyRealEstateTools	www.myrealestatetools.com
Real Estate Webmasters	www.realestatewebmasters.com
A la mode, Inc.	www.alamode.com
RealtySites PLUS™	www.realtysitesplus.com
ActiveAgent™	www.activeagent.com
PropertyMinder	www.propertyminder.com
HouseWeb	www.houseweb.com
Placester	www.placester.com
Market Leader	www.marketleader.com
BoomTown	www.boomtownroi.com
Squarespace	www.squarespace.com

IDX Solutions (Internet Data Exchange)

Market Leader	www.marketleader.com
BoomTown	www.boomtownroi.com
IDXCentral	www.idxcentral.com
Diverse Solutions	www.diversesolutions.com
Zurple	www.zurple.com
Placester	www.placester.com

Virtual Tours

RealBiz Media Group	www.realbizmedia.com
Obeo	www.obeo.com
Paradym	www.paradym.com
TourFactory	www.tourfactory.com

Agents also use Facebook's video feature to create virtual tours.

CMAs

PropertyMinder	www.propertyminder.com
ToolkitCMA	www.toolkitcma.com
Cloud CMA	www.cloudCMA.com
Top Producer®	www.topproducer.com
Realtors Property Resource®	http://blog.narrpr.com
Altos Research	http://altosresearch.com

e-Newsletter Services

MailChimp	www.mailchimp.com
Constant Contact	www.constantcontact.com
The Personal Marketing Company	www.tpmco.com
BombBomb (video email)	www.bombbomb.com
JiveSystems (video email)	www.jivesystems.com

Interactive Voice Response

Proquest Technologies	www.proquesttechnologies.com
Listings-to-Leads	www.listingstoleads.com
ArchAgent	www.archagent.com
iHOUSEweb	www.ihouseweb.com

Lead Generation and Management

Market Leader	www.marketleader.com
Listings-to-Leads	www.listingstoleads.com
REDX (FSBOs/Expireds)	www.theredx.com
ArchAgent	www.archagent.com
Placester	www.placester.com

Software for Financial Management

Quicken	www.quicken.com
QuickBooks	www.quickbooks.com
Money Plus Sunset	www.microsoft.com/money
Mint	www.mint.com

Software for Client Contact Management/CRM

Several programs that provide lead-generating services also have CRM included.

Top Producer®	www.topproducer.com
Wise Agent	www.thewiseagent.com
Cross Coaching Toolbox	www.crosscoachingtoolbox.com
AgentOffice	www.agentoffice.com
Outlook	www.microsoft.com/outlook
Market Leader	www.marketleader.com
Diverse Solutions	www.diversesolutions.com
Brevity	www.brevity.com
BoomTown	www.boomtownroi.com
HouseWeb	www.houseweb.com
Zurple	www.zurple.com
Placester	www.placester.com

Sites for Your Professional Profile

realtor.com	www.realtor.com
Zillow	www.zillow.com
Trulia	www.trulia.com

Sites for Clients to Use and to Give Reports to Clients

PropertyMinder	www.propertyminder.com
Toolkit CMA	www.toolkitcma.com
Cloud CMA	www.cloudCMA.com

Digital Signatures and Online Transactions

DocuSign	www.docusign.com
dotloop	www.dotloop.com

For Real Estate Statistics to Use in Presentations

National Association of REALTORS®, *Profile of Home Buyers and Sellers*, www.nar.realtor.org/research. This report is published every year from extensive surveys of buyers and sellers done by NAR. These reports and others from NAR are a treasure trove of buyer and seller habits and should be used in your buyer and seller presentations. Also, NAR publishes special reports periodically. Check back often (http://www.nar.realtor.org/research-and-statistics).

Realtors Property Resource® (RPR®), http://blog.narrpr.com

Top Producer®, www.topproducer.com

ToolkitCMA, www.toolkitcma.com

Altos Research, http://altosresearch.com

HouseLogic, http://houselogic.com

Trend Reports

- *Swanepoel Trends Report*, Stefan Swanepoel, www.retrends.com
- *Game Plan—How Real Estate Professionals can Thrive in an Uncertain Future*, Ian Morris and Steve Murray
- Inman Select, *How to Fix New Agent Onboarding*, www.inman.com. See Inman for new reports coming out regularly.
- National Association of REALTORS®, *Home Buyer and Seller Generational Trends Report 2016*, www.nar.realtor/research
- *The Real Estate Professional*, http://therealestatepro.com

Of course, see your MLS and your newspaper for local trend updates and statistics.

■ Other Resources

Cloud Sites to Store and Share Files

Dropbox	www.dropbox.com
Box	www.box.com
Google Drive	www.google.com

Surveys

SurveyGizmo	www.surveygizmo.com
SurveyMonkey	www.surveymonkey.com

Blogging and Blogging Platforms

ActiveRain	www.activerain.com
WordPress	www.wordpress.com
Blogger	www.blogger.com
Squarespace	www.squarespace.com
GoDaddy	www.godaddy.com

Color Printing

Expresscopy	www.expresscopy.com

Send and Share Large Files

Hightail	www.hightail.com
Dropbox	www.dropbox.com
Google Drive	www.google.com

Store and Edit Pictures

Google Photos	www.google.com
Flickr	www.flickr.com

INDEX

Notes